National Education Policy 2020

Paving ways for Transformational Reforms

Editors

Pankaj Arora
Haneet Gandhi

SHIPRA

Rs 550; US$ 22

ISBN: 978-93-91978-23-5

2025 Impression
(2023, 2022 PoD, First Published in 2021)

National Education Policy 2020:
Paving ways for Transformational Reforms

Published by:
SHIPRA PUBLICATIONS
LG 18-19, Pankaj Central Market
I.P. Ext., Patparganj, Delhi 110092, India
+91 11 47322068; 96500 28065, 9810522367
info@shiprapublication.com
www.shiprapublication.com

This book is dedicated to

our beloved ones,

Mrs. Bimla Arora, Mrs. Bhagwan Devi,
Dr. Virender Kumar Arora & Dr. Nisha Singh,

who left us for Heavenly Abode during
the journey of writing this book.

Contents

Professor M. Jagadesh Kumar
Vice Chancellor

जवाहरलाल नेहरू विश्वविद्यालय
Jawaharlal Nehru University

Foreword

Being informed of and conscious about the status of education in India for the past so many years, I was pleased when the Government of India shared its vision for improving the education system of India through National Education Policy, 2020. We know NEP 2020 offers suggestions for making our country prosperous and self-reliant. The policy envisions the youth as thoughtful, learned, informed and critical beings. Indeed the policy offers many promising proposals for overhauling the entire education structure of the country.

For a non-expert, decoding any policy is not a simple task. It is not easy to comprehend a policy, understand its connections to the existing scenarios and offer suggestions for its smooth implementation. Often we need help from learned scholars to explain the intents of the policy in a simple, understandable and actionable way. This tough task has been undertaken by Professor Pankaj Arora, Professor Usha Sharma and Dr. Haneet Gandhi who have taken the initiative of bringing out a volume of two books on NEP 2020. The editors have done a magnanimous work of reaching out to some of the veterans in the field of education and having compiled their thoughts and suggestions on the implementation of NEP 2020.

A very important aspect of NEP pertains to the practical aspects related with how to implement the policy's recommendations. Every chapter of the book offers a well-researched, deeply profound insight on issues emanating from NEP 2020. The authors have put across unbiased factual information with ample scope for discussion and deliberation on the implementation of the policy in a time-bound yet effective manner. They also suggest certain actionable plans for effective reach-out throughout the country. Some challenges in meeting the targets of the policy are also highlighted.

Reading these two books was both enjoyable and insightful to me. I can see that these volumes will be very enriching for national and state curriculum makers, educationists and all associated with the field of Education. Since these volumes have been conceptualised in both Hindi and English, it will reach out to a large number of stakeholders, benefit them in drawing theoretical and practical ideas for the fulfilment of NEP 2020.

Congratulations to Professor Pankaj Arora, Professor Usha Sharma and Dr Haneet Gandhi for the bringing out this volume!

With best compliments!

Professor M. Jagadesh Kumar
Vice Chancellor
Jawaharlal Nehru University
New Delhi-110067

June 21, 2021 [International Yoga Day]

प्रो. धीरेन्द्र पाल सिंह
अध्यक्ष
Prof. D. P. Singh
Chairman

सत्यमेव जयते

विश्वविद्यालय अनुदान आयोग
शिक्षा मंत्रालय, भारत सरकार
University Grants Commission
Ministry of Education, Govt. of India

Message

It gives me immense pleasure as I pen-down my message for the edited book on National Education Policy 2020. At this juncture, when we are ready to embrace the National Education Policy with open arms, this book will show us the steps for achieving the goals that have been set ahead by the policy, especially for overhauling the education system for a better India. The editors of the book, Professor Pankaj Arora, Professor Usha Sharma and Dr. Haneet Gandhi had been very thoughtful in bringing out two volumes, one in Hindi and other in English to benefit a large number of scholars.

A quick glance on the chapters of the books narrates the journey that the editors would have taken while contextualizing these books. Each chapter has been chosen mindfully, synchronizing to the themes of NEP-2020. The books are nothing less than a vivid bouquet of ideas, suggestions and challenges, since every chapter has been carefully crafted by eminent educationists who are familiar with the education system of our country.

I congratulate the editors and authors for bringing out such a valuable resource at a time when it is needed the most.

Best wishes for successful publication of the Book

(D.P. Singh)

New Delhi
21st June, 2021
[International Yoga Day]

बहादुरशाह ज़फ़र मार्ग, नई दिल्ली-110002, Bahadur Shah Zafar Marg, New Delhi-110002
दूरभाष Phone: कार्यालय Off. : 011-23234019, 23236350, फैक्स Fax: 011-23239659, e-mail : cu.ugc@nic.in | web: www.ugc.ac.in

Professor V. K. Malhotra
Member Secretary,
Indian Council of Social Science Research

Indian Council of
Social Science Research

Message

It gives me immense pleasure as I pen-down my message for the two edited books on National Education Policy-2020. At this important juncture, when the whole nation is keenly waiting for the implementation of the National Education Policy, I believe this book will be able to indicate the steps for attaining the goals set under the policy, especially those emerging out of the need to overhaul the education system for a new and much advanced India.

The editors of the book, namely, Professor Pankaj Arora, Professor Usha Sharma and Dr. Haneet Gandhi have been quite thoughtful in bringing out these two volumes, one in Hindi and other in English, for the benefits of a large number of scholars across the country. A quick glance on the chapters of the books narrates the journey that the editors have voyaged while contextualizing these books. Each chapter has been chosen consciously to synchronize well with the themes of NEP-2020. Since every chapter has been painstakingly authored by eminent educationists who are familiar with the education system of our country, the books appear to be nothing less than a vivid bouquet of well-crafted ideas, implementable suggestions and likely challenges.

The book has attempted to open up a debate on the 'Indianisation' of the Indian Education System in the backdrop of recent writings of the thinkers and eminent educationists who have been deeply concerned about the aberrations that occurred due to the colonial impact on our education system.

The book aptly highlights the role and importance of Indian higher education and the need for its restructuring on philosophical base and also from the point of view of contents. The editors have made appreciable efforts in bringing out the essence of the NEP-2020 through the write-ups aiming at establishing

Indian ethos based vibrant education system for transforming the nation and improving the curriculum and pedagogy in order to inculcate a deep sense of reverence towards the fundamental duties and constitutional values, bonding with the nation, and a conscious awareness of one's roles and responsibilities in an ever changing world.

I must congratulate the editors and authors who have succeeded in the phenomenal task of encompassing all major thematic areas of the NEP-2020 in just one volume and making the book very valuable resource at an appropriate time.

With Best Compliments!

Professor V. K. Malhotra
Member Secretary,
Indian Council of Social Science Research,
New Delhi-110067

June 21, 2021 [International Yoga Day]

About the Book

National Education Policy 2020, a long awaited document to give a new vision and mission to the Indian education, was released by the Government of India on 29 July 2020. After 34 years, we have witnessed a reformatory document that recommends overhauling the entire education for a better future of the country. The Policy not only envisions a new education structure, it also offers a robust vision for encouraging the youth to recognise and respect Indian culture and values, make connections with the scientific world and prepare for global challenges. This education policy seeks to establish new dimensions of inclusion, innovation and institutionalisation in the Indian educational system. The policy urges to strengthen the processes that must be undertaken to educate the youth rather than on paying attention to the outcome; thereby emphasising on "how to learn" over "what to learn".

The arrival of National Education Policy 2020 also brought with it a 'box' of many possibilities, challenges and solutions, which need to be kept in mind. The most important among them is the urge to preserve the heritage, culture and art of our country. Efforts have also been made to think deep about school education and higher educationto be close to'ground reality'. Implementation of policy points is complex in itself, but at the same time it also requires that the thematic concepts are clearly understood.

As per our past experience, we had noticed that whenever education policies were announced in the past, such as those of 1968 and 1986, the students, researchers and teachers of the educational world struggled hard to decode the tenets of the policies. They found it difficultto decipher the understated aspects, often mentioned as 'reading in between the lines' and to critically review them. We all know that education policies are often not written in an easy-to-comprehend language and style, at least at the face value, so it is very important to decode them for an easy comprehension, telling people what lies "between the lines" to enable them think and review critically. The same concerns were seen after the release of NEP 2020 also.Soon after the release of the new education policy, efforts to understand it started pouring in through webinars, discussion forums, print and social media. Educationists were seen engaging in deliberations and debates. However, all such efforts were being held in a scattered manner. A need to compile such deliberations and debates was felt. A large community of readers, policy-makers, students and scholars, intellectuals and others wished to have a resource that provided a comprehensive outlook on the various aspects of Policy along with shared directions for its implementation. They were eagerly waiting for a book that presented the opinions of experts on the implementation of NEP 2020. Realising this responsibility, the editors of the current book thought of bringing out this publication wherein scholars who have been actively deliberating on Indian education for a long time can share their views, deliberations, concerns and suggestions. The editors were fortunate in this endeavour as very soon a suitable group of authors could be identified and they consented whole-heartedly to write chapters in the area of their expertise. A specific purpose of the present book is to help students, researchers and teachers in the field of education to have a detailed understanding of the various contexts and proposals of education policy and to clarify their views in the context of education policy.The genesis of this book thus emerged. This book in your hand, '*National Education Policy 2020: Towards Constructive Reforms*' offers a anthology of views, debates and suggestions on various aspects of National Education Policy 2020.

It also gives us pleasure to share with youthat all the authors of the book and both members of the editorial board are not only continuously associated with the education world for more than 15 years, they are also actively involved in their research and knowledge dissemination. All the chapters of the book are authored by experienced subject-experts, educationists in their respective fields of knowledge and people involved at the national-level policy making. Each author has placed a mark in the educational world from their scholarship. While writing the chapters, every author analysed at least one dimension of the policy, conducted an extensive research in that area thereby presenting their views after deep reflection. The authors of each of the chapters included in the book have tried to elaborate and deepen the relevant aspects of education with utmost sincerity and analytical point of view which will surely benefit teachers, teacher-educators, policy-makers, community members as well as all the stakeholders. One of the main objectives of writing this book is to analyse every paragraph of the Education Policy with a critical lensand present it as a rich reading material for our readers.

Covering the expanse of the educative world, this book has witnessed a long journey of contemplation. All the chapters were developed through several rounds of discussions, dialogues and peer-review so that the readers are offered avenues to think afresh about education. Whether it is about the Indianness of India's education or its language, art and culture, mathematics, science or technology, higher education or pre-primary education, all themes have been covered in the textbook. The readers will get opportunity to get acquainted to teacher-preparation and teacher-education, children's childhood and youth's literacy, inclusion and holistic education, vocational and professional education, research and life-long learning, and digital world entering education – all have played an important role in nurturing the core concept of education. To bring coherence in chapters, the experts were requested to write their views, suggestions and concerns on Education Policy as a roadmap.Each chapter follows the following format of writing:

- Introduction to the aspect shared in NEP
- Perspectives on the aspect presented in the previous education policies

- Present status
- Suggestions given in the NEP
- Roadmap for implementing the aspect
- Critical points, perspectives and suggestions.

The book comprises of 21 chapters and each chapter covers an important aspect of NEP. The first chapter titled, *National Education Policy 2020: Charting its Uniqueness and Recommendations* explicates the salient aspects of the policy through three sections on School Education, Higher Education and Teacher Education. The next chapter, *Language, Education and Language Policy of Education*is a very significant chapter as it emphasises on the identity of any 'nation' fundamentally getting reflected from the lifestyle, culture and language of its people. The chapter encapsulates the 'linguistic scenario' of the country and its role in education. One would agree that in the context of education, it is necessary to understand that learning is never an accumulative concept nor of cumulative nature; and teachers have a crucial role to play in building such ethos. Chapter three of the book, *Creating and maintaining the honour of Teachers: A Profound Vision of NEP* talks about the education, roles and responsibilities that NEP assumes for the future teachers. Continuing on the spirits of learning, the next chapter, *Children, Childhood and Education* recognises the fact that for the education of the children of our country, it is important to understand the nature and characteristics of the Indian children and the conditions in which they live. The author of this chapter critically questions how basic education and lives of children have been a neglected area so far. Chapter 5, *A Site for Curriculum and Pedagogy* presents connections with past policies to analyse the future prospects and reforms in the Indian school education.Two chapters of the book, namely *Inclusive Education for Equity and Equality,* and *Equity and Inclusion in Higher Education* provide various criteria for identifying the socio-economically disadvantaged groups and people with disabilities. The authors of these chapters suggest various strategies and initiatives that should be taken both at school and in higher education for achieving equitable and inclusive education. The new policy has tried to address the concerns of schools by proposing to establish school complexes or clusters. Chapter 6, *Decentralisation of Schooling through School Complexes and Clusters* shares in detail how this idea will transform the education scenario. The next chapter of the book, *Indianness in Education: Foundational Key for a Self-Reliant India* urges on imbibing 'Indianness' as a quintessential component of the educational discourse. The next two chapters, namely *Reading and Writing: A Strong Foundation for Literacy* and *Foundational Numeracy: A Quintessential Ingredient for a Developing Nation* are about enhancing and developing a conceptual understanding of foundational literacy and numeracy among teachers. Throughout the policy there is a strong emphasis on adopting multidisciplinary approach in education at all levels. The chapter *Multidisciplinary Approach to Education: Effective Teaching-Learning Routines* captures the nuances of multidisciplinary approach with illustrative examples. Another aspect that has emerged strongly in the NEP is that of vocational education. The chapter, *NEP 2020 Recommendations on Vocational Education: A Critical Analysis, and the Way Forward* shares a realistic picture of the status of vocational education and also recommends ways on imbibing lifelong learning of such courses. The chapter, *Pursuits of Strengthening Academic Research* brings to the fore the missing link between industry and academic research that has resulted in creating a lacuna in acknowledging some of the significant researches. The author shares how NEP will strengthen researches in India. There are three chapters in the book, namely, *Genesis, Current Status and Future of Higher Education in India, Structure and Paradigm of Indian Higher Education System,* and *Governance and Leadership in Higher Education* talk aboutaims, objectives and changes that are necessary and desirable for the functionary and jurisdiction of universities and Higher Education Institutes in India. The chapter titled, *Rise and Future of Professional Education in India* explicitly expresses the concern related to agricultural universities, law universities, health science universities and technical universities. NEP 2020 is a vision document and intertwines all the aspects of education for a growing, glowing India. The next chapter, *NEP's Vision on Strengthening Adult Education and Lifelong Learning* mentions the role of ODL programmes at school level by NIOS and SIOS to address adult literacy. India is a global technology leader in information and communication. The Digital India Campaign is helping to transform the entire nation into a digitally empowered society and knowledge economy. The chapter, *Preparing for E-Education through Online and Digital Resources* mentions nuances of Digital India as envisioned in NEP. The Government of India has envisaged inculcation of SDG 4 and its goals in NEP 2020 through effective recommendations concerning the entire educational structure. The last chapter of the book, *Education for Sustainability: One of the Pillars of Quality Education* explains the idea and mission of India for a sustainable India.

The proposed book will help the readers form an informed opinion about the Indian educational system and at the same time try to understand the possibilities for future generations. The chapters are written in such a way so as to help readers relish every aspect of NEP with a distinct flavor of critically.

We are also glad on the timing of this book. This time of the year is most appropriate to launch the book as we have completed a year of the launch of the National Education Policy 2020 and many aspects of the policy have already started to be implemented all across the country. We hope, the discussions presented in the book will help the readers to dig deeper intothe recommendations and 'ground' implementation of the policy. This book provides an opportunity to all the stakeholders to maintain the element of 'education' while discharging their respective responsibilities. The basic objective is to make every effort to makeeducation accessible to all children.

Hope you will benefit by reading this book as it clarifies your thoughts to become a resource for future reference in your journey in the field of education.

Your suggestions and comments are welcome!

Professor Pankaj Arora • Professor Haneet Gandhi

15.08.2021 (Independence Day)
New Delhi

1

National Education Policy 2020: Charting its Uniqueness and Recommendations

Pankaj Arora

The moment we hear the word 'Policy', our attention immediately shifts to the contexts under which the mentioned 'Policy' would have been conceived. Policies can be agents of change having the potential to transform the lives of citizens for generations. The National Education Policy of 2020 is an appropriate example in this regard. Like the Industrial Policy of 1956, the National Educational Policies of 1968 and 1986, the Economic Liberalisation and Reform policies of 1990, the National Education Policy 2020 aims to make India a progressive, conscientious and humane society with a strong cultural fabric. In order to understand the impact of the Policy on the Indian Education system, it is important to look at the policy document through a lens so as to ascertain whether the document paves the way for a robust, growth-centred, culturally rich and diverse, inclusive society. It is also important to envision if the policy connects India and the young Indians with the global scenarios of developmental goals.

On its part, the National Education Policy 2020 envisages multidisciplinary educational institutions where the rigid silos around subject disciplines are broken and the education is viewed as being multidisciplinary and inter-disciplinary in nature. As a change-maker, it abolishes the hierarchies amongst different subject disciplines like sciences, management, engineering and gives equal emphasis to social sciences and language education. In these multidisciplinary educational institutions, every subject will be important and the teaching will also be held in an inter-disciplinary way. The path of inter-disciplinary research will also be paved. In the education policy, importance has been given to Indian knowledge and traditions, as well as cultural values and Indian languages. In the new education policy, there is a possibility that in the coming times we will be able to joyously celebrate our knowledge and be proud of it by not just being a mindless follower of any foreign knowledge. The provision of the National Research Foundation provides a foundation for the research process carried out by these disciplines and institutions. This education policy has raised the importance of bringing

Professor, Department of Education [CIE], University of Delhi, Delhi

the global values of the Indian Constitution to the students with prominence. These constitutional values, along with global values like equality, social justice as well as fundamental duties should be effectively delivered to the younger generation and all these have been advocated to be associated with lifestyle.

The National Education Policy 2020 recognizes the importance of teachers and teacher-education and recommends the need to work on both of them. Kothari Commission in 1964-66 followed by Chattopadhyay Commission of 1983 recommended extensive reforms in teacher-education but due to the changed political conditions, the recommendations of these commissions could not be implemented effectively. The Education Policy of 1986 also reduced the importance of these significant commissions. In the race for materialistic economic resources, concern for the ever-disappearing dignity and respect of teachers also forms an integral part of new policy of education. A teacher, at the ground level, forms a crucial connection who will give shape to this education policy and be instrumental in the effective implementation of the education policy. NEP seeks to attract talented, bright young minds to the profession of teaching.

Providing quality education to the students is an important and necessary aspect that the education policy aims to create for not only the marginalised communities and sections but also for the inclusion of children with special concerns and attention.

To understand the broader aspects of the National Education Policy 2020, it is being presented here in three sections–1. School Education; 2. Higher Education; and 3. Teacher Education

School Education

The first eight chapters of the education policy present various important aspects proposed in the context of school education of India. After independence, various education commissions and committees have reported the concerns related to school education with a focus on bringing all children to schools. Although the National Policy on Education 1986 also emphasised this, the Right to Education 2009 was an important milestone in this direction. The NEP 2020 puts forth a new structure that aims to strengthen the Right to Education and help young Indians to secure a stable and better future.

The basic underlying principle of the policy aims at creating conscientious human beings who are capable of rational thinking and action, including compassion and empathy, courage and resilience, scientific thinking and creative imaginations. The education policy talks of the preparation of positive people who can recognise and play a vibrant role in building an inclusive and pluralistic society, as also laid down in the Constitution of India.

New Structure of School Education

The vision of the National Education Policy is to promote an educational system which is in synchronisation with the Indian values and will contribute to develop equitable knowledge and society by providing high quality education to all. The education policy proposes to integrate the fundamental rights and constitutional values in the curriculum and teaching methods in school education to awaken youth about their role and responsibility as a citizen in the changing world. It also strengthens the 10+2 school education structure and introduces a new school education structure of 5+3+3+4.

Based on this policy, all children between 3 to 18 years of age will be brought under the school education. The Right to Education Act, 2009 ensured education of children from the age of six years to 14 years as their fundamental right. This education policy also provides opportunities for the children under the age of six years in the formal education system. The proposed structure of school education talks of the first five years as the foundation of education, akin to Gandhi's idea of basic education. Research from the field of neuroscience and psychology tells us that 85% of the brain develops in children up to the age of six years. By linking it to an education system that finds its genesis in a multi-dimensional, game-based, activity-based learning environment, the National Education Policy 2020 aims to enrich the younger generation of India with an education that is rich in culture, knowledge and experience.

According to the policy, early childhood education will be provided to the children up to the age of eight years. This education will be in two parts with the aim of achieving maximum results in the development of early literacy and numeracy. It is targeted to reach all students universally for which Anganwadi centres will be upgraded with trained workers/teachers. Efforts will be made to implement early childhood education through Ashramshalas in the remote, backward and tribal districts. The newly proposed Ministry of Education will function with the NCERT to ensure that all students develop the capacity to carry out basic operations in terms of numbers, which form the basis for life-long learning.

In order to achieve the objectives of the basic literacy and numeracy by the year 2025, the governments of the states and union territories will make plans to implement it by identifying the intentions in a phased manner. A national repository of high quality resources will be made available for basic literacy and numeracy on platforms such as The Digital Infrastructure for Knowledge Sharing (DIKSHA). Recruitment and training of teachers will be ensured on priority. The National Policy on Education aims to achieve a 100% gross enrolment ratio from pre-school to secondary school level by 2020, that includes reducing the dropout rate of students.

The new structure of 5+3+3+4, presented in the education policy, is for pre-school, preparatory level, middle level and secondary level for children between the age of 3-8 years, 8-11 years, 11-14 years and 14-18 years respectively. The period of five years of basic education is the time of perception building and the development of content and pedagogy with the help of corresponding activities. This is a stage of conceptual knowledge in elementary education, and there will be promotion of teaching through dialogue in the classroom, including reading, writing, speaking, art, language, etc.

Secondary level education which is of three years, is the stage for working on perspectives and beliefs. This will be taken up in science, mathematics, arts, sports, humanities and professional subjects with interesting ways of pedagogy. Thereafter, it will be followed by four years of multidisciplinary studies at secondary school level. At this stage, flexible choice of subjects will be made available to students taking into account their abstract knowledge, critical thinking and life aspirations.

Home Language / Mother Tongue, Multilingualism and Various Professional Skills

Multilingualism and the power of language have been given its due importance in school education. Young children will be educated in their home language / mother tongue or the language spoken by the local community. Realising the sensitivity of the three-language formula, it has been said that it should be implemented through the education policy, but at the same time, the need to make it flexible has also been acknowledged. No language will be imposed on any state. Students will be able to choose the languages themselves and two out of three languages will be Indian; later in Class VI or VII, students can also change their language.

The education policy seeks to implement the three-language formula, keeping in view the need for promoting multilingualism and national integration in accordance with the provisions of Indian Constitution. For the first time in independent India, a policy has aimed at standardising the Indian sign-language all over the country and developing its course material at state and national level.

Today's era is the era of Artificial Intelligence and robotic science. Connecting important contemporary subjects like environment, health, organic-learning, etc. to students' knowledge, development and the academic pursuit in this regard will be promoted. Adolescent boys and girls from Class VI will be introduced to various vocational skills. Vocational education opportunities will be provided to them during school vacation. Some vocational programmes will also be developed through online education. The education policy has presented an agenda before NCERT which is to prepare a new comprehensive National Curriculum Framework for school education, NCF-2021. Textbooks will be written at national level and will include the local content.

Comprehensive Evaluation

Along with all of the above, quite detailed suggestions have been given for the evaluation of school students. One of the main recommendations is that the IQ (Intelligence Quotient) based examination system (which is primarily meant to evaluate cognitive domain) will be replaced by an EQ (Emotional Quotient) based comprehensive assessment model, aimed at evaluating students' competencies.

School-cluster Model

Another important change in the context of school education is the introduction of 'School-Cluster Model'. This model has the potential to promote resource sharing as well as optimum use of the administrative expertise. This suggestion of the school cluster seems to actualise the 'Common-School System' which was one of the important recommendations of Kothari Commission, 1966. As per this suggestion in NEP, schools at different levels of education will be in the same or adjoining premises. Here, administratively, the Principal of the higher school will ensure the optimum use of all available resources. This would include resources of sports, music, and art as well as sharing of some of the key laboratories.

This way, we can see that the first eight chapters of the Education Policy give importance to almost all aspects of school education and explain each one of them in detail. The suggested changes in the school education ranges from its structure, teaching styles, the preparation of textbooks and importance to be given to languages. The proposal of the NCF-2021 would help in making it a holistic education policy. The education policy seeks to change the basis of assessment, give importance to board examinations (twice in a year) and eliminate the culture of coaching throughout the examinations and entrance-based admissions. The goal of egalitarian and inclusive education presents a roadmap to formulate plans at the state level, keeping in mind the need and contexts of children from socially and economically diverse backgrounds, including transgender and children with special needs.

Higher Education

Section II of the National Education Policy is presented in a total of 11 chapters (9–19). Each chapter discusses a crucial aspect related to 'higher education' of our country. Considering the needs of the 21st century, quality higher education can develop from a democratic, just, socially conscious brotherhood which would promote social welfare, a sense of justice, freedom and equality for all. Higher education with vocational, technical and professional subjects which are necessary for the 21st century will provide a satisfactory life to the younger generation and enable their economic independence.

The education policy aims at providing equal opportunities for inclusive quality higher education with aspirations for transforming the higher education system and adding fresh momentum to it. Higher education will take place in multidisciplinary and holistic universities and colleges. In these multidisciplinary institutes, students will have freedom to choose subjects that suit their own academic tastes and professional needs.

Students will be able to choose their subjects for their graduation and further education in accordance with their choice and abilities. This will also break the hierarchies of stream-based subjects in higher education. All subjects are important and their selection should be tailored to the student's own interests.

This policy will prevent fragmentation of higher education by developing higher education institutions as large and multidisciplinary clusters/knowledge hubs. Examples are given from ancient universities like Takshashila, Nalanda, Vikramshila, etc. where thousands of students from India and other countries used to take lessons on life and develop multidisciplinary perspectives. It is also proposed that in a phased manner, universities will be given graded autonomy.

Autonomous Students / Autonomous Teachers / Autonomous Institutions

The education policy of 2020 has given freedom to students to choose their subjects as well as the freedom to regularise their higher education. The ever-increasing dropout rate at the university level was not only a waste of a student's personal resources and time, but was also becoming a serious concern at the national level. The present education policy gives multiple options to students so as to help them continue their studies. One important option is the proposed change in the duration and structure of degree programmes. Students will not only be able to choose major and minor subjects according to their interest, but will also get the opportunities to experience holistic and multidisciplinary education. If for any reason a student drops out of her/his course of graduation, s/he will be awarded a certificate based on the duration of studies s/he has invested in. Thus, there will be a provision of pursuing one-year studies leading to certification, a diploma based on 2-year studies and a bachelor's degree on 3-year studies. A 4-year undergraduate student will take advantage of specialisation and research-based courses to acquire a 4-year bachelor's honours degree.

The students will be able to resume their studies at any point of time to complete the academics wherever they had to leave incomplete. This provision has been prepared on the basis of multi-entry / multi-exit scheme which is an innovative idea of NEP 2020. The credit of all the studies that a student has done will be preserved in her/his digi locker. The number of credits will increase as the student goes on to do further studies and will qualify her/him for certificate, diploma, degree, etc. Higher education institutions have been aimed to become multidisciplinary institutions by 2030. Simultaneously, the Gross Enrolment Ratio (GER) has been proposed to be increased from 26.3% in 2018 to 50% by 2035. In order to enhance the reach of higher educational institutions, provisions of SDG4, promotion of open and distance education (ODL) and online education will be promoted. It is important to mention here that in this regard the UGC Resolution, 2020, Gazette of India has already been announced on 4 September 2020.

It is important to understand the concept of autonomy for teachers too. The education policy gives freedom to teachers of the universities to develop various specialisation-based curriculums. Teachers have autonomy to develop need-based new academic fields and to also apply those specialised courses at an individual level. Such autonomy will now be available to teachers of universities. This will not only open new avenues of learning and teaching but will also open new avenues of expansion of knowledge through research.

Another important dimension of NEP 2020 is the new regulatory system which will grant graded autonomy to the educational institutions with the aim to empower and authorise them. This will also pave ways for promoting innovation and making institutions more responsible. Many large universities in India are burdened with affiliated colleges. A lot of energy and resources of these universities get absorbed in conducting examinations for these affiliated colleges and declaring their results. On the other hand, these affiliated colleges keep focusing on increasing the enrolment level of students to generate more fees. Little attention is given to improving the condition of labs, sports facilities or even faculty development. It's time these colleges start owning responsibility and accountability. As per the new education policy, after attaining autonomy, these colleges will not only have to update their courses and conduct examinations, they will also be given the responsibility to give degrees and make their degrees significant in the students' community and job market. These colleges will have to raise their academic standards and maintain them at a regular basis. In the present context, this culture of affiliated colleges has been promoting the ill-practice of license-raj and have become centres of different types of corruption. In such a situation, if they are given autonomy then along with the students, the society and education at large will improve manifold.

Liberal Arts and Research

Holistic and multidisciplinary education has potential to develop all the capabilities of human beings in an integrated manner, be it intellectual, aesthetic, social, physical, emotional or moral. This type of education can become a means for a well-balanced person who could be equipped in the disciplines of humanities, sciences, language, social science along with possessing abilities in professional and technical knowledge. The person will surely be possessing competencies of the 21st century as s/he will be fluent in her/his behavioural skills (soft skills), communication, discussion, and debates. The policy envisages a liberal education structure that will enable a creative combination of subjects for study. The choice of multiple entry and exit will promote the young generation to the possibilities of life-long learning beyond conservative disciplinary boundaries. The policy also talks to promote quality research at Ph.D level, at the same time it proposes to do away with the M.Phil programme, which according to me should have been done long back.

The nature of universities will be redefined as 'research-intense university' or 'teaching-intensive university'. Start-up, industry based research and innovation based research will be promoted in all the institutions of higher education. In order to promote international education, transfer of credit to the research sector will be made flexible. At the same time, flexible rules will be prepared to facilitate scholars from other countries as well. The meritorious students for higher education and research will be inspired through a number of schemes. The establishment of the National Research Council (NRC) would entail a comprehensive approach and a collaborative approach to research and innovation. The nature of research must be valued for the solution of social problems. It should be leading to intellectual satisfaction along with recognition and progress of the country. In the midst of all this, Indian knowledge, India culture, Indian languages and Indian values will also be given priority.

Regulatory System of Higher Education

Education policy suggests refurbishing the regulatory system of higher education under the principle of 'light but tight' and having a facilitative approach. The Higher Education Commission of India (HECI) will be set up for higher education regulation and there will be four vertical regulatory agencies under it which will be assigned specific regulatory work. Such a structure will be helpful to eliminate the clash of mutual hits between different roles. It will establish the principle of separating the roles and functions of each from the other. It also aims to empower higher education institutions by focusing on some basic issues.

The national responsibilities and accountability associated with this will be in line with higher education institutions. There will be no distinction between public and private educational institutions.

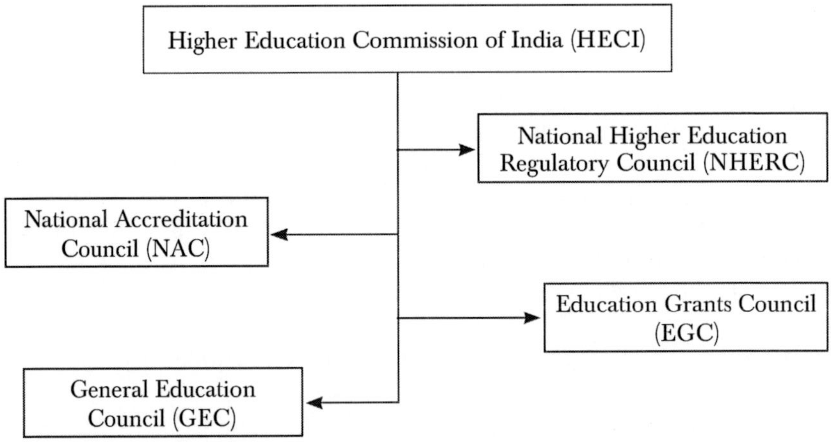

Effective administration and leadership for higher education institutions will also be promoted. Thus, the second part of the Education Policy 2020 presents detailed views and recommendations on almost all aspects of higher education.

Education and Teacher Education

If 'education' is a discipline?

When we hear or read the word 'education', immediately the image of a school flashes into our minds. This is a common visual perception related to education. However, if our vision gets confined to education only within the school boundaries, then we need to rethink, as this would be a limited approach. We need to think of education beyond the four boundaries of a 'school'. Many such experiences are part of the world of education. Sometimes personal, sometimes collective! There are a number of conflicting situations where there is often a discussion on 'education', but the education departments of universities, with their little recognition, are still struggling for their identity.

Many questions arise in this context. What happens in the education departments of the university? Is there actually some teaching related work taking place? Or has their role been delimited to only administrative departments? It is painful to say that even today clarification has to be given that 'education' is a discipline and in the education departments teaching takes place in the context of B.Ed./M.Ed and research in the area of 'Education'. Even in universities, many people do not know that just as there is a Faculty of Arts or Faculty of Science, there also exists a 'Faculty of Education'. The question arises why do people not consider 'education' as an academic discipline? Perhaps, people of the education sector themselves did not make sufficient efforts to establish education as an academic discipline. Of course, education is an interdisciplinary subject but it was never meant to remain that way. It has now emerged and established as a discipline with its unique identity and epistemology. Those who have failed to regard or acknowledge 'education' as a discipline need to rethink. One of the reasons for this limited viewpoint can be associated with the functioning of the education departments and of all those teaching in the education faculties who have till now not been able to establish education as a discipline. Nearly 60 years ago, when the Kothari Commission talked about establishing 'education' as an academic discipline, the Commission rephrased teachers' preparation from 'teachers training' to 'teacher education'. This was the first important move in accomplishing 'education' as a discipline.

Unfortunately, this problem has been transformed into a 'problem of identity' of an important academic subject. This question arises because no one has ever tried to establish 'education' as an area of teaching/learning or research. For a long time, it has been projected that those who regularly read newspapers or listen to television discussions on current topics are experts of political science, which is not the case as Political Science is a much deeper discipline and not just limited to the understanding of the articles printed in the newspaper or the current debates on television. As a discipline, Political Science includes its own principles, theory and philosophy. Almost a similar debate and struggle is seen with the Education discipline. The worry is not because of the people who declare themselves as educationists with a half-baked understanding of education, but it is more worrying with those who are already working in the field of Education. These should have promoted the sense of curriculum, textbooks, and evaluation methods as envisioned by educationists. We do not have any reservation to accept a very small section of such understandings as an exception. In order to understand the concerns of society, a degree of discipline is not always necessary but the concern increases when a person of Physics declares or is considered to be an expert of Political Science after writing a few articles on politics.

In the same way, the ability to place our views on certain aspects of education can lead us to the illusion of being an educationist. Understanding the mathematics that is used in everyday life and working on your daily maths concerns should not give the illusion of being a mathematician. Similarly, any general knowledge of education or criticism of the system of examination is not adequate to be an educationist. There should be a clear difference between the two things –One is the result of practical common understanding while the other is an expertise based on theoretical studies and research.

'Education' has two distinct forms

'Education' is not only a discipline but it has two distinct forms. One is its 'liberal side' which is taught and studied like any other discipline of social science. Another form of the discipline, 'Education' is a professional face where its primary function is to promote research on various problems associated with educational institutions and students, make teaching more interesting and relating it with contemporary technology. The professional aspect of 'education' interprets the principles of curriculum development, pedagogy and evaluation. The first form of education is promoted by degrees such as B.A. and M.A. (Education); or rather, is studied and taught as a liberal discipline. Its second form, which is professional, is identified by acquiring degrees such as B.Ed., M.Ed., D.Ed. or B.El.Ed. In short, we call it 'Teacher Education', which is the desired professional qualification to become a teacher. M.A. (Education) and M.Ed present liberal side and professional side of education respectively. An obvious question that arises here is that when both are postgraduate degrees, what is the difference between them? To understand their differences, you can take the example of 'psychologist' and 'psychiatrist'. In some form or the other, we all are psychologists – as a teacher, as a parent or as an experienced adult. But a 'psychiatrist' not only provides advice but also provides essential medication. Therefore, these can also be understood as liberal aspect and professional aspect of the disciple of psychology respectively.

Teacher Education

'Education' is an academic discipline and teacher education is its professional face. This face prepares students for a particular occupation. Akin to how teacher education is seen worldwide. India also needs specific professional regulatory institutions to promote professional education and to ensure its qualitative improvement from time to time. Parallels can be drawn from Medical Council of India for medical education, Bar Council for legal education and AICTE for engineering education. These regulatory bodies consist of administrators and subject-specific experts. These professional regulatory bodies not only allow relevant teaching institutions to meet the needs of a particular profession but also redefine the needs and challenges of that professional course from time to time. Similarly, National Council of Teacher Education (NCTE) was established in the year 1993 by an Act of Parliament for the regulation of teacher education institutions. However, till date, there is confusion about the structure of the NCTE, whether it is administrative or academic? If we look at the leadership of this institution, we would find that sometimes the chairperson of this institution is a teacher-educator and sometimes it is a bureaucrat.

Since its inception, most of the attention and energy of NCTE institution has been expended in accrediting newly opened institutions of teacher education. Though there are four regional offices of this institution, their focus is more on recognising new B.Ed institutions and inspecting their infrastructure. The institution does not have a single permanent academic member or academic unit to attend to the important work such as improving the nature of teacher education programmes and upgrading them according to the needs of the time. NCTE depends on the cluster of borrowed experts for its core mandate of maintaining the quality and regularity of teacher education.

Although the 'cluster of borrowed experts' is a harsh term, the reality is even harder! The quality of 'teacher education' is the key to the entire education system. It is through quality teachers that we can effectively reach the students in schools and make our classroom a centre of interesting, innovative and critical pedagogy. One of the main reasons for the steady decline of the teacher education institutions is the faulty criteria adopted for recruitment and promotion of the teacher educators, which at present is determined by UGC. In 'teacher education', the standards of recruitment and promotion have been kept at par with any other discipline of social sciences. This, too, is one of the main causes of continuous qualitative deterioration in teacher education.

Now that the new education policy has been announced, NCTE has to understand its larger role which is both academic as well as administrative. It will have to make desired and unavoidable changes in the recruitment and promotion rules of teacher-educators, keeping in mind the specific needs of the teacher-education curriculum, school-internship as well as activities of teacher-education institutions. These changes should not only motivate teacher-educators but will also be acceptable in their professional growth.

We all know that a 'teacher' is the centre point who will embody all these reforms and far-reaching goals on the ground. In such a situation, it becomes very important to understand how the new education policy considers 'teacher education'. In this policy, instead of the existing 17 types of teacher education programmes, three major programmes have been given space. 4-year Integrated Teacher Education Programme (ITEP) which undertakes teacher education for primary, upper-primary and secondary-school education. This 4-year ITEP invites young students, after Class XII, who aspire to become teachers at school level. Being associated with teacher education, I can say that this change will prove to be a milestone in improving the state of teachers in India. With this proposal, now qualitative changes can be made in teacher education which have been pending for years. At the same time, youngsters who intend to join school teaching after completing their 4-year graduation or post-graduation will be invited into the teaching profession through one-year B.Ed programme.

The New Education Policy also paves the way to phase-out the present 2-year B.Ed programme by the year 2029-30. The 2-year B.Ed programme, which has always been under various question marks since its inception (2015) and has never been able to give any results as per its claims will cease to continue. In the context of teacher education, it will be important that its regulatory body (NCTE) be strengthened. This institution should not only work to give recognition to new teacher-education institutions but to also contribute in developing quality programmes for Teacher Education.

In bringing these reforms, NCTE has not only to understand its important role, but has to also make meaningful efforts without any delay. Some of them would be:

- Establishing 'education' as an important academic discipline.
- To review administrative and academic activities in teacher education institutions frequently.
- To adapt the work-culture and needs of teacher education institutions by redefining rules of recruitment and promotion of teacher educators. This is a broad educational reform that is absolutely necessary.

Conclusion

In the end, I would say that no policy is complete or good by itself. In due course of time, we should keep an eye on those many new aspects that will be opened and demand focus. Many would require changes as per the situation and time. It becomes crucial that while determining the Plan-of-Action for National Education Policy 2020, we should be restrained, sensitive and keep the windows open for future needs so that even after 15-20 years, this education policy shall remain as meaningful as it is being seen in today's context.

2

Language, Education and Language Policy of Education

C.K. Saluja

"At Cambridge University, a Professor was drowned deep into his studies in his room. An English soldier arrives in the room, and straightaway accuses the Professor of not contributing in the ongoing war against the Germans, in which the soldier and his colleagues were taking part. With a calm composure, the Professor asks the soldier–'Who is he fighting for?' The soldier replies rather quickly that he is fighting for his nation. The scholar then asks–'the nation for which you are shedding your blood, what that nation actually is?' The soldier replies that the country is the land and its people. On further inquiry, the soldier reveals that he wishes to save his culture too. The Professor says that he too is contributing to the culture of the nation. The conciliated soldier respectfully salutes the Professor and retreats from the room avowing to defend the cultural heritage of his nation with greater might."

[Quoted from a Supreme Court verdict (1994)]

The above quote is absolutely valid as the identity of any 'nation' is fundamentally assumed to get reflected from the life-style of the 'people of that nation'. Further, it is also true that the life-style of a nation is treasured in the sagas of the 'glorious literary traditions' of that nation. This glorious tradition expresses itself through the medium of language and literature as both are interlaced. In fact, literature reflects life and provides a creative basis for the 'educational tradition' for a nation. It is worth noting that the role of 'language' is not just limited to mere notification of the content by some subject-expert or through a subject-matter. 'Language' not only expresses the rich and collective life-style of a society, it also serves as a guiding light. For this reason, the issue which emerges repeatedly in the new National Education Policy 2020, is associated with the 'Indian languages'. By doing a detailed observation of the education policy, one gets a clear sense that the ultimate crux of this education policy is encapsulated in the 'linguistic scenario' of the country.

Acharya Vinoba Bhave has written about 'Basic Elements of Education' in one of his books, *Thoughts on Education.* It states, *"English rule continued here for more than a century, but science could not spread much in Hindustan. This was because all the science was captivated in the English books. Science, in real life, is related to the universe. There can be science in agriculture. There can be science in the act of cooking. There can*

Former Professor, Department of Education (C.I.E.), University of Delhi, Presently Academic Director, Samskrit Promotion Foundation, New Delhi

be science in the cleaning. In this manner, all the different parts of life require science. Since they didn't know English, millions couldn't learn science. Now, after a hundred years, it's being voiced that there is a paucity of science books in native languages. Who is guilty? Is it a crime on the part of those native languages or it's the crime committed by those who did wrong planning all these years?... If science wouldn't get connected to the mother-tongue of the learner, it would perish on its own in the very mind of the educator. We are committing a blunder. We are not thinking that if something as crucial as science won't be accessible in our native languages, how would it spread?"

(*Thoughts on Education,* Vinoba, p. 54, Sarv Sewa Sangh Prakashan, Varanasi, 7th ed., December 2016)

On one hand, the question raised by Vinoba ji in the above mentioned article is deeply connected with language-related plans proposed by policy-makers time and again with the aim of national development. On the other hand, this question also expresses the need to resort to the promise enshrined in the preamble of Indian Constitution as–"Justice-social, economic and political; Liberty of–thought, expression, faith, religion and worship; Equality of–honour and opportunity; and to achieve all these, and to ensure the dignity of the individual, and unity and integrity of the nation, Fraternity."

The Preamble of the Indian Constitution lays the foundation for the social, economic, political and social philosophy of India and seeks to articulate the various provisions of the Indian Constitution that aim to build India as a complete sovereign, socialist, secular and democratic republic with a basic objective of building an egalitarian society. It is important to note that the provision of the right of children to compulsory and free education as a fundamental right is also provided in the Constitution under Article 21 (A). This clearly implies that education is the basic foundation or means for a person to live a dignified life.

According to the Universal Declaration of Historical Human Rights adopted in the United Nations General Assembly in 1948, "Everyone has the right to education". Article 26 of the same declaration states, "Everyone has the right to education. Education shall be free, at least in the elementary and fundamental stages. Elementary education shall be compulsory." And also that "Education shall be directed to the full development of the human personality and to the strengthening of respect for human rights and fundamental freedoms." It is clear that in this statement there is a sense of building an egalitarian society and a honourable life of every person.

Stating the scenario of the new education system of India, the committee believes that "the vision of India's new education system has accordingly been crafted to ensure that it touches the life of each and every citizen, consistent with their ability to contribute to many growing developmental imperatives of this country. We have proposed the revision and revamping of all aspects of the education structure, its regulation and governance, to create a new system that is aligned with the aspirational goals of 21st century education, while remaining consistent with India's traditions and value systems." (Vision of education system in India, Draft National Education Policy 2019, page 24)

In the Preamble of the Constitution, along with mentioning India as sovereign, socialist, secular and democratic republic it also identifies justice, freedom, equality and fraternity as four pillars of Indian sovereign. Later, the words 'socialist' and 'secular' got added to the Preamble of the Constitution in 1976 through the 42nd Constitution Amendment Act. Due to this addition, the effects or implications were re-considered. Although it is clear that they have a special place and importance in individual and collective terms, various judgements in the court had to highlight these terms. They echoed that the term socialism is inherent in the sense of 'equalitarian collectivism' and the attainment of these four basic values of justice, equality, freedom and fraternity contained in the Preamble of the Indian Constitution are manifested in various provisions of the Constitution.

Language-related questions in the form of language policy are also associated at both individual and collective levels to the basic elements of the attainment of these four values. It is the language through which an individual seeks social, economic and political justice, freedom of thought, expression, faith, religion and worship, equality of dignity and opportunity; and in all of these lies the dignity of an individual and unity and integrity of a nation. It is clear that the 'question of language' associated with freedom to understand and express is basically a question of the fundamental right of a human being. Article 19 related to freedom of expression in the Indian Constitution is a strong proof of this fact. Articles 343–351 of Part 17 of the Constitution, divided into four chapters are entirely related to the State's language policy (Official Language):

(1) Language of the Union
(2) Regional languages
(3) Language of Supreme Court and High Courts and
(4) Specific instructions.

Apart from this, Articles 14, 21, 29, 30, 46, 120, 210 and the Eighth Schedule of the Indian Constitution are also directly or indirectly related to the language policy. Various judgements rendered by the courts give a clear reference to the fact that the question of language in India is theoretically linked to social justice as a fundamental right. Its relation is directly related to the individuality of an individual and, then subsequently, to the larger society. This is the reason why the courts, especially the Supreme Court, have tried to clarify various provisions of the Indian Constitution giving importance to the individual's fundamental right. In addition, the 'Fundamental Duties' as 'Part 4 (A)' to the Constitution under the 42nd Act of the Constitution Amendment, is the strongest evidence of this fact. It is evident that a well-organised and orderly social life becomes mandatory to comply with them. This is the reason that basic values like 'justice, freedom, equality and fraternity' have a special place and importance in the Preamble of the Indian Constitution. In our Constitution, they have not only been given a special and important place but an attempt has also been made to clarify what the future form of Indian society should be like! Initial words of the Preamble of the Constitution, 'We, the people of India' lead us to ponder what 'we' and 'people of India' can ultimately mean! The use of these two words indicate the characteristics of the Indian land as a nation and of the people living in it! In the judgement made by the Supreme Court in 1994, there was an attempt to make it very clear that the words 'we, the people of India' were directly used to identify India with its pride. Therefore, it becomes imperative for Sanskrit to have a special place in India's education policy. According to the Supreme Court, *'The source of our culture will dry up if we discourage the study of Sanskrit (Article 3) ... Without studying Sanskrit, it is not possible to clearly understand the Indian philosophy on which our culture and heritage is based.'*(1994 (6) SCC Report)

The various provisions of Article 51 (A) relating to fundamental duties of the Indian Constitution, especially provision (a), (b), (c), (d), (e) and (f), help us to realize our duty towards harmony in the diversity of India and also towards the preservation of India's rich culture and values. According to Article 51 (f), it is the duty of every Indian to "honour the rich heritage of our composite culture and preserve it." It is clear that *'education and culture'* are basically integral parts of life and national identity. If the ideals of life can be determined by culture then education carries out the role of the practitioner to achieve those ideals. This form of life is basically the determinant of national consciousness. However, the linguistic barrier in the Indian educational system is a sign of the fact that the education system operating in India could not be 'Indian' even while it is being *'practised in India'*. In India, education did not take its *'national'* form, even though in the Delors Report which was set up internationally in the context of education for the twenty-first century has tried to make clear that education should stand on the following four basic pillars based on the Indian philosophy of education:

- Learning to know (Education for knowledge)
- Learning to Do (Education for Karma)
- Learning to Live Together (The spirit of education to live together is basically dependent on the Rigvedic proclamation 'Samgachdhvam samvadadhvam')
- Learning to Be (Education to be a human).

It is clear that the origin of the education system of any nation is inherent in the culture of that nation, and in turn, the origin of that culture lies in the language / languages of that nation. That is why the education policy of every nation lays emphasis on language education. In the absence of this, the education system of any nation will not be able to attract the people of its nation, as a result of which theory will remain alienated from the national identity. In fact, in any nation the question related to language is essentially a fundamental question related to human rights of its citizens. At the international level, 21st February is celebrated as 'Mother Tongue' day which indicates this fact. It is also important to note that the cultural background of any person, considered as identity, is directly related to the language. Articles 28 and 29 related to the education of minorities in the Indian constitution reflect this fact. The Indian education system is highly specialised due to its multi-lingual distinctiveness. Specific attention and priority should be given to this and its essential goal and task should be understood. Therefore, after attaining independence, the dream of development of the nation should have been embraced by the recommendations of education policy with clear language policy while adopting the great culture of the nation. But the formulation of the first Indian education policy as the basis of the language policy of independent India came almost 20 years after attaining independence and in this too, the aspect of 'language policy', was interpreted as '*Three Language*' Formula, which was seen as impractical. It remained limited to calculations only. It should be clear that language policy cannot be limited only to 'how many and which languages should be taught, especially in a diversified nation like India where we have so many languages and dialects *(chaar kos par paanee badale aath kos par baanee), The taste of water changes at every four miles, while dialects change at every eight miles).* Also, despite the same culture, the reorganisation of states' happened on the basis of language. As a result, this formula has not been implemented since then.

While on one hand, Sanskrit is considered as the basic language of Indian culture, its importance is felt not only in India but also at a global level. Therefore, it is our constitutional obligation to enrich the vocabulary of Indian languages. There has been hesitation to place Sanskrit in the language policy, however on the basis of various arguments, efforts have been made to include it in the 'language policy'. Article 351 of the constitution declares very clearly that "*It shall be the duty of the Union to promote the spread of the Hindi language, to develop it so that it may serve as a medium of expression for all the elements of the composite culture of India and to secure its enrichment by assimilating without interfering with its genius, the forms, style and expressions used in Hindustani and in the other languages of India specified in the Eighth Schedule, and by drawing, wherever necessary or desirable, for its vocabulary, primarily on Sanskrit and secondarily on other languages.*" (Article 351; Constitution of India)

It is important to note that Sanskrit occupies a special place in the list of different languages enumerated in the Eighth Schedule of the Indian Constitution and has the responsibility of making the national language (or languages) of India flourish. However, it has to go through a long struggle to get a place in Indian education policy. The Supreme Court had to order that Sanskrit reading and teaching should be managed in the school curriculum. According to the recommendations of the Supreme Court and other various commissions / committees, it is recommended that in view of the highest development of Indian languages, Sanskrit must be promoted as it is the base for all Indian languages. Sanskrit should have been in the education system for a long time.

It is important to note that the core of modern science and knowledge remains in culture. It can be clearly understood from this point of view that culture is a very broad concept. Under it, the entire life-style gets contained. It also remains the basis of modern science. It is clear that to understand modern science, it is imperative to understand the long tradition of science. From the Indian point of view, Sanskrit is the basis of this tradition of knowledge which can enrich Indian languages by creating vocabulary of different types of cognitive subjects, and by using these languages as the medium of instruction, the process of education can be made smooth and accessible.

It is a matter of significant attention and consideration that children, being aware in their everyday language as well as mother tongue, are literate before school. In the National Curriculum Framework (2005), it was expressed very clearly by referring to "*areas of curriculum, school stages and assessment*" that "the child naturally acquired language from his home and social environment". Children have an innate ability to language learning. Most children have full linguistic ability by assimilating language complexities and rules before they start formal education. Even children with different talents, who cannot speak, develop equally complex alternative signs and symbols for their expression. "It is clear that on this basis, the formal process of their education can take place in the mother tongue. It is also true that a child is not a 'blank slate' before school admission, as some learning paradigms have pre-conceived it. From this point of view, the language and policy of any nation is considered to be the most important, primary, and basic part of the education policy of that nation. As indicated, it should have become a matter of highest priority in terms of compliance with the democratic process after attaining independence.

Even though 22 Indian languages were constitutionally recognised in the Eighth Schedule of the Constitution (initially this number was 15), no Indian language was given required recognition at the higher educational level. It is clear that there is a relationship between higher education and research. Good understanding and quality of research has a deep relation with good understanding and authority of language. Quoting the statement of National Policy on Education (1968), the Supreme Court in one judgement said that – "Research in Indology, humanities and social sciences will receive adequate support. To fulfil the need for the synthesis of knowledge, inter-disciplinary research will be encouraged. Efforts will be made to delve into India's ancient fund of knowledge and to relate it to contemporary reality. This effort will imply the development of facilities for the intensive study of Sanskrit and other classical languages. An autonomous Commission will be established to foster and improve teaching, study and research in Sanskrit and other classical languages." (Article 5.33; National Policy on Education, 1986, cited by Supreme Court, 1994)

Although various institutes, directorates, language academies, commissions, committees, etc. have been formed from time to time for the development of various languages in India, there has been a lack of teaching or course material at all levels in Indian languages in academic terms. In this whole perspective, 'What is the place of Indian languages?' has been a very challenging question in the form of language policy or language education in the Indian education system. It is clear that the new National Education Policy of India 2020 looks at the challenge of the language in the context of these points. This education policy considers language as 'power' and believes that language is a powerful means for the empowerment of an individual.

The policy also proposes restructuring of the school education sector. In its proposed 5+3+3+4 school structure it considers language as the basis for pre-school education – 'to make basic literacy and numeracy the highest priority so that all children can acquire basic learning skills like 'literacy and numeracy' up to class 3 '. According to National Education Policy 2020 'children should not only learn, but more importantly learn how to learn.' It emphasises perceptual understanding, developing creativity and logical thinking, indicating the need and importance of the child's 'language of thinking' in the context of giving importance to life skills such as mutual communication, cooperation, group work and flexibility. A larger role of language is seen in this policy. This policy mainly outlines the role of language in the following ways –

- In the context of Indian Constitution under the Preamble 'justice and equity'
- Equality of opportunity
- Denying discrimination based on language
- Personality base
- Medium of basic education including higher education
- Interaction with teachers
- Teacher education
- Bilingual curriculum
- The basis for continuous learning
- The basis of the Indian knowledge tradition
- Cultural Rights and foundation
- The basis of social coordination and society
- Right to expression on the basis of Article 19 of the Constitution.

Although language-related discussion appears 'scattered' in this policy, its specific mention appears in Chapter Four. Chapter 22 of the policy is entirely related to the promotion of 'language, art and culture'. It also has a specific implication that the question of language cannot be separated from the question of 'culture and art'. Various main aspects related to the language of the policy can be summed up in the following points –

- Early five-year basic education has been seen as language education only.
- Recognition of language as synonymous with 'power' as a source of knowledge.
- From this point of view, classifying language as a process of empowerment of an individual.
- Flexibility in Three Language Formula so that children can choose the language themselves.
- Specific provisions for teaching cultural / classical languages –
  "*India will similarly expand its institutes and universities studying all classical languages and literature, with strong efforts to collect, preserve, translate, and study the tens of thousands of manuscripts that have not yet received their due attention.*"(22.16).
- Although mother tongue has been discussed for elementary education, it has also been suggested to adopt it at a higher level.
- Establishment of 'Indian Institute of Translation and Interpretation' at the national level for the creation of high-level content in Indian languages –
  "India will also urgently expand its translation and interpretation efforts in order to make high quality learning materials and other important written and spoken material available to the public in various Indian and foreign languages. For this, an Indian Institute of Translation and Interpretation (IITI) will be established." (22.14).
- Strengthening language departments in multi-dimensional form in terms of research etc. in universities –
  "Strong departments and programmes in Indian languages, comparative literature, creative writing, arts, music, philosophy, etc. will be launched and developed across the country, and degrees including 4-year B.Ed. dual degrees will be developed in these subjects. These departments and programmes will, in particular, help to develop a large cadre of high-quality language teachers – as well as teachers of art, music, philosophy and writing – who will be needed around the country to carry out this Policy. The NRF will fund quality research in all these areas." (22.9)
- Establishment of language related new organisation –
  "it is also proposed that a new institution for Languages will be established." (22.16).
- Language as a cultural necessity –
  "Cultural awareness and expression are among the major competencies considered important to develop in children, in order to provide them with a sense of identity, belonging, as well as an appreciation of other cultures and identities. It is through the development of a strong sense and knowledge of their own cultural history, arts, languages, and traditions that children can build a positive cultural

identity and self-esteem. Thus, cultural awareness and expression are important contributors both to individuals as well as societal well-being." (22.2)

- Scheme for updating dictionaries.
- To make language pedagogy more experiential –
  "*The teaching of all languages will be enhanced through innovative and experiential methods, including apps, by weaving in the cultural aspects of the languages – such as films, theatre, storytelling, poetry, and music – and by drawing connections with various relevant subjects and with real-life experiences. Thus, the teaching of languages will also be based on experiential-learning pedagogy.*" (4.21)
- Promotion of text-related activities for practical development of languages –
  "*Language-teaching too must be improved to be more experiential and to focus on the ability to converse and interact in the language and not just on the literature, vocabulary, and grammar of the language. Languages must be used more extensively for conversation and for teaching-learning.*" (22.7)
- Promotion of foreign languages in terms of global cultural introduction –
  "*In addition to high quality offerings in Indian languages and English, foreign languages, such as Korean, Japanese, Thai, French, German, Spanish, Portuguese, and Russian, will also be offered at the secondary level, for students to learn about the cultures of the world and to enrich their global knowledge and mobility according to their own interests and aspirations.*" (4.20)
- Promote communicability in the target language.
- To give priority to the study of comparative literature.
- Practice and training in creative writing.
- In order to promote Indian cultural and linguistic development, teaching of Sanskrit has been recommended as a first language, bringing it into mainstream and transforming Sanskrit Universities into a multidisciplinary institution related to higher education –
  "*Due to its vast and significant contributions and literature across genres and subjects, its cultural significance, and its scientific nature, rather than being restricted to single-stream Sanskrit Pathshalas and Universities, Sanskrit will be mainstreamed with strong offerings in school – including as one of the language options in the three-language formula – as well as in higher education. It will be taught in interesting and innovative ways, and connected to other contemporary and relevant subjects such as mathematics, astronomy, philosophy, linguistics, dramatics, yoga, etc. Sanskrit Universities too will move towards becoming large multidisciplinary institutions of higher learning. Departments of Sanskrit that conduct teaching and outstanding interdisciplinary research on Sanskrit and Sanskrit Knowledge Systems will be established / strengthened across the new multidisciplinary higher education system. Sanskrit will become a natural part of a holistic multidisciplinary higher education if a student so chooses. Sanskrit teachers in large numbers will be professionalised across the country in mission mode through the offering of 4-year integrated multidisciplinary B.Ed. dual degrees in education and Sanskrit.*"(22.15)

- In this view, it is important to consider the strengthening of Sanskrit in relation to Sanskrit and Indian languages.
- Establishment of Language Academies and development of new words and vocabulary–
  "For each of the languages mentioned in the Eighth Schedule of the Constitution of India, Academies will be established consisting of some of the greatest scholars and native speakers to determine simple yet accurate vocabulary for the latest concepts, and to release the latest dictionaries on a regular basis." (22.18)
- Scholarships for the study of languages and encouragement to use –
  "*Scholarships for people of all ages to study Indian Languages, Arts, and Culture with local masters and/or within the higher education system will be established. The promotion of Indian languages is possible only if they are used regularly and if they are used for teaching and learning. Incentives, such as prizes for outstanding poetry and prose in Indian languages across categories, will be established to ensure vibrant poetry, novels, non-fiction books, textbooks, journalism, and other works in all Indian languages. Proficiency in Indian languages will be included as part of qualification parameters for employment opportunities."* (22.20)
- High level use of technology for language teaching.
- Plans for conservation, development and promotion of Indian languages.
- Students have the opportunity to choose the route for their own learning.
- Wide use of technology for removing language related barriers and development of 'sign language' of disabled students –
  "Indian Sign Language (ISL) will be standardised across the country, and National and State curriculum materials developed, for use by students with hearing impairment." (4.22)
- Respect for localism in the context of the Concurrent List of Constitution.
- Establishment of inclusion by language.
- Use of Indian languages in terms of qualitative enhancement of education.
- Management of funds through 'National Research Establishment' for research in Indian languages –
  "Universities and their research teams will work with each other and with communities across the country towards enriching such platforms. These preservation efforts, and the associated research projects, e.g., in history, archaeology, linguistics, etc., will be funded by the NRF." (22.19)
- *Efforts to preserve and promote all Indian languages including classical, tribal and endangered languages will be taken on with new vigour. Technology and crowdsourcing, with extensive participation of the people, will play a crucial role in these efforts.*(22.17)

  Apart from the above, several more points can be identified in the policy promoting Indian culture and language –

- Provision for reading and learning additional Indian language at foundational level.
- Creation of multidisciplinary institutions as well as multi-lingual institutions.
- Planning of specific schemes for the development of Indian languages.
- Role of languages in integration and integrity of knowledge.
- Role of languages in the development of intellectual, social, aesthetic, physical, emotional and morality under multi-dimensional education.
- Development of bilingual courses in the context of Indian languages up to graduation level.
- Preference for teachers teaching in the mother tongue of the students.
- To provide specific training for teachers teaching in mother tongues.

Summarising, one can say that in the National Education Policy 2020 an attempt has been made to look at the context of language in a very comprehensive manner. Referring to the importance of Indian languages, it is believed that "*Indian languages are some of the most expressive and scientific in the world, containing much of the world's great literature and knowledge. They are also truly functional languages, many spoken by lakhs if not by crores of people, and represent the culture and heritage of entire regions and generations, and of centuries if not millennia. True inclusion and preservation of culture and traditions of each region, and true understanding by all students in schools, can be achieved only when suitable respect is given to all Indian languages, including tribal languages. It is thus absolutely critical to preserve the truly rich languages and literatures of India, just as other technologically advanced countries (such as South Korea, Japan, France, Germany, Holland, etc.) have so deftly preserved their languages in the face of internationalisation.*" (Draft New Education Policy, 2019)

The question of language policy is fundamentally connected to the 'humanistic approach to education'. Therefore, there is a need to always look at its dimensions in a very comprehensive manner. Its education often begins in both formal and informal forms, in the family itself, with the birth of the child, and continues to spread momentarily lifelong. While its relationship is inseparably linked to the constantly changing needs and daily activities of the individual, stability, effervescence and variability of the culture always irrigate its foundation. While its vocals continue to inspire the singing of efforts to vocalise the free or bound speech of the advocates, the audience's irrational boundaries or presuppositions keep it in place. While its oral form keeps on singing the saga of its independent nature, its written form always engages in efforts to tie it. It is true that the 'language' confined in the broad dimensions of education carries the responsibility of making it strong and articulate. And, it is also true, the language that lifts politics is always hurt by the weapons of political vices. Thus, it is ironic that language, which gives the basis of a person's daily bread-butter, starts losing its shine owing to its 'daily bread-butter'. There are so many such questions, which have to be questioned and hunted for answers in the language policy. This is why the policy of language that gives the ability to express oneself cannot be counted even in the calculation of some languages. Language policy requires a serious perspective of 'consciousness'. Language is not merely a structural formation of letters, words, sentences, etc., but it is a strong basis for the empowerment of the creative power of a 'person'.

These entire perspectives require a vibrant environment to give a strong foundation to the Indian education system. It is clear that the communicability and practicality of any language depends on its communicative form. This livelihood depends only on the communicativeness of the language. Commissions, committees and policies related to education have continuously hinted at making the methods adopted for the reading of languages be made more and more alive, but in this context, there was no concrete implementation policy. It requires a mental ground and commitment. These tasks can be proven in a planned way.

It should be clear here that according to the decision of the Supreme Court, the fundamental right related to life conferred under Article 21 in the Constitution of India means 'right to live a dignified life' and right to free and compulsory education under Article 21 (A) means 'quality education' for all, based on the principle of equality. From the point of view of the child rights, children must get opportunities for expressing their affection, playing games, provision to pure food and water, security, pure environment etc. These are now part of the fundamental rights of the child. It is also worth noting here that Chapter six of the *The Right of Children To Free And Compulsory Education Act, 2009* discusses the measures to be taken for the protection of children. It is clear that child rights or human rights have a direct and strong connection with the language policy of the nation. Therefore, the language policy of the nation cannot ignore them. This is the essence of this policy.

It is true, as has been made clear, that the main function of the language is to establish communicative relations between the people of the nation. Therefore, the language policy of the nation should also be tied and paged in this mutual affection, not by the 'principles of partition'. This becomes even more important in the Indian diverse linguistic landscape. This diverse linguistic scenario should be synonymous with mutual learning and teaching, not malicious conflict. Every word of every language not only sings songs of the living stories of thousands of years of feeling of thousands of people but brings the world in the form of a composite culture. In the context of India, this expression proves more significant. Only the language and policy of the nation can become the light of this composite culture and can show the affectionate path! Lighting the path of education can make it meaningful! This is where the 'functioning' of this policy is placed.

Our National Education Policy of 2020 is trying to cater to these vital questions in itself. Its meaning lies in shaping its implementation by all of us. It reminds us again and again that – Keep in mind that 'language policy' is made for children, and that children are not to be granted for language policy.

3

Creating and Maintaining the Honour of Teachers: A Profound Vision of NEP

Pawan Sinha

Education, Learner, School and Teacher! All these words related to any education system are not just words, but imbibe a whole tradition and entire philosophy within themselves. It has a tradition because since the advent of human life, there has also been 'education'! This means that 'education' is the process of knowing, learning and inculcating it into one's life. In the whole process of life, humans continued to learn new things, kept learning and tried to imbibe the same in the life which they knew and learnt. It is a 'Philosophy' because it gives the vision to understand life and the world! This is the same life and world in which 'education' is used or the education helps in 'grooming' the life and the world.

In the context of education, it is necessary to understand that learning has never been an accumulative concept nor of cumulative nature, the nature of learning or its ethos has never been argumentative. This limit of learning is neither for the learner nor for the teacher! Both have to continue learning and this continuity is also necessary because there is continuity in life too! That is why it is constantly being reiterated that the history of education and its tradition is as old as the history of human life! Rabindranath Tagore also believes that "*A teacher cannot truly teach until he studies himself, a lamp cannot ignite another lamp until it continues to burn itself.*" It is a very big responsibility of a teacher – to 'update' his concepts about education itself and to 'explain' the true meaning of education to the society and the nation as well. Somewhere this responsibility of a teacher also becomes the responsibility of teacher education!

The question is also about the quality of school education, and as soon as this question arises, the picture of a teacher comes in front of the eyes. Another important point to consider is that as the 'education' and 'schooling' are different, similarly education is neither limited to the boundary of the school nor 'confined' within the boundary of the school. Similarly, the kind of emotions, understanding, perspective and 'sustenance' required to be an effective teacher is neither limited nor 'confined' within the realm of teacher education! As a person, the teacher also continuously learns and develops feelings from the surroundings, community and events occurring around him/her! If a person has all the positive concepts related to life and has a 'lively'

Associate Professor, Moti Lal Nehru College, University of Delhi and Founder, Paavan Chintan Dhara Ashram, Gaziabad

attitude towards facing and resolving the complexities of life, then such a person, such a teacher will also adopt a 'lively' attitude towards children's education and will never 'quit'! This vision towards teacher, education and learner is helpful in understanding the point that a teacher has a very pivotal role in children's education and it is constantly influenced by the teacher's personality, education and his morale! In this sense, we should all have a deep sense of responsibility towards the teachers!

As we know, the biggest responsibility of ensuring the quality of schooling is on teachers! Some important points of thinking or pondering questions arise in the context of a 'teacher'! Can anyone become a teacher or be a teacher? Can anyone be made a teacher? Is 'teacher hood' inherent in teachers or can 'teacher hood' be developed? Is 'Right' of being a 'Teacher' possible? These questions are also related to the teacher's education, their place, honour and importance! The higher the position of the teacher in a society, the higher or paramount it is, that society and nation is considered more developed. A person can become anything in life and the role of teacher can never be negated in this process of 'becoming'. So 'Creator' is more important than 'Creation'. Although it is believed and is also true that one cannot teach anyone anything, the responsibility of learning is 'on the learner'. But it is equally true that when the appropriate and conducive environment is available for the learner, learning becomes relatively simple and interesting. The role of a teacher is that of a facilitator or a resource–to provide motivation to the learner and to create a conducive learning environment! In this view, the teacher's position in the society is of utmost honour.

The National Policy on Education 1986 also states clearly – "The status of teachers in a society reflects their cultural-social vision." It has been said that no nation can rise above the level of its teachers (National Education Policy, 1979: 9.1). It is true that the status of teachers must be elevated! After all, it is a question of the life of a child.... After all it is a question of the life of many children.... After all it is a question of the life of many generations.... Ultimately it is a question of the whole nation and the 'life' of the nation! In fact, the kind of personality a human child attains, they create a similar society and that society creates the same kind of nation. Only a strong personality can strengthen a society and a nation!

Teacher Education and Various Policies and Commissions

In the scenario of education which appears after the attainment of independence, in addition to establishing the importance of education, special emphasis has been laid on the importance of teachers. Yes, it is a different matter that varied commissions and policies continue to emphasise differently about the responsibilities, duties, functions, education, recruitment, salary, etc. of the teacher. But this much is certain that along with the education of children, teachers and their education have been a major concern in all education policies and commissions. University Education Commission (1948-49) and Secondary Education Commission (1952-53) – both have emphasised on increasing the quality of education. So that education can be made useful for the nation, society and the individual and for this, the role of teacher has been appreciated. In its document, the University Education Commission (1948-49) expresses its concern for the teacher's education and the knowledge he has learnt – "It is unique that the school teacher keeps on teaching on the basis of knowledge acquired by him / her by the age of 25 and is not able to acquire any new knowledge apart from his experiences. For this, it is necessary that the teacher should be informed about the new knowledge from time to time, only then he can do full justice to his / her duty." This concern of the University Education Commission (1948-49) indicates that it is very important for teachers to be updated. Whatever knowledge a teacher acquires in his 'time' seems incomplete and meaningless for 'today's time'. Therefore, the need is that teachers have to learn continuously and keep updating themselves, only then they can match their 'steps' with 'speed and stride of time'! The University Education Commission (1948–49) reviewed the existing teacher training programmes with full sincerity and suggested that teacher training programmes should be flexible and according to local conditions. Remodelling of courses, selection of appropriate schools for practical training and recommendation of more time for school practice are the main concerns of this Commission. The biggest achievement of this Commission was to rename 'Teacher Training' and the new name was 'Teacher Education'!

The Secondary Education Commission (1952-53), which made various recommendations regarding the training of teachers and their conditions of service, recommended equal pay for equal work and qualifications and asserted that teachers should get that much decent pay scale that their respect can be maintained in society. Teachers should not be allowed to teach tuition, keeping in mind the point that the teaching profession should not become a medium to earn money. Highly emphasising the complex nature and deep understanding of teaching, the Commission recommended that only qualified and trained teachers should be appointed for educating the children.

Is it possible that if we invest more and carefully in teacher education, then we will be able to see positive results in school students? The Kothari Commission (1964–66) linked the education of teachers with schooling, stating that "for qualitative improvement in education, it is imperative that teachers have a proper programme of professional education. The return on expenditure on training of teachers will be quite valuable, as the result of improvement in education of millions of students will be much less than the amount of economic expenditure. ... . There is a need for large-scale organisation of programmes of in-service education so that every teacher can receive two-three months of in-service education after every term of five-year." Regarding the teaching profession, the concerns of the Kothari Commission are welcome, because the more and more planned the investment in teacher education, the better results are seen in the development of children. This means that the more qualified, capable and resourceful the teachers become, they will be able to involve school children in their sense of responsibility in a more informed and serious manner. In addition, keeping in view the possibilities of research in the field of education, emphasis has also been laid on continuous training of teachers and it is recommended to be included in in-service training every five years. The manner in which the Kothari Commission has emphasised the qualitative improvement and training in teacher education expresses the concern of the Commission towards the enrichment of the capacity of teachers.

The National Commission for Teachers (1983–85), based on teacher and teacher education, states clearly in the preface of its document that "the nation must become fully committed to the welfare of the teacher and enhance his reputation in the society. In return, the teacher should dedicate himself to his/her duties." While this Commission provides autonomy to teachers on the one hand, on the other hand it also promotes commitment through 'dedication to duties'. This Commission organises education, teachers and prestige in a well-thought system and sees it as an important link for the development of the nation. The teacher's position in the entire educational system is sure and respected. Equally important is the Commission making special provisions for the position/person which is so important. This Commission is completely dedicated to the teacher and puts every aspect of it before everyone – with recommendations!

The National Teachers Commission (1983–85), like all policies and commissions, has also emphasised the prestige and economic needs of the teacher. At the same time, the Commission does not restrict teacher's skills to only teaching the subject, but also gives importance to their role in character-building and development of values among children. This point is an extension of the teacher's field of work and also mandatory! Expressing its aspiration for this point, the document elaborates that talented people should come in the field of education so that the talent of children can be enhanced, nurtured and help can be provided to these children for the development of a strong character. The important recommendations made by the National Teachers Commission (1983–85) in relation to teacher education are as follows –

- 4-year integrated training course after senior secondary level which will include graduation and training.
- Extending the duration of the one-year B.Ed. course through two summer months and ensuring that the academic session is of 220 days with longer working hours.
- Teachers should be selected on the basis of certain factors, such as better physique, linguistic ability, ability to communicate, general awareness about the world, positive attitude towards life and ability to develop good human relations!

The due importance given to the careful selection and teaching practice of teachers which is evident in the recommendations of the National Commission for Teachers (1983-85) is reflective of its educational vision and concern!

The National Education Policy (1986), which gives the highest importance to the honour of teachers, asserts that "no nation can rise above the level of its teachers". It becomes clear by itself that teachers have the main role in the process of nation-building, this role goes beyond the future development of the learners and extends to the society and the nation. This statement is very important and inspiring in itself. This statement gives dignity to 'being a teacher'. It also mentions the granting of full autonomy and independence to teachers by stating that "*Teachers should have the freedom to innovate, to devise appropriate methods of communication and activities relevant to the needs and capabilities of and the concerns of the community*" (National Policy on Education 1986: 9.1). This refers to the ability of teachers to improve their classroom processes and make appropriate decisions about teaching and learning practices. The recommendations for transparency in promotion of teachers and to create appropriate opportunities for their advancement double the importance of teachers. "*Teacher education is a continuous process and its pre-service and in-service portions are inseparable.*" All these points refer to policy concerns and practical solutions. One of the most important things– the closure of sub-quality institutions is necessary so that quality in teacher education can be ensured which has a direct impact on school education. Continuing education of teachers is another important point of this policy which has been reiterated by other policies and commissions in other words.

Acharya Ram Murthy Committee (1990) was appointed by the Government of India in 1990 to review the National Policy of Education (1986) and the major suggestions regarding teacher education by this committee were: i) First Degree Course in Teacher Education should not be provided in correspondence mode. ii) More institutions should be encouraged to introduce an integrated curriculum of four years of education in the pattern of regional colleges. iii) The practice of using teacher-training institutes as a dumping ground for unwanted employees should be stopped. It is a very important point that teacher-training institutes need to be seen as extremely dignified centres. This will have a double benefit. One, only those people will come to this field who can perform well in this field and second, it will ensure the quality of teacher education as well as school education.

The Education without Burden (1993) report also expressed concern about the attitude of teacher-training and teaching-training institutions and it was asserted that measures should be taken to improve teacher training and to create an educational environment. There has also been a lot of emphasis on improving the educational environment. The committee believes that "*previous efforts to improve teacher training programs and institutions have proved successful in limited quantities. Overall, teacher training still remains separate from mainstream education. In most places in-service training has also become a ritual that lacks the ability to motivate anyone along with lack of educational content*". The concern of this report is absolutely legitimate that in-service training should not become a ritual. Special efforts are required for this and these efforts should be honest.

National Education Policy 2020 and Teacher Education

The kind of concerns about teachers and teacher education displayed by the National Education Policy 2020 are undoubtedly praiseworthy and need of the hour! It is not that the points of view mentioned in the National Education Policy 2020 were not the part of any previous policy, but rather that all the 'valid' and 'necessary' points have once again been emphasised and 'warned' that if teachers do not get their respectable place, then it is not only 'harmful' for the teacher, but also 'fatal' for the society and the nation. The answer is found in the National Education Policy 2020 itself – "*Teachers truly shape the future of our children – and, therefore, the future of our nation. It is because of this noblest role that the teacher in India was the most respected member of society. Only the very best and most learned became teachers. ... The high respect for teachers and the high status of the teaching profession must be restored*" (5.1 page 20). After careful consideration of these mentioned points, it is understood that respect of teachers is also necessary so that only good and learned people become teachers. Another meaning of this is that 'becoming a teacher' is not an "open invitation" to everyone, nor can everyone be a "teacher"! In these lines two words need to be looked at and those are the words – teachers 'were' respected members and 'revived'. The first word 'were' refers to the golden past of the teacher, and the second word 'revived' demands to restore the same golden past. 'This is really important!'

Recruitment and Posting

The National Education Policy 2020 makes special provisions in the context of recruitment and posting of teachers and special care has been taken of rural teachers in these provisions. A logical reason has also been provided that in rural areas only a sincere student will be able to complete 4-year integrated B.Ed. and after successfully completing the degree, local employment can be boosted. Local teachers will be able to do the work of teaching in the local language. This will also provide excellent teachers in those areas where they are most needed. The recommendation to increase the housing allowance to encourage working in rural areas is appreciable and should be welcomed.

The policy also expresses concern on the harmful practice of excessive transfers of teachers and recommends the stoppage of this practice. Excessive transfers have a negative impact on the relationship between the teacher and the community. The policy recommends an online software-based system in order to maintain transparency in transfer. This recommendation regarding transfer is a good step but its implementation will not be easy, because even after special provisions, there is a shortage of teachers in rural areas, which this policy also indicates.

In the process of recruitment of teachers, efforts are being made to ensure the presence of excellent teachers by recommending teacher eligibility test (TET) or NTA examination, interview, teaching performance in class at all levels of schooling, these are excellent efforts but maintaining its objectivity is a complex challenge! But there is a commendable effort in this – to give importance to the local language. This will enable quality and meaningful dialogue between children and teachers.

To ensure an adequate number of teachers in subjects, it is recommended to recruit them in a school or school complex. It is not as simple as it seems in reading and listening, because recruiting teachers of the subject in the same school might make it difficult to maintain the 'system'! This 'concern' of the policy that the vacancies of teachers should be filled immediately is valid. This will enable the maintenance of the quality of education.

Work Culture and Environment during Service

This attempt of the policy to materialise the concept of inclusive community will give true meaning to education. This policy talks about radical changes in the work environment and culture of the school. The availability of adequate physical resources, internet, toilets, clean and attractive spaces in schools is an imperative in the concept of school, which the new education policy addresses well. This policy emphasises the learning of all children, with a strong and safe learning environment for all children and teachers, including differently abled children. The policy also emphasises on special care for safety, health in schools in the in-service training. Putting so much emphasis on 'safety' in schools and training schools, is a need of time and a primary concern. It is good that National Education Policy 2020 looks at linking education to society and takes initiative to change education to suit the nature of society!

Often, teachers have a 'valid' complaint that they are 'surrounded' by a variety of 'responsibilities' which are non-academic and that their large amount of time is wasted in fulfilling them! The new education policy 'exempts' teachers from non-academic tasks and states that "*tasks that are not directly related to teaching will not be allowed to be done ... so that they can fully concentrate on teaching-learning work.*" This long-awaited recommendation is undoubtedly a 'great relief' for teachers, as well as will positively affect school education.

This policy addresses the very sensitive issue of teaching, to enable teachers to make their teaching effective and to have the autonomy to determine the curriculum and teaching method. It is the teacher who knows the children of his class and school best and is familiar with all their strengths and weaknesses. Such a close relationship with children creates harmony between the two. This harmonious relationship between teacher and learner is the purpose of any education system and also the need! Teachers have been expected to emphasize on all-round development of children, with a focus on socio-emotional aspects, along with teaching. Teachers can do this – for this, the nature of teacher education will also have to be determined in a similar manner.

Continuous Professional Development (CPD)

As was already clarified earlier, the teacher himself/herself has to learn continuously, so that he/she can keep himself updated and get acquainted with innovation. The National Education Policy also makes diverse provisions for the continuous professional development of teachers and talks about attending workshops from the local level to the international level. It also recommends the provision of an online teacher development module. The policy clearly states that teachers should participate in a continuous professional development programme of about 50 hours each year for their own professional development. These programmes will emphasise the understanding and application of innovations, whatever new concepts are there for professional promotion of teachers. For this development of teachers, the selection of subjects and the medium should be chosen thoughtfully. The administration of any school and that administrator or leader is expected to have the capacity to lead, as this affects the entire educational system. That is why the National Education Policy 2020 emphasises continuous learning of heads or principals of school complexes so as to enhance their leadership capabilities. They will also participate in a continuous professional development programme of about 50 hours each year. This will strengthen the entire education system and teachers will also get the requisite support to work under efficient leadership and solve their problems.

Career Management and Progress

This policy, emphasising the recognition and promotion of excellent teachers, recommends the creation of a strong merit-based tenure, promotion and salary system. Emphasis has been laid on the vertical mobility of teachers on the basis of career growth and merit. With this, they will also be able to cooperate in the school administration system. This is a commendable step of the policy which will encourage teachers to do better.

Professional Standards for Teachers

The qualities that are expected in a teacher become his/her standard level. This policy will be formulated by the National Council of Teacher Education for the preparation and development of a general guiding set of National Professional Standards (NPST) for NCERT, SCERT, teachers of all levels and teachers from all regions by 2022 and in 2030 promotion and salary at the national level will be managed on the basis of professional standards. This NPST will also inform the design of pre-service and in-service teacher programmes. Along with this, the promotion and increment of teachers will also be done on the basis of this NPST. Setting standards for teachers will bring quality in teaching. This is an important policy effort.

Special Teacher

Education is the fundamental right of every child. In this context, it is necessary to make efforts to facilitate the learning of differently abled children who have difficulty in learning. Therefore, in some areas of school education, emphasis has also been laid on the need of additional special teachers who have full knowledge and skills of the special needs can take special care of the differently abled children. In order to meet the demand of such teachers, the policy suggests that secondary expertise can be developed after the preparation of pre-service teachers. However, in an inclusive classroom or education system, every teacher should have enough ability to meet the needs of his students.

Perspective about Teacher Education

As it was clarified earlier, teachers are the axis of any education system; their abilities, their sensibilities and skills play an important role in 'building' the learner and education system and providing them 'perfection'. Due to this, specific recommendations have been made regarding teacher and teacher education in the policy of education. Keeping the demand of excellent quality teachers at the centre, the National Education Policy 2020 makes a variety of recommendations. The details of which are as follows:

- By 2030, teacher education will be included in multidisciplinary colleges and universities and a department of education will be established which will provide B.Ed., M.Ed. and Ph.D. This recommendation of this policy ensures quality material and training for teachers in future. By doing this, the supply of excellent quality teachers will also be ensured.
- This policy, which recommends different types of undergraduate courses at different stages, wants to ensure that by 2030 B.Ed. courses should run smoothly in multidisciplinary institutions. A bachelor's course in education will be a 4-year integrated B.Ed. which will also include practical practice training in the form of pupil-teaching. For the students who have obtained a bachelor's degree in any other subject, B.Ed. programme will be of two years. For those learners, one-year B.Ed. will be there who have obtained a four-year multi-graduate degree or a postgraduate degree in a specific subject and wish to become a teacher of that specific subject. Recognised multidisciplinary institute of Open Distance Learning (ODL) can provide better quality B.Ed. course through mixed or Open Distance Learning (ODL mode) for students of far-off inaccessible geographical locations and serving teachers who wish to enhance their qualification. This recommendation, inviting various 'gates' to 'enrol' and become 'excellent teachers' in the programme, emphasises practical training and teaching practice in school.

- To accommodate oneself with changing times and technological development it is necessary that this technique is imparted in teacher training to address the basic needs and basic issues of education, such as – pedagogy in relation to fundamental literacy and numeracy, multi-level teaching and evaluation, teaching differently abled children, teaching children with special interest or talent, use of educational technology and learner-centred teaching, etc. Also, this policy emphasises practical training in classroom education in local schools. It also specifically recommends that while teaching subjects, the fundamental duties of the Indian Constitution (Article 51A) and other constitutional provisions should also be emphasised. In addition, it also recommends making environmental education an integral part of the school curriculum. The idea that teachers should be taught fundamental duties in teacher training –strengthens the process of building society and nation. This recommendation of linking 'teaching of subjects' to the civic life of the learners is exemplary. It really gives education its meaning.
- Promoting local arts, agriculture, sports, carpentry, etc. through short-term local teacher-education programmes and recommending the appointment of these people as 'master instructors' in school premises will act as a bridge between teacher education and school education. At the same time, Indian knowledge, tradition and culture will get a boost and Indian businesses will get an opportunity to revive.
- After the basic training of being a teacher, if one wants to study in a specific field of work in this field, then short-term certificate courses will also be widely available, such as teaching of students with special needs, courses to promote one from primary to secondary level. This provision in teacher education will not only give teachers an opportunity to enhance their professional abilities, it also 'protects' from the frustration, depression that may arise from years of teaching the same thing at the same level. Adopting to the ever evolving technology will also help teachers to stay updated and meet the needs of the time.
- The work of suggesting those studies, research, documentation and suggestions which are working at international level and can be useful in 'Indian context' will be done by NCERT. This statement of the policy is noteworthy that "... *will recommend that what can be learned from these can be incorporated into the practices being implemented in India*". This statement indicates that there is always a need for Indianisation of teacher education!
- The National Curriculum for Teacher Education will be prepared by 2021 based on the principles of National Education Policy 2020, by and in consultation with NCERT, which will be shared with various partners and finalised by mutual consultation. Expected amendments will be made every 5-10 years to address the newly emerging complexities of teacher education.

- Strict action will be taken against 'Sub-standard Stand Alone' teacher education institutions and if necessary, they will be closed. This will be the most 'appreciable' step when 'stand-alone' teacher education institutions with a tendency to earn will be controlled. This will bring the required quality in teacher education!

It is clear from this discussion that the National Education Policy 2020 has a serious approach towards teacher and teacher education and similar seriousness is evident in their approach of implementing all the recommendations. In order to take care of the honour and position, prestige of teachers, the policy frees them from all non-academic tasks. At the same time, it ensures that those who come in the field of teacher education should be sensitive, good and learned and who can shape the future of the learners. This policy shows full agreement that the quality of schooling depends on the quality of teachers and hence teacher-education cannot be compromised in any way. The close observation and recommendations of each stage of the journey of teachers from their preparation of becoming a teacher to their classroom teaching helps to understand that teachers and their education is not only a process of human formation rather it is the process of building society and nation directly or indirectly. The way in which the local teachers have been given place in teacher education, due to this the 'distance' created by the language will be reduced as well as there will be an increase in employment in the local areas. This policy, which promotes the freedom of teachers from non-academic activities, emphasises on the learning of teachers also along with that of the learner. This 'honour' given to teachers in various policies looks good on paper, but neither did we instil in the teachers the courage to teach in their own way keeping in mind the needs of their children, decide their way of working on their own without rigidly following the textbooks, set the date of assessment according to their own choice, nor the skill and capability through which they can 'handle' any emergency situation. Although this cannot be generalised, the situation is almost the same. The National Policy on Education 2020 is committed to once again 'creating and maintaining the honour' of teachers. But this honour is also the responsibility of the teacher himself/herself. While the establishment of departments of education in multidisciplinary colleges and universities needs to be done at a rapid pace, there is also a need to keep its socio-cultural perspective at the centre while creating a new framework of teacher education.

Policy is good, recommendations are also commendable ... Just, education-policy needs to make sincere efforts to implement them!

4

Children, Childhood and Education

Usha Sharma

> "He will educate himself on his own. A plant grows itself, does the gardener grow it? He just provides the necessary environment to it, it is the plant itself that does its own growing"
>
> (*Education, Swami Vivekananda*)

This line by Swami Vivekananda about the growing of a plant holds true in educating a child as well. *"You cannot teach a child. He will educate himself. Your task is to provide an appropriate environment."* This is the essence of children's education and pedagogy. If children get a good upbringing in the early years of life then they will become better people and better citizens. In this way, children's education is linked to their 'good upbringing and suitable environment'. It is the responsibility of 'all' to provide or arrange for the good upbringing and suitable environment of the child. When we say 'all' it includes all the persons associated with the child – parents, family, neighbourhood, friends, schools, teachers, educational administration, education officers, policy-makers, society and nation! The reason for this is that education is a shared responsibility and can and should be carried out jointly. Another significant point in relation to children's education is–the concept of children and their childhood! If we consider children to be 'mini-adults', then all our educational activities and pedagogies will be planned accordingly.

Children and Their Childhood: Children are not Mere Numbers!

For the education of the children of India, it is important to understand the nature or basic characteristics of the Indian children and the conditions in which they live. The geographical, social and cultural variations in which Indian children live in, facilitates the development of their basic nature and tendency. But yes, like every child in the world, Indian children also want affection, safety, education, protection, and they too have immense possibilities to learn. There is a need to understand their potentials and give them a suitable environment to grow. "*The child also educates himself. But yes, you can help him in progressing in his own way.*" This line, in essence, indicates the responsibility of all of us– 'elders', who are engaged with the child in one way or the other. There are many children in the country who do not even have the basic

Professor and In-charge, Cell for National Centre for Literacy, NCERT, New Delhi facilities of life and we can often see them around us; sometimes working at a shop or at a crossroads or on the footpaths!

One More Point... Children are not Numbers!

Children are not numbers....! Yet, statistics related to children tell us that "*Even today, millions of children do not have pens in their hands. They are loaded with litter ware and junk sacks.*" According to a report published on the World Against Child Labour Day, i.e., 12 June 2020, many poor children do not even get two full meals a day due to poverty. From a very early age, children begin to struggle with hunger, and their parents also 'push' them into this struggle and put them into labour or work. They also suffer torture and suffering at the places where they work, and at times become 'victims' of exploitation and sexual harassment. While struggling with hunger, the childhood of children gets burdened under the 'harsh realities of life'. Statistics also show that *'many children in the age group of 5 to 17 are engaged in such works that deprive them of a normal, happy childhood, such as – integrated education, health, care, leisure time or basic freedom of life.'* According to a report released by the United Nations, a total of 152 million children in the world are engaged in child labour. According to the International Labour Organization, out of these 152 million children involved in child labour worldwide, 73 million are engaged in hazardous work. These hazardous works include manual cleaning, construction works, agriculture, mining, factory work, hawking and domestic help. In the last several years, the number of children between the age group of 5 and 11 years who have been found to be involved in dangerous activities has increased to 19 million. The census of 2011 shows that in India about 43 lakh children work as child labourers. According to UNICEF, India alone accounts for 12 per cent of the total child labour present worldwide. And if we dig further to the reports collected by several non-government organisations which give non-official statistics, there are about five crore child labourers in India.

Children are not numbers! Yet, statistics related to children indicate that seven out of every 10 children working in India work in the fields. A report released by *'CRY-Child Rights and You'* on Child Labour Prohibition Day (June 12), published in *Digital Bureau Amar Ujala*, New Delhi on June 12, 2019, cites the 2011 census of children and expresses the concerns related to children, their childhood and safety while stating that 62.5 per cent of children under the age of 18 work in agriculture or other related occupations. Out of 4,03,40,000 working children and adolescents, 2,52,30,000 children are working in the agriculture sector. According to the International Labour Organization, about 15.2 million children in India are working as child labour. Out of 10 labourers, seven children work in agriculture. A similar picture has emerged from the current trends in India that more than 60 per cent children are working in agriculture or other related activities. The International Labour Organization states that farming is the second most dangerous occupation worldwide. The main reason for this is that farming work has its own challenges, such as spray of pesticides and use of equipment such as hammer, plough, etc. which can hamper the development of children. It can have negative effects on their body. Not only this, an analysis of the 2011 census data showed that most of the children working in the fields are unable to study. Out of 4,03,40,00 working children and adolescents in the age group of 5-19 years, only 99 lakh children are able to go to school, i.e., 24.5% of working children go to school. In other words, three out of every four working children lose his/her right to education. Despite the provision of right to education, very few children working in the fields are able to continue their education.

Children are not numbers! Yet, statistics related to children depict that "*at least 95,000 children have died or been injured since 2005. Thousands of children have been abducted and millions of children have been denied health services by attacking hospitals.*" In one of the reports of 'Save the Children' it is stated, "*According to the data of 2018, one in six children worldwide is living in conflict zones.*" Overall, this number amounts to a total of 41 crore 50 lakh. This figure is double than the data received in 1995. They also state, "*girls are at a much higher risk of sexual and gender-based violence, including forced marriages. Boys face the risk of murder, crippling, kidnapping and conscription in armed organisations.*"

Children are not numbers! Yet, statistics related to children suggest that the lack of child nutrition in India has increased alarmingly, affecting the growth of children. According to the National Family Health Survey (NFHS) (2019) India has the highest number of underdeveloped children (stunted height and weight as per their age) in the world. In 18 out of 22 states of India more than a quarter of children under the age of five are underdeveloped (having stunted height compared to their age). Statistics related to the weight of children when compared to their corresponding age also reveals that Assam has the highest (25%) rate of children whose weight is less as compared to their age, especially among the children up to five years of age. Bihar's condition is most pathetic in terms of prevalence of underweight children who are under five years of age. 41% of children in Bihar are underweight, relative to their age. The health of children is as important in their life as is their education. Nutritional deficiency affects their health and health affects their cognitive development! Therefore, the nutrition of children is very important for the 'nourishment' of their life.

Children are not numbers! Yet, statistics related to children indicate that many children have been affected in the Covid-19 epidemic. Even though lots of efforts were being taken to develop a system of online education, due to the varied socio-cultural environment in which children thrive, many children have been found to be deprived of their studies in online classes. According to a report of the United Nations, about two-thirds of the children between 3 to 17 years, i.e., about 1 billion 30 crore children, do not have adequate facilities to get connected to the internet. This is one of the major reasons for their interrupted education. This situation gets worse in rural areas. The coronavirus epidemic has severely affected the nutrition, health and education of children. Not only this, UNICEF also believes that with the disruption of health services and increasing poverty resulting from epidemics "*the future of an entire generation is in danger*". Interruption in the basic services and increasing poverty rates are the biggest danger for children. The longer this crisis will last, the deeper will be its impact on children's education, health, nutrition and welfare. Nearly one third of countries have faced decline in access to health services by at least 10%, including vaccination and maternal health services. It is stated that in India almost 26.5 crore children got deprived of the food which they used to have as midday meals. Due to closure of school, 33% of the school-going children were affected. According to UNICEF, the number of children living in poverty without access to education, health, housing, nutrition, sanitation and water globally is expected to increase by 15% by the end of this year.

Children are not numbers! Yet statistics related to children suggest that there is an increase in the number of child sexual abuse. According to a report published in *Navbharat Times* on 18 March 2018, based on the data shared by the National Crime Records Bureau (NCRB), there has been an 11% increase in crimes against children in India between 2015 and 2016. There has been an increase of 12,786 cases of crime against children across the country. While the number of crimes against children was 94,172 in 2015, it rose substantially to 1,06,958 in 2016. The abuse and exploitation faced by children adversely affects their childhood, and also has a negative effect on their mind and brain. The age in which the hands of children should have paper-pen, the age in which they need the abundant affection, love, protection, safety and conducive environment, in that delicate age they have to face the harshness of life and many times they are not even able to say anything about it. This is really an alarming situation!

Among all these statistics related to children, there is another data which gives a little hope amidst the above stated gloomy states. This data is related to the mortality rate of infants. In recent years, the government has reported a decline in child and infant mortality in India. According to the Population Division of the Department of Economic and Social Affairs of UNICEF, World Health Organization (WHO) and the World Bank Group, the mortality rate (infant mortality) of children under five years in India was 126 in 1990, which has come down to 34 in 2019. The number of deaths of children under five in India in 2019 was 8,24,000, compared to that of 34 lakhs in 1990. In this way, an annual reduction of 4.5% has been recorded in the deaths among children during 1990 to 2019. According to the report, child mortality in India (death per 1,000 live infants) was 89 in 1990, which has come down to 28 in 2019. Last year, 6,79,000 infants died in 2019 as compared to 24 lakhs in 1990.

This whole discussion related to children indicates that children, who we consider to be the future as well as assets of any country, have to be protected for both, their life and their childhood. Only when we ensure the safety of children, we will be able to make an effort in improving their education as well.

Children, Care and Education: Constitutional Provisions and Others

Education in itself is a vast concept and includes every dimension of life! In similar terms, life is also a vast concept that includes every dimension of education. The nature and characteristics of education is such that it expects quality along with continuity. Education in the early years of life also demands a variety of expectations and provisions. Early Childhood Care and Education (ECCE) is an important stage in the life and educational journey of any child. Basically, early Childhood Care and Education covers the life period of a child up to eight years of age since their birth. It is the period of rapid development of the brain and are also the years on which the child's lifelong development depends. The concept of ECCE incorporates a set of those investments and processes that ensures the fulfilment of subsequent needs of social, emotional and cognitive development of young children. It includes health, nutrition, care and learning opportunities of the early years. Recognising the importance of Early Childhood Care and Education, the Indian Constitution has also made provisions to cover all the dimensions related to a child's life:

- *Article 21 (a) – The State shall provide free and compulsory education to all children of the age of six to fourteen years in such manner as the State may, by law, determine.*
- *Article 23 – Traffic in human beings and beggar and other similar forms of forced labour are prohibited and any contravention of this provision shall be an offence punishable in accordance with law.*
- *Article 24 – No child below the age of 14 years shall be employed to work in any factory or mine or engaged in any other hazardous employment.*
- *Article 39 (e) –that the health and strength of workers, men and women, and the tender age of children are not abused and that citizens are not forced by economic necessity to enter avocations unsuited to their age or strength.*
- *Article 39 (f) –that children are given opportunities and facilities to develop in a healthy manner and in conditions of freedom and dignity and that childhood and youth are protected against exploitation and against moral and material abandonment.*
- *Article 47- Duty of the State to raise the level of nutrition and the standard of living and to improve public health. The State shall regard the raising of the level of nutrition and the standard of living of its people and the improvement of public health as among its primary duties, and, in particular, the State shall endeavour to bring about prohibition of the consumption except for medicinal purposes of intoxicating drinks and of drugs which are injurious to health*

According to the Constitution of India, Article 21 gives the fundamental Right to Live, and the life that should also be dignified, i.e., it is important to have quality of life, otherwise "*life of many is passing on the footpaths only*!" Along with the Right to Live, Article 21A gives the fundamental Right to Education – "*The State shall provide free and compulsory education to all children of the age of six to fourteen years in such manner as the State may, by law, determine.*" Article 45 of the Indian Constitution was amended (86th Amendment) which focused on Early Childhood Care and Education to state, "*The State shall endeavour to provide early childhood care and education for all children until they complete the age of six years*". The word 'endeavour' in this Article has caused concern in the minds of all those who are extremely concerned and reflective about the care and education of children. In this sense, the responsibility of the teacher and the school has shifted to the family and family members. In fact, we all have responsibility for the care and education of children – family, parents, teachers, schools and communities! Different policy makers and stakeholders are also part of this responsibility.

Early Childhood Care and Education: Policy Based Efforts

As has been previously elucidated, early childhood, defined as a period of eight years from the time of birth of the child, is a peak time for significant growth along with mental development. During this phase, children are highly influenced by the surroundings and the people associated with them. According to UNESCO, "*Early Childhood Care and Education is more than the initial stage for preparing the child for formal schooling. This emphasises on child's inclusive and all-round development, in which pertinent efforts are made to fulfil the child's own social, emotional, cognitive and physical needs. ECCE formulates a solid and comprehensive foundation for lifelong learning and well-being. It believes in a unified and holistic paradigm and follows the life-cycle approach.*" Thus, ECCE represents a continuation of the entire childhood from pre-natal stage till the time of eight years of age of the child. It is more than preparing for primary school! It aims for the holistic development of the child's social, emotional, cognitive, and physical needs so as to create a solid and broad foundation for their lifelong learning and well-being. Alongside, ECCE is capable of caring and integrated upbringing of the future citizens, there are endless possibilities in this context.

If we look in-depth, Human Rights and Child Rights cannot be ignored while making the efforts for the education of children. The Article 26 of the Universal Declaration of Human Rights (1948) clearly states – "*Everyone has the right to education.*" Child Rights (1989) also provides the space for Right to Education to the child along with Right to Health and Nutrition. Many rights related to the lives of children have been discussed in the Child Rights, which recognises the presence of children, their development and the responsibility of elders towards them. The following child rights can be seen to understand this–

Article 24	Good quality health care services for better health, primary health care, potable water, nutritious food and clean environment, pre-natal and post-natal health care of mother, preventing infant mortality and child mortality.
Article 27	Physical, mental, spiritual, moral and social development of children to achieve better life standards, better material facilities of nutrition, clothing and housing, etc.
Article 28	Equal right to education, free primary education, higher education, vocational education.
Article 29	Education should be such that it develops the personality and talent of the child as much as possible.
Article 30	The child has the right to learn and use the language and customs of his family, whether or not it is the language and customs of the majority of the people of the country.
Article 31	The child has the right to rest, play and participate in a wide range of activities.

National Education Commission (1964-66): The Commission emphasised that children should be provided pre-primary education of 1 to 3 years and should be given admission in Class I only after completing six years of age. All children should be given education in their mother tongue only in primary classes. It is an important recommendation of this commission that children should not become part of formal class at a very young age.

National Children's Policy (1974): The policy was adopted on 22 August 1974 to address the challenges related to children's lives. The main goals of this policy were–

- Reducing Infant Mortality Rate
- Reducing Maternal Mortality Rate
- Reducing Malnutrition among children
- Making efforts for universalisation of Early Childhood Care and Education
- Achieving 100 per cent access and retention in schools including pre-schools
- Complete abolition of female infanticide, child marriage and child labour and ensuring the survival, development and protection of the girl child.

Special provisions were made for the protection, care and education of children in this national policy.

Integrated Child Development Services (ICDS) (1975): The Government of India launched a centrally sponsored scheme in 1975-76 namely, the Integrated Child Development Services (ICDS) with the objective of holistic development of children and empowerment of mothers. The main objective of this scheme is to nurture children in the age group of 0-6 years and to lay the foundation for proper psychological, physical and social development of children with the aim of holistic development of children and empowerment of mothers. At the same time, adequate efforts are also being made to reduce the rate of mortality, illness, malnutrition and school dropout. Work is also being done to ensure the proper health and nutrition of the mothers. The Integrated Child Development Service has four distinct components –

1) Early Childhood Care Education and Development (ECCED)
2) Care and Nutritional Counselling
3) Health Services
4) Awareness and Community Mobilisation, Advocacy and Information, Education and Communication.

The objectives of the Integrated Child Development Service are mainly achieved through Anganwadi workers.

National Education Policy 1986: The NEP 1986 made several important recommendations in the context of childcare and education. These recommendations are as follows –

- "... *specially emphasises investment in the development of young children, particularly children from sections of the population in which first generation learners predominate.*" (5.1)
- "Recognising *the holistic nature of child development, viz., nutrition, health and social mental, physical, moral and emotional development, Early Childhood Care and Education (ECCE) will receive high priority and be suitably integrated with the Integrated Child Development Services programme, wherever possible. Day care centres will be provided as a support service for universalisation of primary education, to enable girls engaged in taking care of siblings to attend schools and as a support service for working women belonging to poorer sectors.*" (5.2)
- "*Programmes of ECCE will be child-oriented, focused around play and the individuality of the child. Formal methods and introduction of the 3R's will be discouraged at this stage. The local community will be fully involved in these programmes.*" (5.3)
- "*A full integration of child care and pre-primary education will be brought about.....In continuation of this stage, the school health programme will be strengthened.*" (5.4)

The National Policy on Education (1986) makes practical recommendations by familiarising the socio-cultural conditions of India and calls for the development of the all-round personality of children, whether they are child care centres or nutrition, health! If we consider, then it is evident that many of those things which are being said in the 1986 policy are the same as have been shared in 2020 policy. This means that not much has changed in the arena of education.

Learning without Burden (1992): It expresses concerns about starting education from an early age and states that "*Despite official stipulations that no textbooks be used at this stage, pre-school teachers and parents in the urban centres are feeling 'compelled' to burden the young child with textbooks and the formal learning they represent.... The pernicious grip of this false argument manifests itself in absurd and of course deeply harmful practices in pre-school and primary schools, such as early emphasis on shapely drawing, writing and memorising information. Intrinsic motivation and the child's natural abilities are being smothered at a scale so vast that it cannot be correctly estimated*" (Learning Without Burden, 1992, p. 14).

This policy suggests that there is a need for the formulation of regulatory mechanisms for nursery schools and to rigorously follow the same. It states that, "*a) Appropriate legislative and administrative measures be adopted to regulate the opening and functioning of Early Childhood Education Institutions (pre-schools).... It should be ensured that these institutions do not perpetrate violence on young children by inflicting a heavy dose of 'over education' in the form of formal teaching of Reading, Writing and Numbers....The practice of holding tests and interviews for admission to nursery class be abolished...(b) Norms for granting recognition to private schools be made more stringent*" (Learning Without Burden, 1992, p. 26).

National Early Childhood Care and Education Policy (2013): This policy expresses concern on the care and education of children. Mentioning the assurance of adequate care and education in primary years of children as the priority of India, gives rise to many possibilities. In order to achieve the right to free universal pre-school education, it is also necessary to ensure comprehensive access to integrated services. Balanced parenting by parents and caregivers is also being marked as important. Apart from this –

- "*The vision of policy is to achieve holistic development and active learning capacity of all children below six years of age by promoting free, universal, inclusive, equitable, joyful and contextualised opportunities for laying foundation and attaining full potential.*" (4.1)
- *The following base standards would be non-negotiable for promoting quality ECCE and shall be made mandatory for all service providers rendering any kind of ECCE service.*
  - ✓ *Adequately trained staff*
  - ✓ *Age and developmentally appropriate, child centred curriculum transacted in the mother tongue/local vernacular*
  - ✓ *Adequate and safe drinking water facilities*
  - ✓ *Adequate developmentally appropriate toys and learning materials*
  - ✓ *A safe building which is within easy approach. It should be clean and should have surrounding green areas*
  - ✓ *Adequate and separate child-friendly toilets and hand wash facilities for girls and boys*

- ✓ *Separate space allocated for cooking nutritionally balanced meals and nap time for children*
- ✓ *Immediate health services in terms of First Aid/Medical kit available at the centre*
- ✓ *The adult/caregiver: child ratio of 1:20 for 3–6-year-old children and 1:10 for under 3s should be available at the ECCE Centre. Children should not be unattended at any given point of time.*

All these points indicate that ECCE is an important concept and venture that should be taken care of.

National Children's Policy (2013): It also recommends that survival, nutrition, development, education, protection and participation are the undeniable rights of children. It also gives guidelines to states to ensure mental health care, post-natal care and nutrition of children. It also discusses the *provision for the right of the girl child to life, survival health and nutrition* (4.4). The National Children's Policy (2013) states that states should take all necessary measures to *provide universal and equitable access to quality Early Childhood Care and Education (ECCE) for optimal development and active learning capacity of all children below six years of age.* (4.6 (i))

Education for all: The Global Monitoring Report (2008): The report also emphasised that programmes that include nutrition, health, and cognitive components have a positive impact over a child's well-being. However, the latest report in 2015 suggests that the services of Early Childhood Education (ECE) have also expanded significantly (UNESCO, 2015). With this expansion, the movement has been made towards improving the quality of ECCE and making it free and compulsory, especially for underprivileged children. Therefore, equitable and primary investment in the quality of ECCE services and programmes became a matter of significant concern. Recognising this, the World Education Forum 2015 adopted the 'Incheon Declaration for Education 2030', which provided for at least one year of free and compulsory quality pre-primary education and encouraged quality early childhood development, care and access to education for all.

In terms of its educational objectives, the National Education Policy 2020 states that "*The purpose of the education system is to develop good human beings capable of rational thought and action, possessing compassion and empathy, courage and resilience, scientific temper and creative imagination, with sound ethical moorings and values. It aims at producing engaged, productive, and contributing citizens for building an equitable, inclusive, and plural society as envisaged by our Constitution*" (NEP 2020, pp. 4-5). To achieve this greater objective, it is necessary to focus on the upbringing and environment of children even before the academic life and to provide them a better environment in which they can develop their abilities to the optimum level. As a result of this, the first principle among the basic principles of the National Education Policy 2020 is based on the acceptance, recognition and striving for the development of unique abilities of every child. The document strongly supports the need to make teachers and parents sensitive towards the child's capabilities! Paying full attention to the all-round development of the child means taking care of every aspect of his personality. This need has been articulated in the first chapter of the National Education Policy 2020. It is also known that this policy has introduced a new structure of the school system: 5 + 3 + 3 + 4, i.e., three years of pre-school education in the first five years and Class I and II in the next two years! Education from Class III to Class V in the next three years. After this, education from Class VI to Class VIII in the next three years, whereas education from Class IX to Class XII is included in the next four years. Early Childhood Care and Education is in fact the foundation of learning where the child needs the utmost care. But it does not mean that children do not need care after this age or stage, rather it means that this stage of life is very complex, important in terms of development and learning. Efforts made at this stage of life are helpful in learning and living a better life. A brief description of the provisions made by the National Education Policy 2020 for early childhood care and education is as follows.

National Education Policy 2020 for Early Childhood Care and Education

Universal Early Childhood Care and Quality Education

The first six years of life are important in terms of education and for living a normal life, because the rate of growth in these years is much faster than any other stage of development. Research in Neuro-science confirms the importance of early years in a child's life, especially when the child is six years old. 85% of brain's development has already taken place before the age of six. Research also suggests that brain development is not only influenced by the quality of health, nutrition and care, but the quality of the socio-environmental setting also influences the development of the child in these early years. The National Education Policy also cites the same point and gives importance to Early Childhood Care and Education (ECCE), and makes provisions for such an education system for children which can provide them better nutrition, health, education and environment during this age. Not only can equity be established in society through ECEC but also a comparatively better positive long-term outcome can also be achieved in children through this than the later interventions. That is why the policy sets the goal that universal Early Childhood Care and Quality Education will be achieved before the year 2030.

Creative Pedagogy for Holistic Development

Since Early Childhood Care and Education (ECCE) is a sensitive phase that affects the later years of life, the emphasis has been made on providing education to children of this age informally through play-methods. Under ECCE, if children are taught with multi-dimensional and multi-level, play-based, activity-based and discovery-based learning methods, then better results will be achieved. It is certain that the informal method works at this stage. In creative pedagogy, children are given opportunities to become actively involved and to learn through varied kinds of stimulating activities. Children's language, number sense, various types of indoor and outdoor sports, drama, music and social work, personal and public hygiene, etc. are included in this creative pedagogy. Jean Piaget also emphasises that children construct knowledge on the basis of their socio-cultural experiences. All the aspects related to ECCE also indicate its flexibility in which the socio-cultural perspective of children is taken into consideration. Provision of quality education for the health and care of children will have to be made soon – this is the idea of the policy and also the goal!

Outstanding Syllabus and Academic Structure

The National Education Policy 2020 looks at categorising ECCE into two parts – education for children in the age group of 0-3 year and for the children of age group of 3-6 year. In order to achieve the goal of quality education for both, there is a need to create excellent curriculum and educational framework. The policy also mentions the adoption of national and international innovations in appropriate and rational ways. The traditions of child care and education which have been existent from many centuries in India – they also need to be adopted, such as – stories, poems, anecdotes, game songs, art, etc.! Through all this, an effective structure can be given to the education of children. In the policy, on the one hand there are talks about Indian traditions, on the other hand, the indication has also been made to accommodate international perspective. 'What will work' for Indian children and Indian classrooms? – this requires that researchers should be upgraded. The research done in Indian contexts will be helpful in the development and implementation of excellent curriculum and educational frameworks. "After all, Heart is Indian!" (*Akhir, Dil Hai Hindustani*!). The understanding developed from the research done in the Indian background and the educational structure developed from that understanding will also serve as a guide for parents.

High Quality ECCE Institutes

To reach all the children of the country, it is necessary to open high quality centres of ECCE across the country. Parts of the country which are in very remote areas will also be reached. All round development of children will be ensured through a strong ECCE system. According to the National Education Policy 2020, this work will be done in four ways – 1) through already empowered stand-alone Anganwadi system, 2) through Anganwadi co-located with primary school, 3) through pre-primary schools/sections covering at least age 5 to 6 years co-located with existing primary schools, 4) through stand-alone pre-schools! Efforts will be made to ensure ECCE in accordance with the systems and arrangements which would be available in the area. The policy also does not forget to ensure that only the staff / teachers who will be trained in the curriculum and teaching of ECCE are to be recruited in all schools. This is an important point on which the success / failure / results of ECCE depend upon.

High Quality Anganwadi Centres

As has been clarified, high quality Anganwadi Centres will be established across the country. These centres will have trained workers or teachers. Each Anganwadi will be set up as a well-designed, well-ventilated, child-accessible building. The premises of Anganwadi and Primary schools will be integrated and community's/parent's participation will also be ensured. The findings of a research study conducted in Jaipur suggest that there is a difference in the effectiveness of ECCE programs run by the government (Anganwadi) and non-governmental organisations in terms of children's cognitive development and school readiness. The findings of the study suggest that Anganwadis functional under the Integrated Child Development Services (ICDS) programme are lagging behind from the ECCE centres run by non-governmental institutions in terms of ensuring cognitive development and ensuring school readiness among children enrolled in the institutions. Although, infrastructural facilities were not found to be of good quality in the ECCE centres run by the non-governmental organisation, but the situation of Anganwadi centres run by the government was found to be worse. They were not able to meet the educational needs of pre-school children (Kumari, Archana, 2016). It is clear that to achieve the goal of quality ECCE, the goal of infrastructure must also be achieved. The physical environment of ECCE centres is as important as its academic education.

Balvatika (Kindergarten)

Before entering into Class I every child will be enrolled in pre-primary classes or 'Balvatika (Kindergarten)'. These will have trained ECCE teachers and this preparatory class will mainly incorporate play-based pedagogy. The purpose of this 'Balvatika (Kindergarten)' is to work for the development of children's cognitive, emotional and physical abilities, and also to develop foundational literacy and numeracy. There will also be a provision of mid-day meal and health check-up for the children enrolled in 'Balvatika (Kindergarten)'. The provisions made in the policy are ingrained in the fact that all round development of children requires additional support, nutrition and creative pedagogy.

Quality Training

In the process of teaching and learning, it is also important that the teachers themselves are ready for this process. Their own education and training should also be of quality and relevance. The way the policy is looking at ECCE by connecting it to the whole life of the child, it also expects high quality teaching skills from the teachers. The National Education Policy 2020 recommends the training of Anganwadi workers/teachers in a planned manner to prepare ECCE teachers. This responsibility of training has been given to NCERT to prepare a syllabus/pedagogical framework for 10+2 pass Anganwadi workers/ teachers, through which a six-month certificate programme can be provided to them. If the Anganwadi workers/teachers have not passed Class XII or have less qualification then there is a provision of one-year diploma program for them. This training programme will cover foundational literacy, numeracy and other important aspects of ECCE. This training program can be done through digital / distance medium as well as through smart phone. As there are limitations in the availability of facilities so every possible provision has been made for training. The preparation of cadres of qualified teachers through organising training, continuous evaluation, vocational training, guidance etc. by the mentor of the Cluster Resource Centre of the Department of Education, continuous professional development, etc. are other important provisions. All the provisions made in the policy for ECCE related training reflects the genuine thought about its implementation.

Ashramshala

India is a country of diversities and the geographical conditions of the country also vary. Keeping this in view, the policy talks of formulating 'Ashramshalas' in tribal areas in order to promote ECCE in far-flung areas. This work will be done in a phased manner. This is a good initiative and it requires practical thinking, as there is diversity in tribal areas too, they are in different parts of the country. The concept of Ashramshala will be helpful in ensuring the attainment of quality ECCE in the tribal society which is struggling with basic necessities of life. There is a need to provide ECCE to them in their own language and modalities.

Shared Responsibility

As we all know that education is the shared responsibility of all. This is equally true in the context of Early Childhood Care and Education. The policy clearly states that "*the responsibility for ECCE curriculum and pedagogy will lie with Ministry of Education to ensure its continuity from pre-primary school through primary school, and to ensure due attention to the foundational aspects of education. The planning and implementation of early childhood care and education curriculum will be carried out jointly by the Ministries of Education, Women and Child Development (WCD), Health and Family Welfare (HFW), and Tribal Affairs. A special joint task force will be constituted for continuous guidance of the smooth integration of early childhood care and education into school education.*" (NEP 2020, pg. 9) In this way, it is clear that the care and education of children is the shared responsibility of all and the coordination between various institutions, ministries is also required.

In fact, ECCE is the best investment to promote Human Resource Development, gender equality and social cohesion, and subsequently to reduce expenses of remedial programmes. It also plays an important role in addressing educational disparities in the context of underprivileged children. ECCE strengthens the foundations of lifelong learning, determined by the remarkable changes in children's developmental fields. The child needs a caring and stimulating environment in order to develop the full potential of the mind. Early Childhood Care and Education not only has a positive implication from the point of view of personal self-development, but it can reduce social inequality by compensating for vulnerability and disadvantage arising from factors such as poverty, gender, race, caste, and religion. Apart from this, it is a fact that primary education outcomes cannot be improved despite high investment unless quality of Early Childhood Care and Education is not ensured and improved. In this context, a lot of expectations are automatically made from the teachers and parents, that we should understand the children first and foremost! All the processes of education revolve around the child! The child is and must be the axis of all our efforts! But family, teachers, schools, society and policy makers are not free from this responsibility towards children, because education of children is the shared responsibility of all of us!

References

https://navbharattimes.indiatimes.com/india/day-against-child-labour-2020-child-labour-in-india-data-and-all-you-want-to-know/articleshow/76334222.cms, Navbharat.com Updated: 12 Jun 2020

(https://www.amarujala.com/india-news/world-day-against-child-labour-six-out-of-every-10-children-working-in-india-do-wages-in-farms?pageId=2)

https://www.dw.com/hi/युद्ध-के- कारण-बर्बाद-होता-बचपन/a-52360393

https://www.dw.com/hi/बच्चों-के- कद-और-वजन-में-गिरावट-से-जूझता- भारत/a-55978062

https://news.un.org/hi/story/2020/12/1035512

https://www.dw.com/hi/unicef-warns-of-lost-generation-as-virus-harms-childrens-services/a-55659103

https://www.jagran.com/lifestyle/health-india-s-child-mortality-rate-declined-between-1990-and-2019-un-20727362.

Kumari, Archana (2016). *Impact of Quality of ECCE Programs on Cognitive Development and School Readiness of Children, International Journal of Advanced Research* 4(7):1098-1104, DOI: 10.21474/IJAR01/1019, July 2016)

National Education Policy (2020), Ministry of Education, Government of India

5

School: A Site for Curriculum and Pedagogy

Haneet Gandhi

It has always been a dream of all academicians and those associated with the wellbeing of children that education be imparted for every child's interest and functional needs. Eminent philanthropists and social reformers such as Swami Vivekananda, Mahatma Gandhi, Rabindranath Tagore, Aurobindo Ghosh, John D.V., Maria Montessori believed that education should be imparted through amalgamation of activities such as arts, sports, painting and such so that the holistic development of the child can be ensured. These educationalists have also remarked how children are sensitive to language so as to emphasise that all kinds of formal schooling must be done through their mother tongue. Teaching in the mother tongue of the child ensures a rich and socially viable individual. These reformers have always held a thought that the creation of good human beings can only be achieved through education, and only through meaningful education we can build a strong nation. All education-philosophers propagated a strong and profound education policy that can help a nation attain the heights of prosperity. Only by an inclusive, better quality education a nation can make its youth capable of realising freedom, both mentally and physically, prosperity and self-reliance. Inspired by the ideas and recommendations of these Indian educational philosophers and reformers, the new education policy, i.e. the National Education Policy 2020 has been conceptualised.

On 29 July 2020, the Government of India launched a new nation-wide policy in education, titled National Education Policy 2020. After incorporating more than two lakh suggestions on their earlier published draft (Draft, National Education Policy 2019) this education policy was formulated to make it more holistic and inclusive. In this entire process of making the policy, people from all sectors were consulted for their views and suggestions. Stakeholders from Gram Panchayats to Zilla Parishads, Anganwadi teachers to Universities, Philosophers to general public, Academicians to Industrialists, all were invited. Summarily one may say, this education policy is a result of shared opinions, suggestions and advice from many.

After 34 years, India has seen a policy of education. In these past 34 years, many things have changed. We, as a nation and the entire global, as a whole, have advanced in terms of science, technology, economy, demands and needs. Coping with these changes and to propose a futuristic vision for the Indian Education system, the new policy proposes several recommendations.

Professor, Department of Education [CIE], University of Delhi, Delhi

One of them is related to school education. The policy strongly recommends overhauling of the educational structure in schools. The new National Education Policy 2020 has introduced 5+3+3+4 structure in place of the existing 10+2 school structure. It also proposes inculcation of Indian knowledge and languages instead of alienated foreign knowledge.

Some of the salient recommendations which the policies have made for strengthening the school education system in India are discussed. The author presents connections with past policies to analyse the future prospects of Indian school education. And brings out the practical and idealistic ideas of the past policies to make connections with new reforms.

The Earlier Policies

After India›s independence, the strongest path that our academicians, thinkers and national leaders took in shaping the foundation and future of the country was strengthening the education system. Soon after the independence, in November 1948, Radhakrishnan Commission was constituted with an aim to strengthen university level education in India. The commission observed that since the future construction of the country is actually happening in schools, it is difficult to make any effective changes in higher education without improving the school education structure. After this, the Secondary Education Commission was established in 1952 under the chairmanship of Dr. Mudaliar. This commission introduced a number of effective recommendations, such as adopting a diverse curriculum, introduction of a three-tier undergraduate course, conducting secondary education in two parts, objective testing methodologies, secondary education to be connected with primary education, core and optional subject areas etc. After taking in these suggestions and recommendations, the Kothari Commission was established with a view of understanding the entire structural system of education and to find solutions to the problems for the educational structure of the entire country. The Kothari Commission laid special emphasis on building social efficiency, national integrity and establishing a socialist society. It thus proposed a 10 + 2 + 3 structure for the education system in India. The commission also promoted tri-lingual formula in schools, continued science and technical education till higher level, and inculcation of moral and social values at all levels. Based on these recommendations, an education policy was published in 1968 with the aim of making a commitment to national development and for preparing skilled youth. This National Education Policy was implemented in May 1986, and is still holding the reins of education in India. In fact, in August 1985 a document called 'Challenge of Education' was prepared in which various people from various sections of India (intellectual, social, political, vocational, administrative, etc.) gave comments and suggestions on the course of education that must be adopted for a bright India. And, finally in 1986 the Government of India published 'National Education Policy'. The most important feature of this policy was uniform educational structure for the entire country, which was the 10 + 2 + 3 structure.

Putting special emphasis on child-centred pedagogy, the National Education Policy 1986 stated that the method of imparting education at the primary level should be child-centred and activity-based. First generation learners should be allowed to grow at their own pace and there should also be a system of supplementary and remedial education for them. As children grow older, cognitive elements will grow in them and through practice they will eventually acquire formal abstract skills. In addition, the policy also gave specific guidelines to ensure basic, essential facilities in all schools under the Operation Black Board campaign. The campaign was targeted on provisioning basic education to all children across India. It was about provisioning schools with basic infrastructures, necessary facilities and teaching materials. Thus, the NPE 1986 started sowing the seeds for improving the condition of primary education in India.

Another aspect for which the National Education Policy 1986 can be complimented is its views on inclusive education. The policy clearly states that children who have dropped out of school in the middle, or live in areas where there is no school or are engaged in work, and girls who cannot go to school full-time, must be brought back to school through multidimensional and systematic informal education. The policy clearly perceives a disconnect between formal and informal education. For children, learnings gained from their background and that given in formal settings must be seamless, in a continuum. In this regard, it states that non-formal education must be placed equivalent to formal education. Access to the formal system should be made for the children who pass through the informal system. An educational system like the National Centric Curriculum should be designed so as to bridge informal experiences with formal knowledge.

An amalgamated intermix of science, humanities, computers was introduced to make the curriculum diverse and broad. In support of this, the policy states that at the level of secondary education, students should begin to acquire knowledge in specific areas of sciences, humanities and social sciences. For a broader perspective, children should be equipped with necessary computer-related and vocational skills. Perhaps, while formulating the policy, the policy makers had realised by soon there would be an upsurge for computer-based skills in India. They, therefore, emphasised incorporating computer education and computer-based skills in school education. Along with this, the policy also recommended putting vocational skills in the ambit of school education. It directed inclusion of vocational subjects in the general curriculum at the school level. For a well-organised, planned and rigorously implemented programmes, vocational education must be of utmost importance. This would definitely need educational restructuring. Subjects like agriculture, marketing, social services, health related courses and such must be offered at the higher secondary level. It further stated that the responsibility of establishing vocational courses or institutions will be on the government, and certain public and private sectors can be consulted while doing so. Special steps must be taken for women and other sectors who are already in the deprived zone. Appropriate programmes will have to be started for the differently-abled. Courses and programmes will be redesigned to meet the demands of people who have special abilities. There should be a spectrum of specialisations. Students will have to be given more flexibility in deciding the courses they would like to pursue in future. The policy recognised special emphasis on promoting linguistic ability.

After the 1986 National Education Policy, the National Curriculum Framework (NCF) 2000 and 2005 came into existence. These were conceptualised for implementation of policy at school level. The curriculum frameworks paved ways for defining the curriculum, its effectiveness and pedagogy at school level. The frameworks made a note that the curriculum must be designed in such a manner that the people who study it can develop acumen to raise their voices against inequality to bridge the social, cultural, emotional, and economic needs of the country. NCF 2000 further stated that any curriculum has three pillars – Relevance, Equality and Excellence. For effective teaching at the school level, these three pillars must be taken into cognizance. NCF 2000 also clarifies that school curriculum must aim to provide useful avenues to the learners to acquire knowledge, develop understanding, hone their skills and adopt a positive attitude for the overall development of their personality. The curriculum must provide learning experiences that can encourage the multidimensional aspects of the child such as linguistic intelligence, logical mathematical intelligence, spatial intelligence, physical intelligence, musical intelligence, interpersonal intelligence and naturalistic intelligence. The policy identifies these eight types of intelligence as key aspects to be developed through the educational institutions.

Thus, the purpose of NCF 2000 was to reform the curriculum while meeting the challenges and expectations of the future by incorporating overall development and equity of the child and inculcation of values in the society. Keeping with these objectives, the NCF 2000 also urged to make pedagogy multi-dimensional and to link it with the contexts. It commented that pedagogy is not just about teaching; it is also a passage for enculturating children within the prevailing contexts and milieu. The pluralistic nature of Indian society should also be reflected in pedagogical practices of the schools. As stated earlier, NCF 2000 highly emphasized on vocational education for promoting skillful youth. It stated that India's future lies in making our youth skilled and professional and for this the subjects will have to be chosen from both, general and vocational fields. Schools in which vocational courses are taught should have their own training and production centres. These centres must provide opportunities for students to acquire the necessary qualifications based on real-life experiences expected at the workplace. In order to make the education process of the child meaningful and joyful, concerns of reducing the burden of education were highly expressed in the document. It urges on making Indian knowledge and its traditions a part of the school education. Infant education and care is of utmost importance to a developing country like ours. Under the Integrated Child Development Scheme, pre-school education through Anganwadi was promoted. It was believed that such an education will prepare young children for a further formal school system. To reduce the burden of the curriculum and to broaden the intellectual development of children, it remarked that this issue cannot be solved by only reducing the size of textbooks; the solution of this issue has to be found in its entirety. Memorisation of redundant concepts, complex ideas that are beyond the intellectual capacity of the child, tendency to rote learning and unnecessary pressure on homework will have to be removed. It is time to move away from the tyranny of rote, mindless learning. Creating a general plan of study for the primary and secondary levels that emphasises on 'how to learn' will be most suitable for students in terms of content and learning methods. Emphasis was laid on adopting the Swadeshi curriculum so as to link the curriculum to the Indian knowledge and traditions. Emphasising the Swadeshi curriculum, it has been said that the students must be aware of the progress that was made in the country in the past in various fields of knowledge. In addition, knowledge of Loka-cultures and its taste, folklore, traditional dance styles, costumes and instruments should be made an essential part of the school curriculum.

Thus, we see that NCF 2000 offers suggestions for radical change in curriculum and pedagogy in a comprehensive manner for the establishment of Indian education system whereby celebrating the spirits of democracy, equality, equity and most importantly, Indianness.

The National Curriculum Framework 2005 also suggested adopting empirical pedagogy and meaningful experiential learning as part of the school system. Education should be constructive, child-centred and drawn from the child's milieu. It recognised pedagogy as a resource for increasing the child's creativity. The document believed that teaching must be done in a dialogical manner, as a two-way process whereby the students must be given space and opportunities for self-expression and reflection. Teaching should be in a dialogical manner and not in the usual unilateral style. This way of interaction will increase the confidence and self-consciousness of the child. In addition to giving recommendations on the pedagogy to be adopted, the framework also suggested various methods for evaluation and assessment. It urged on reforming the traditional ways in which assessments were being done. The framework stated that intelligence is multidimensional and therefore, pedagogy and assessment must also be enriched to incorporate the multidimensionality of every child to its fullest. Excellence in diverse fields should be recognised and respected.

School Education as per National Education Policy 2020

The new education policy, known as National Education Policy 2020, was formulated in June 2017 under the chairmanship of former ISRO chief Dr. Kasturirangan. This is the country's third national based education policy. In this policy, special emphasis has been given to equality, quality, responsibility and accessibility of education for all. A landmark leap that this policy takes is in redefining the school education system. Instead of the 10+2 school education structure, it proposes the structure of 5+3+3+4. This policy is committed to reforming the education system of the country. It has laid down its recommendations for quality pre-school education to higher education.

In order to promote and preserve linguistic diversity, the policy emphasises on adopting mother tongue, or local or regional language as medium of instruction up to Class VIII. Language has been given its due place in the policy as it proposes promotion of ancient Indian languages by establishing institutes such as 'Indian Institute of Translation and Interpretation', 'National Institute for Persian, Pali and Prakrit' among the higher educational institutions of the country. These institutes will be entrusted with the tasks of preservation and development of Indian languages. It has been suggested to strengthen and promote local as well as vernacular languages through these institutes.

The policy recognises the value of pre-schooling and recommends that three years old children be given relevant pre-school education in their foundational stage through the Anganwadi, Balwatika, play schools, etc. The National Education Policy 2020 envisions a continuum between pre-school and post-school higher education of the child. It envisions that the curriculum and pedagogy at all levels must be interconnected and should be such that the translation of children from one stage to another becomes seamless. The policy clearly states that the pedagogy of the whole school will be directed in such a way that the overall development of the students can be done. High level skills like logical thinking, creativity, spirit of cooperation, team work and such must be developed. It also states that to develop mindfulness towards social concerns, a sense of responsibility through multilingualism and digital literacy must be constructed. Aim of schooling should be to equip the students in all academic as well as non-academic areas. Thus, there must be an amalgamation of subjects like sports, science, arts, language, literature, moral understanding, etc. This will widen the possibilities for the children. That is, the new education policy envisions a curriculum and pedagogy for the overall development of children, skillful youth and creation of digital India. School syllabus should be intertwined with vocational education with future potential skills, experience-based and logical thinking pedagogy.

The policy has made notes of the faulty systems of examinations and assessment that are currently being followed in the nation. It proposes establishment of a new national assessment centre called PARAKH. The institute being software based will harness the benefits of artificial intelligence for devising formative and adaptive assessment in schools.

According to the National Policy on Education 2020, vocational education will be started from the sixth grade onwards so that children can learn at least one skill before leaving the school. Apart from this, there will be no strict classification between science and social sciences and students will be allowed to study a wide variety of subjects. Earlier, subjects were grouped in 'streams', but with the implementation of NEP 2020 this practice will change. Students who wish to pursue engineering will also be able to study music and arts. It proposes establishment of institutes in the lines of the National Science Foundation which will include, in the curriculum, areas of sciences as well as social sciences. The policy also emphasises learning the basics of mathematics and Sanskrit in the first and second grades and enhancing understanding in these two areas by the end of fifth grade.

The NEP 2020 strongly envisions making the education system digitised. It states that digital literacy will be integrated for all students in basic level education. Pedagogy and assessment will have to be devised on the basis of availability of the digital facilities available at the school level. High level computational thinking, programming and other computer based activities will be included at the school level. Thus, the policy proposes to prepare the youth for an emerging digital India. The youth so prepared will not only know the potential problems but will also be able to present solutions. It envisions that with this digital India, the criterion of ethics will also be advanced for the youth. The policy recognises the worth of incorporating moral values along with digital literacy. In this context, it states that ethics must be taught from the early years onwards to the higher classes. Such an induction will prepare children to be good people, develop good character, lead a productive life and contribute positively to the society.

The National Policy on Education 2020 is committed for the development of a variety of skills in the Indian youth. It therefore proposes building vocational education and its associated institutional structure for the social utility. Incorporating and integrating professional education within mainstream education is indeed an appreciable move. The National Education Policy 2020 is committed to promoting vocational education at the secondary level. It instructs encouragement of local knowledge of the rural and tribal areas along with imparting technical training through a structured curriculum support. This includes creation of institutions such as the Center for Traditional Mediation, Center for Wildlife Conservation, and increasing economic prospects in the extinct folk genre to make younger people skilled and professional. It quotes that only five per cent of people in the age group of 19-24 years in India get vocational education. As a result, the number of unskilled and semi-skilled youth in India is increasing. The corrective efforts given in the National Education Policy 2020 will make India more economically and technically independent in the coming years. Also, the demand for skilled Indians in the global market and income level will increase gradually.

Along with these significant recommendations, the National Policy on Education 2020 also presents a blueprint for promoting Indian languages and Indian knowledge tradition among the youth. In this context, the policy clearly states that Indian literature and tradition encompass profound and deep knowledge in many disciplines and fields which needs to be unearthed.

Subjects such as mathematics, philosophy, art, logic, zoology, ecology, medicine, management, music, yoga, biology have deep rooted connections in the ancient Indian knowledge systems. Studying these subjects through the traditional Indian ways will help in transferring our culture and knowledge from one generation to another. We should seek avenues so that all relevant aspects of the Indian knowledge and tradition are accurately and scientifically incorporated into the school education at all classes. Indian languages, Indian knowledge and philosophy are being emphasised through the National Policy on Education 2020. Many changes have been proposed in the policy for the spread of Vedic mathematics, Indian philosophy, and Indian languages and traditions.

Road Map Ahead

Although the new policy of education is rich in its ideology and recommendations, it is speculated that the government may face some challenges in implementing it in true spirit. One such challenge could be related to promotion of online education, e-learning and e-content which will increasingly become the future of digital India. As per a recently released government report, only 9.85 per cent of public schools have computer facilities and only 4.09 per cent schools are provided with internet accessibility. In such a situation, to fulfill its dream of creating digital youth, the government will have to first ensure all required facilities in the school complexes.

Another challenge that we could face will be at the level of Anganwadi education. According to a report, three lakh sixty-two thousand nine-hundred forty Anganwadi centres do not have basic infrastructural facilities such as toilets and clean water; therefore, education in these centres would be questionable. Before thinking of education, provisions of basic hygiene and health will have to be made. It is necessary to ensure basic facilities and requirements before thinking of education in any way. Only then we will be able to fulfill the dream of giving proper education to crores of young children of the country.

In the end, one may say that apart from these sporadic challenges, overall the new National Education Policy 2020 gives bright hopes for a good educated futuristic India. As a document, it offers many promises and strong recommendations for strengthening the school education system of the country. This policy strongly acknowledges Indian cultural roots and Indian knowledge tradition, with a view to creating the future of youth keeping in view the global prospects.

It can be said that the National Education Policy 2020 is a co-mixture of both ideal, ground realities and futuristic demands. The government's will power and real reforms in the education system can provide a new direction to education in India. The formulation of education policy after so many years is a proof that India will soon rise towards a bright and promising future.

6

National Education Policy 2020: From the Lens of Inclusion

Yukti Sharma

An Overview

The policy has discussed inclusion in the context of issues of equity, social justice and equality which is in consonance with the key ideas about inclusion and inclusive education at the international level. The policy strongly asserts for inclusive and equitable education with the premise that education has an instrumental role in establishing an inclusive and equitable society. Thus, although it's a policy in education but it associates education vis-à-vis inclusion to the larger society. Hence, while discussing inclusive education reference is given to all levels of education. Also, the policy envisions to bring inclusive changes both in the education system as well as in the institutions that are engaged with education. The policy discusses the conceptual idea of equitable and inclusive education and explicitly states the various expectations from it. The idea of inclusion as stated in the policy has a broader connotation as it very vividly presents the diversity that exists in India and the need of social inclusion. Thus, it provides various criteria for identifying the socio-economically disadvantaged groups of people in Indian apart from people with disabilities. In response to the exiting situation in India the policy recommends various strategies and initiatives that should be taken at both the school as well as in higher education for achieving equitable and inclusive education. Thus, the chapter is divided into sections where each one discusses the above-mentioned key ideas stated in the policy substantiated with excerpts from the policy.

Towards Equitable and Inclusive Education

The policy strongly recommends inclusion as the fundamental principle. Hence it is asserted in the policy that full equity and inclusion should be the cornerstone of all educational decisions to ensure that all students are able to thrive in the education system. According to the policy these fundamental principles should not only guide the education system at large but also the individual institutions within it. This is aligned to the global education development agenda that is reflected in the goal 4 (SDG4) of the 2030 Agenda for Sustainable Development which was adopted by India in 2015. The goal

Professor, Department of Education [CIE], University of Delhi, Delhi

seeks to *"ensure inclusive and equitable quality education and promote lifelong learning opportunities for all"* by 2030. The policy acknowledges that education is the single greatest tool for achieving social justice and equality. Education is a great leveller and is the best tool for achieving economic and social mobility, inclusion, and equality. Hence, the policy envisions that Inclusive and equitable education is although an essential goal in its own right but it is also critical to achieving an inclusive and equitable society in which every citizen has the opportunity to dream, thrive, and contribute to the nation With this as one of the rationale for inclusive education, the Policy reaffirms that bridging the social category gaps in access, participation, and learning outcomes in school education should continue to be one of the major goals of all education sector development programmes. Hence it contends that the education system must aim to benefit India 's children so that no child loses any opportunity to learn and excel because of circumstances of birth or background. (Ref. 6.1, p. 24). Thus, the policy recommends social inclusion and not just the inclusion of children with disabilities which is in tandem with the international evolving idea of inclusion. In this context, the new education policy very explicitly states that all students, irrespective of their place of residence must be provided a quality education system, with particular focus on historically marginalized, disadvantaged, and underrepresented groups. The policy specifically states that the appropriated initiatives must be in place to ensure that all students from the above discussed groups, despite inherent obstacles, are provided various targeted opportunities to enter and excel in the educational system.

This shows that the policy recognizes and is responsive in the following ways:

- It acknowledges the huge diversity that is present in India as well as within Indian population.
- It is aligned to the international perspective of inclusion and to the SDG4 to which India is a signatory. Thus, the policy intends to meet the goal which is an International commitment on the part of India.
- It contends that education is a fundamental right in itself for all humans but at the same time it has a vital role in addressing issues of social justice, equity, as well as social and economic mobility. Thus, it rationalises the larger role and importance of inclusive education.
- It recommends the education system to focus on all kinds of exclusionary processes thereby attending to all groups who need to be included in the system as well as in the society. They may be disadvantaged or may be marginalized or may be underrepresented for any of the social, economic, political or any other reason.
- It specifically advises 'quality education' for all which means that by inclusive education the policy expects a quality education for all citizens and not simply a mere entry into the system. It asserts that learners from all groups should be provided opportunity to enter as well as excel

in the education system. The entry has been to some extent assured by the RTE, 2009 and RPWD, 2016 Acts but what is more important is the engagement of the learners after they get entry into the institution. The policy is therefore accentuating on the phrase 'quality education'.

The Idea of Socio-economically Disadvantaged Groups (SEDGs) and Subsequent Deliberations

The policy has introduced the concept of Socio-economically disadvantaged groups (SEDGs). It has recommended various ways in which Indian population can be broadly categorized such as gender identities that particularly include female and transgender individuals, socio-cultural identities like Scheduled Castes, Scheduled Tribes, OBCs, and minorities, geographical identities like students from villages, small towns, and aspirational districts, disabilities including learning disabilities, and socio-economic conditions like migrant communities, low income households, children in vulnerable situations, victims of or children of victims of trafficking, orphans including child beggars in urban areas, and the urban poor. The policy has shared various concerns regarding the SEDGs. Such as the policy has highlighted that while overall enrolments in schools decline steadily from Grade 1 to Grade 12 but this decline in enrolments was significantly more pronounced for many of these SEDGs, with even greater declines for female students within each of these SEDGs and often even steeper in higher education. Thus, the policy examines the impact on enrolment rate of learners who belong to SEDGs. Its further correlation is that the enrolment rate is even less if the child belongs to more than one SEDGs that is if the learners is belongs to a low-income background and is also a female. The literature too recognises this correlation, and these students are generally identified as doubly disadvantaged. Also, the policy observes that the disadvantage is more noticeable at higher levels of education as the enrolment rate goes down precipitously (Ref. 6.2, p. 24).

The policy specifically deliberates on the status of education of some of the SEDGs in terms of their enrolment and retention rates. It recognises that there is multiplicity of factors, including lack of access to quality schools, poverty, social mores and customs, and language have had a detrimental effect on rates of enrolment and retention among the Scheduled Castes. Thus, the policy recommends that bridging these gaps in access, participation, and learning outcomes of children belonging to Scheduled Castes will continue to be one of the major goals. The policy mentions that Other Backward Classes (OBCs) which have been identified on the basis of historically being socially and educationally backward also need special focus (Ref. 6.2.2, p. 25). It specifically states that the tribal communities and children from Scheduled Tribes face disadvantages at multiple levels due to various historical and geographical factors (Ref. 6.2.3, p. 25). Also, the policy recognises that the since the tribal communities and their culture don't find representation in school education hence their children often find it irrelevant and foreign to their lives, both culturally and academically. They state that although various programmatic interventions for children from tribal communities are currently in place, but still special mechanisms need to be made to ensure that children belonging to tribal communities receive the benefits of these interventions (Ref. 6.2.3, p. 25). Thus, the policy highlights the concern regarding implementation of the existing interventions and their impact. The policy also recognizes relative underrepresentation of the minorities in school and higher education. In response to this the policy acknowledges the importance of interventions to promote education of children belonging to all minority communities, and particularly those communities that are educationally underrepresented (Ref. 6.2.4, p. 25). Last but not the least, the policy makes a special mention of Children With Special Needs (CWSN) or Divyang and the importance of creating enabling mechanisms for providing them the same opportunities of obtaining quality education as any other child (Ref. 6.2.5, p. 25). Thus, it shows an acceptance of the idea of CWSN and the concept of 'enabling mechanism' signifies that the policy takes on from the perspective if social model of disability where the society is considered to be disabling rather than the individual.

Specific Recommendations for SEDGs

The policy has given specific attention to each group of SEDGs by discussing about each one of them and the concerns related to them. The policy has recommended for giving focused attention on reducing the social category gaps in school education.

- *Early Childhood Care and Education (ECCE):* The policy is responsive to the early childhood care and education for the children belonging to SEDGs. Hence, it suggests that the critical problems and recommendations regarding ECCE, foundational literacy and numeracy, access, enrolment and attendance discussed in Chapters 1-3, are particularly relevant and important for underrepresented and disadvantaged groups. Therefore, the measures from Chapters 1-3 will be targeted in a concerted way for SEDGs (Ref. 6.2.3, p. 25).
- *Identifying and Strengthening existing Policies and Schemes for SEDGs:* The policy advises that it is essential to identify the existing policies and schemes that were effective in increasing the enrolment if children of SEDGs in schools. Such as, targeted scholarships, conditional cash transfers to incentivize parents to send their children to school, providing bicycles for transport, etc., that have significantly increased participation of SEDGs in the schooling system in certain areas. These successful policies and schemes must be significantly strengthened across the country (Ref. 6.2.4).
- *Undertaking research to assess the effectiveness of various measures for SEDGs:* The policy suggests that research should be undertaken to find out

which measures were particularly effective for certain SEDGs. Some instances quoted in the policy are:

- o Providing bicycles and organizing cycling and walking groups to provide access to school have been very effective.
- o Schools providing quality ECCE is very useful specially for children of families that are economically disadvantaged.
- o The counsellors and/or well-trained social workers that work with and connect with students, parents, schools, and teachers in order to improve attendance and learning outcomes have been found to be especially effective for children in urban poor areas (Ref. 6.5, p. 25).

- *Identifying Special Education Zones (SEZs)*: The policy observes that the data shows that certain geographical areas in the country contained significantly larger proportions of SEDGs and identifies some geographical locations as Aspirational Districts which require special interventions for promoting their educational development. Hence, the policy recommends such regions should be declared as special education zones so that intensive and concentrated efforts should be made to improve the educational situation there (Ref. 6.6, p. 26). This shows that the policy acknowledges the existing disparities within the educational status of the various regions in the country considering the vastness and the diversity of the country. At the same time, it also gives arecoomendation in this regard to address the issue.
- *Free boarding facilities in schools*: The policy recommended that free boarding facilities would be provided to students especially for girls that are as per the standard of Jawahar Navodaya Vidyalayas. The policy recognises various challenges that students might be facing in relation to the various factors that effect their access to the school. Such as many students may not have a school near to their house and may have to travel a long distance. Also, some belonged to socio-economically disadvantaged backgrounds and hence was not possible to attend the school regularly. The policy in the context of double disadvantage that girls from socio-economically disadvantaged backgrounds experience, suggests that Kasturba Gandhi Balika Vidyalayas should be strengthened. At the same time the policy also ensures that the sttudents who are facing any kind of disadvantage vis-à-vis their education should be given opportunity to engage in quality education. One such recoomendation is related to building up of additional Jawahar Navodaya Vidyalayas and Kendriya Vidyalayas would be built around the country (Ref. 6.9, p. 26).
- *Conserving the insights and practices from Alternative Schooling*: The policy encourages to derive insights from alternative education for establishing inclusive education. Thus, establishing that inclusive education is the amalgamation of learnings from both special and general education that

align to the principles of inclusion. At the same time, it seems that the policy discourages any kind of existence of a parallel system of education by bringing alternate schools with the larger school education system. Also, it attempts to create channels for children from these schools to access the higher education. Some suggestions in this regard are (Ref. 6.15, p. 27):

- o Including the alternative schools by aligning the subject and learning areas with those prescribed by the NCFSE to make opportunities of higher education accessible to their learners.
- o Provision of financial assistance to alternative schools for introducing science, mathematics, social studies, Hindi, English, State languages, or other relevant subjects in the curriculum, as may be desired by these schools.
- o Encouraging students of these schools to appear for State or other Board examinations and assessments by the National Testing Agency (NTA) to facilitate their enrollment in higher education institutions.
- o Orientation of teachers to new pedagogical practices.
- o Strengthening of the libraries and laboratories by making available relevant books and teaching-learning resources.

- *Response to girl's education in the country:* The policy has strongly noted that about half of all SEDGs is represented by the women as they are part of all the disadvantaged groups. The policy recommends the following in this regard:
  - o The policy additionally recognizes the special and critical role that women play in society and in shaping social mores; therefore, providing a quality education to girls is the best way to increase the education levels for these SEDGs, not just in the present but also in future generations (Ref. 6.7, p. 26).
  - o The policy thus recommends that the policies and schemes designed to include students from SEDGs should be especially targeted towards girls in these SEDGs (Ref. 6.7, p. 26).
  - o The policy advises the Government of India to constitute a 'Gender-Inclusion Fund' for building the nation 's capacity so that equitable quality education fcould be provided to the groups that face disdavnatge due to gender. It includes both girls and transgender students. According to the policy this fund should be used for provisioning that supports the students in gaining access to education such as the provisions of sanitation and toilets, bicycles, etc. Alos, the funds should be used by the stated in addressing the gender related issues specific to the local contexts. On the same lines, the policy recommends the development of 'Inclusion Fund' schemes for other SEDGs. The policy through the funds aims to

eleminate the disparities w.r.t education of the disadvantaged groups to a large extent (Ref. 6.8, p. 26).

- *Provisioning for Children with disabilities*:
  - The policy strongly recommends the inclusion of children with disabilities and their equal participation from the foundational stage to higher education. Thus, it specifically states that the inclusion of children with disabilities in ECCE should be ensured. The policy is completely aligned to the idea of inclusion as it precisely talks about the participation of children with disabilities in regular school system. In this context the policy refers and quotes The Rights of Persons with Disabilities (RPWD) Act 2016 that defines inclusive education as a '*system of education wherein students with and without disabilities learn together and the system of teaching and learning is suitably adapted to meet the learning needs of different types of students with disabilities*' (Ref. 6.10, p. 26).
  - The Policy refers and recommends following the RPWD Act 2016 has suggested that expert bodies working with people with disabilities should be involved for preparing the National Curriculum Framework. (Ref. 6.10, p. 26).
  - The policy acknowledges various strategies such as one-on-one teachers and tutors, peer tutoring, open schooling, appropriate infrastructure, and suitable technological interventions to ensure access can be particularly effective for certain children with disabilities that have been essential part of inclusive education (Ref. 6.5, p. 25).
  - The policy give due emphasis to barrier free access for all children with disabilities as well as provisioning in terms of resources, recruitment of special educators with cross-disability training and for the establishment of resource centres for integrating children with disabilities into regular school system. In this context, the policy refers to the idea of school complexes also. (Ref. 6.11, p. 26).
  - The policy recognises that different categories of children with disabilities have differing needs and hence recommends accommodations and support mechanisms tailored to suit their needs. It specifically recommends the provisioning of assistive devices and appropriate technology-based tools, as well as adequate and language-appropriate teaching-learning materials (e.g., textbooks in accessible formats such as large print and Braille). (Ref. 6.11, p. 27).
  - The policy identifies the role of NIOS for developing high-quality modules to teach Indian Sign Language, and to teach other basic subjects using Indian Sign Language (Ref. 6.11, p. 27).
  - In case of children with severe disabilities, the policy is equally responsive and derives from the RPWD Act 2016. It acknowledges

the significance of home-based education for children with severe and profound disabilities. A meaningful suggestion in this regard is that the children under home-based education must be treated at par with any other child in the general system for it recommends that the guidelines and standards for home-based schooling should be developed in the light of the RPWD Act 2016 (Ref. 6.12, p. 27).
   - In case of children with specific learning disabilities the policy states that the children should be identified at early stages and their needs should be addressed using appropriate strategies for teaching as well assessement. In this regard, it also specifies the role of National Assessment Centre, PARAKH for formulation of guidelines and recommendation of tools for assessment. (Ref. 6.13, p. 27).
   - The policy recommends that the teacher education programmes should equip teachers with knowledge about strategies for teaching children with specific disabilities (including learning disabilities) along with awareness about children belonging to other disadvantaged groups (Ref. 6.14, p. 27).
- The policy strongly recommends that various efforts should be made to reduce the disparities in the educational status of children belonging to Scheduled Castes and Scheduled Tribes (Ref. 6.16, pp. 27-28).
- The policy also prescribes simple mechanism for easy access and awareness about scholarships, opportunities and schemes for students from SEDGs (Ref. 6.18, p. 28).
- One of the commendations of the policy is that it strongly focusses on developing an inclusive educational school culture and sees it as essential for empowerment of all children as well as for overall transformation of the society. It suggests various ways in which the schools should develop this culture (Ref. 6.19, p. 28).
- The policy recommends that sensitization of the students was utmost important for developing an inclusive culture in the school. Considering the huge divesrity in the country, the policy aptly envisions a school curriculum that includes experiences that nurture various human values and at the same time detailed knowledge about different cultures (Ref. 6.20, p. 28).

Thus, with regard to the provisioning and strategies related to SEDGs, the policy has given very comprehensive and detailed recommendations discussing the needs of each group separately. This shows that the policy is sensitive towards the specific unique needs of each group considering that thee have emerged through their experiences historically. The policy derives largely from RPWD Act 2016 which is the revised PWD Act, 1995 and is in itself a very exhaustive act. While discussing about the context of SEDGs, the act strongly asserts that an inclusive school culture has to be developed for true inclusion of children of these groups into general schools. This shows that the identification of SEDGs is not for segregation but for understanding their current status and needs to include their children in the general education system effectively

The Context of Higher Education

The policy has extended the concern of equity and inclusion in higher education too. It has specifically suggested steps to be taken by Governments that are specific to higher education shall be adopted by all Governments and HEIs. The policy suggests that suitable Government funds should be earmarked for the education of SEDGs and there should be clear targets set for higher GER for SEDGs. It also proposes that gender balance in admissions to HEIs and access by establishing more high-quality HEIs in aspirational districts and Special Education Zones containing larger numbers of SEDGs should be enhanced. As an implication, it suggests that high-quality HEIs that teach in local/Indian languages or bilingually should be developed. The policy specifically recommends that more financial assistance and scholarships to SEDGs in both public and private HEIs should be provided. It suggests that outreach programmes on higher education opportunities should be conducted and provision for scholarships among SEDGs. It also recommends the development of technology tools for better participation and learning outcomes (Ref. 14.4.1, p. 41).

The policy has also given specific suggestions for the HEIs that range from infrastructural to enforcing rules for their protection to curricular experiences. Some steps suggested for all HEIs (Ref. 14.4.2, pp. 41-42):

(a) Mitigate opportunity costs and fees for pursuing higher education.
(b) Provide more financial assistance and scholarships to socio-economically disadvantaged students.
(c) Conduct outreach on higher education opportunities and scholarships.
(d) Make admissions processes more inclusive.
(e) Make curriculum more inclusive.
(f) Increase employability potential of higher education programmes.
(g) Develop more degree courses taught in Indian languages and bilingually.
(h) Ensure all buildings and facilities are wheelchair-accessible and disabled-friendly.
(i) Develop bridge courses for students that come from disadvantaged educational backgrounds.
(j) Provide socio-emotional and academic support and mentoring for all such students through suitable counselling and mentoring programmes.
(k) Ensure sensitization of faculty, counsellor, and students on gender-identity issue and its inclusion in all aspects of the HEI, including curricula.

(l) Strictly enforce all no-discrimination and anti-harassment rules.
(m) Develop Institutional Development Plans that contain specific plans for action on increasing participation from SEDGs, including but not limited to the above items.

Thus, it can be seen that the policy recommendations envision preparing the higher education system towards inclusion too. This shows that the policy itself is inclusive by not restricting the inclusive principles to merely school education as is the case with RTE Act, 2009. There are specific suggestions for macro level where the governments are advised to review and ensure the issues of access, quality, availability of higher educational institutions in their regions. It gives detailed suggestions for HEIs to develop them into inclusive institutions.

Concluding Thoughts

The discussion and the excerpts from the new education policy above shows that the policy has given a detailed discourse on inclusive education and disadvantaged, or marginalised groups of people followed by the recommendations. Thus, the part of policy related to inclusion has been conscripted using appropriate rationale wherever required taking on from the existing researches, Acts or theoretical ideas. The policy recommendations are aligned to the international initiatives in inclusion. As compared to the previous policy, it is based on the broad idea of inclusion that encompasses social inclusion. Also, it reiterates at several places specifically in the context of children with severe disabilities that the education of all children is the responsibility of the state. Hence, the policy sensitively and comprehensively given recommendations for inclusive education that requires a detailed plan for its implementation at various levels and in various ways.

References

National Education Policy (NEP) 2020. Ministry of Human Resource Development (MHRD), Government of India (GOI). https://www.education.gov.in/sites/upload_ files/mhrd/files/NEP_Final_English_0.pdf. Retrieved on Sept. 7, 2021.

The Rights of Persons with Disabilities Act (RPWD) Act 2016. The Gazette of India. Part 2 Section 1. Ministry of Law and Justice (Legislative Department). http://www.upfcindia.com/ documents/rpwd_101017.pdf. Retrieved on Sept. 7, 2021.

The Right of Children to Free and Compulsory Education Act (RTE) 2009. The Gazette of India. Part 2 Section 1. https://www.education.gov.in/sites/upload_files/mhrd/ files/upload_ document/rte.pdf. Retrieved on Sept. 7, 2021.

7

Decentralisation of Schooling through School Complexes and Clusters

Kaushal Kishore[1] and Chandan Shrivastava[2]

After a long gap of thirty-four years, recently, India got its new education policy, titled 'National Education Policy 2020'. Considering school education as the most important segment, the policy has dedicated about 50% of its content to issues related to school education.

In India, we have so many concerns related to school education, such as poor infrastructure, lack of qualified teachers, depletion of students' learning, dropouts, etc. Along with these, the bigger challenge is that all schools are not similar in their resources. Many schools are infrastructurally rich but may have a lack of human resources such as teachers and support staff. On the other hand, we may also find some schools which have more than the required number of teachers as compared to their students' strength. These types of situations are very much true for the common government schools across India if we exclude the schools like *Navodayas* or *Kendriya Vidyalayas.* Another major issue with almost every school is about the decreasing graph in the learning levels of students from early classes to upper classes. It has been found that as the students move from Class I to above grades, their learning outcomes reduce substantially (NAS, 2017). This infers that the present system of schools is struggling to deliver expected levels of learning to its students. All these are prime concerns for the policy makers which demanded an overall transformation of the Indian school system.

The new policy has tried to address these concerns through its various provisions and transformative ideas. School complex or cluster is one of such transformative ideas proposed by it to enhance the quality of schooling by endorsing the idea of grouping of schools wherever possible. According to it, the implementation of school complexes or clusters will help in creating efficient resources and better coordination, functioning, leadership, governance, and management in the school clusters. But, along with progressive dimensions, this idea has also floated many concerns and challenges before academia, such as, what will be the modalities of its execution? Will this really bring quality change in all schools? Is it possible to apply this idea universally in diverse conditions that exist in our country? All such questions are definitely

[1] Professor and Dean, School of Education, Central University of South Bihar, Gaya

[2] Assistant Professor, School of Education, Central University of South Bihar, Gaya

bothering us and it is very difficult to suggest any solution at this juncture. However, we can begin by analysing the core idea of 'School Complex/ Cluster' as conceptualised by the NEP 2020. We can also inquire about the evolution of this idea in the past. This chapter is an attempt to address these points conceptually.

Idea of School Complex and its Historical Backdrop

The core idea of the school complex/cluster is based on the principle of decentralisation of governance. In general, the idea of decentralisation is based on the principle of distribution of authority and responsibility from upper to lower levels in a system. Decentralisation can also be defined as the transfer of decision-making powers from central authority to intermediate authorities, local authorities and educational institutions, in varying degrees (Welsh & McGinn, 1999). Decentralisation of governance can be visualised in many ways from general administrative decentralisation to the transfer of bigger regulatory and financial powers to regional and local levels. It is largely accepted that the process of decentralisation in educational administration may significantly improve transparency, administrative productivity, financial management, and quality and convenience of services. Therefore, a decentralised education system would be more compatible with the local requirements and will greatly address contextual learning challenges.

The school cluster system is one of the modern forms of educational decentralisation that developed in the last few decades which stresses on grouping of those schools which are geographically compatible in order to share educational resources and instructional materials with the purpose of improving the overall quality of education. This kind of system allows neighbouring schools to practise cooperative learning by sharing their educational resources to maximise the extent for common advantages of all schools in the cluster. But, how to create this group of schools in a coherent way needs a lot of planning and ground work. However, the school complex/ cluster systems need to be visibly presented and clarified to build awareness and a sound understanding of its importance, potentials and utility (Dittmar, Mendelsohn & Ward, 2002).

In the past, the idea of school complexes in India was initially brought by the Education Commission (1964-66) in its report. For uplifting the general standards of secondary and primary schools, it was envisioned that a relationship between different educational institutions would improve by establishing 'School Complexes'. In the opinion of the commission, the schools within the radius of about five to ten miles should be linked together to form a 'school complex'. It was assumed by the commission that the group of schools in a school complex can help each other in improving the quality of education, share the aids, library books, laboratory materials, etc. The commission described the working of the school complex in detail and talked about its many advantages, such as breaking the barrier of isolation of schools by making them work together. This will also lead to cooperative efforts to improve different functions of a school. The school complex can be used as a unit for introducing better methods of assessment and evaluation of learners. Through this, the education departments will have space to provide better facilities to schools and to decentralise authority. This was also visualised that the school complex can take up the responsibility of in-service education of teachers in general and the upgrading of the less qualified teachers in particular. The Kothari Commission had, thus, given a very creative idea of improving the standard of schools through their own cooperation in the form of school complexes.

Following the recommendation of Kothari Commission, the idea was implemented by various states on a try-out basis. The Maharashtra Government decided to establish such school complexes in their state by passing a resolution in 1968 to that effect. The Resolution pointed out the isolation of schools and about the limited coordination that existed between the working of secondary and primary schools. It was hoped that the gap can be overcome by making each higher stage responsible for improving the standard of the next lower stage. The plan of action made by the then Maharashtra government was almost the same as mentioned by the Kothari Commission. The state of Bihar also introduced this scheme in its few districts in 1975. There, the school complex was called 'Sankul'. For better implementation, 'Sankul' schools were regularly inspected. Due to this, punctuality and regularity of the teachers increased. This also resulted in guiding teachers for better ways of teaching and using the available resources. The whole set-up was given a formal administrative set-up where the school complexes were required to do many activities such as preparation of annual plan for academic and physical improvement of schools, regular and intensive inspections of the member schools, organisation of student activities, establishing parent-teacher organisations and arranging their meetings, conducting uniform examinations and evaluating the students' performance, and conducting monthly meetings and reviewing the work done. Initially, the scheme showed very encouraging results in Bihar but soon got diluted due to negligence. Similarly, in Uttar Pradesh, the scheme was implemented on a trial basis in three blocks consisting of four school complexes each which were expected to undertake lots of academic activities together. However, the idea remained limited to a small geographical area and could not scale up (Sinha, 1981).

In Rajasthan, the scheme of the school complex was introduced on a voluntary basis with a view to improve the standard of the school education. The complexes were established only where the Headmasters volunteered. Initially the number of the complexes was about seventy in 1967 which doubled by 1972. The scheme was also introduced in the state of Haryana in 1969-70 with just six school complexes. In a study, it was found that the scheme had presented a very dynamic approach to solve the problems of school education in the State. Many other states also benefited from the scheme. For illustration as an extension to this scheme, junior basic training schools and other higher secondary schools were made centres for the in-service training in Haryana; and in Tamil Nadu, the scheme was introduced in a huge magnitude of about two thousand school complexes. There, one high school was linked with three to four middle schools in the locality. These middle schools were connected with ten to twenty primary schools. As an innovative practice, the state of Tamil Nadu also established college-school complexes (Singhal, 1983).

In this way, many states have made several plans to implement the idea of school structure on an experimental basis. This is also true that the idea was not taken with intensity in due course, however, it is also visible that the states have not completely side-lined it. Many states have assimilated the idea of school cluster with their existing model. For instance, Bihar has made a cluster of schools with about fifteen to twenty schools together and a dedicated cluster resource centre is also established for proper coordination and organisation of academic activities among the schools of such clusters. But we need to reflect, that did we efficiently implement this idea or it is still unutilised. The National Education Policy 2020 has created a new opportunity to revisit this idea of School Complex/Cluster for its implementation in contemporary time. The policy document is very elaborative to discuss its needs and benefits which should be holistically understood and discussed.

Need for School Complexes/Clusters in India

Before proposing the idea of a school cluster, the NEP mentions some key data to provide a picture of ground reality of schools in India. It quotes U-DISE (2016–17) and says, about 28% of government primary schools and 14.8% of upper primary schools in India have a total number of students below thirty. And, the average number of students per class at the elementary level (primary and upper primary, i.e., Grades I–VIII) is near 14, with a notable proportion with a number of students below six. This is also alarming that we still have about one lakh single teacher schools as per data of year 2016–17 and maximum of them are primary schools. Economically, these small school sizes are very suboptimal and even operationally, they are poor in terms of deploying teachers or generating physical resources. This is also crucial that in these schools, teachers often teach multiple grades at a time, as well as multiple subjects, including subjects in which they have no expertise, and physical resources are simply not available across schools. Therefore, this system of isolated small schools leads to a negative impact on education and the teaching-learning process. Small schools also increase systemic challenges for governance and management. But can we really get rid of small schools? This is a very valid question because the Right to Education Act has made certain norms for elementary schools to provide reachable access to schools for the children of concerned age groups. The schools cannot be closed just because they are having small numbers of students and teachers. Although consolidation of schools is an option which is often discussed and debated but it must be carried out very judiciously. The NEP underlines that it may be done only in such cases when it is ensured that there will be no impact on access. In place of this, the isolated schools can be made bigger by grouping them together with neighbouring schools as proposed in the progressive idea of school complex/cluster by the NEP. The geographical dispersion, challenging access conditions, availability of teachers etc. must be taken into consideration while implementing the idea.

The NEP discusses five key objectives behind the intervention of school complex/cluster.

- The first objective is to ensure that every school has an adequate number of teachers, counsellors and staff (shared or otherwise) to teach all subjects including art, music science, sports, languages, vocational subjects, etc.
- The second objective talks about rich resources (shared or otherwise), such as a library, science labs, skill labs, playgrounds, computer labs, sports equipment and facilities, etc.
- Third objective stresses on building a sense of community to remove the isolation of teachers, students, and schools, through joint professional development programmes, sharing of teaching-learning content, joint content development practices, holding joint activities such as art and science exhibitions, sports meet, quizzes and debates, and fairs.
- Fourth objective is about collaboration and support across schools for the quality education of children with disabilities. And
- The fifth objective is talking about better governance of the schooling system by decentralising all greater decisions, to principals, teachers, and other stakeholders within each group of schools. Such a group of schools should also be treated as an integrated semi-autonomous unit. These objectives are expecting the schools to function very differently.

School Complexes/ Clusters

Now, the question is how schools should be grouped in a school complex/ cluster and in which way. In this context, the NEP 2020 has proposed the grouping of one secondary school together with all other schools offering lower grades in its neighbourhood including *anganwadis*, in a radius of five to ten kilometres. This must be underlined that the grouping of schools as 'School Complex/Cluster' is not understood as physical shifting of schools but sharing of resources across the complex to have a number of other benefits. For example, this will lead to improved support for children with disabilities across schools. More topic-centred clubs and events, better incorporation of art, music, language, vocational subjects, physical education, and other subjects in the classroom can also be visualised. Grouping of schools will also enhance the use of ICT tools to conduct virtual classes, better student support, enrolment, attendance, and performance through the sharing of social workers and counsellors, and School Complex Management Committees (rather than simply School Management Committees) for more robust and improved governance, monitoring, oversight, innovations, and initiatives by local stakeholders (NEP 2020). Therefore, the focus of the entire exercise of grouping the schools is for the benefit of all.

This is also welcoming that the NEP is not excluding private schools from the idea of school complex/cluster. In this context, the policy suggests twinning or pairing of one public school with one private school across the country, so that such paired schools have space to meet and interact with each other, learn from each other, and also share resources to each other, if possible. In addition, best practices of private schools can also be documented, shared, and institutionalised in government schools, and vice versa, where possible. The idea is to vanish the polarity between public and private schools so that they can work together and have co-existence.

Creating Vibrant Community of Teachers for School Complexes/Clusters

As mentioned earlier, lack of vibrancy is the root of poor performance of schools in our country since even potential teachers also do not work efficiently in a demotivated environment. Therefore, formation of school complexes could go a long way towards preparing vibrant teacher communities. Deployment of teachers to school complexes may automatically lead to creation of healthy relationships among concerned schools which would help in creating a more vibrant teacher knowledge base. Also, teachers will not remain isolated any longer at their very small schools. They will become part of a larger school complex community, sharing best practices with each other and working collaboratively to ensure that all children are learning. Many academic events will be organised together where all have to participate and celebrate. This togetherness of schools has a lot of possibilities to pull-up a low performing school and make it better. Sharing of possible human resources as well as movable materials will serve the needs of isolated schools. The School Complex Development Plan (SCDP) will be created by the concerned principals and teachers together with the involvement of school management committees. The plans will comprise human resources, physical resources and infrastructure, learning resources, improvement initiatives, school culture initiatives, financial resources, teacher development plans, and educational outcomes.

Now, changing the role of principals and teachers is another key issue for effective implementation of the school complex/cluster system. They must be capacitated for the new role and challenges. To address this, the NEP proposes to have modular leadership/management workshops and various online development opportunities through different platforms for continuous improvement of their professional knowledge and skills. It is expected from them to have a minimum fifty hours of continuing professional development

(CPD) modules per year, covering areas such as content, pedagogy, leadership and management, etc. This is highly important for an ideal implementation of a school complex/cluster system since the onus is on the teachers. So, along with other planning, the focus must be on proper capacity building of teachers and principals.

A Mechanism of Autonomy and Interdependence Among Schools

At present, schools have very little autonomy to innovate and establish their identity. They are demoralised due to following routine orders and have no vibrancy of work. By grouping, the governance of schools will be also improved and would become far more efficient and self-reliant. The NEP reiterates that the school complex/cluster will have significant autonomy to innovate towards imparting integrated education and to experiment with curriculum, pedagogies and other activities in consonance with the National Curricular Framework (NCF) and State Curricular Framework (SCF). This will surely help in creating a unique identity of schools within their complex/cluster. This can be possible that many schools may emerge as a specialised centre of any activity or learning. The autonomy and decentralisation of power will boost them to take initiative at their level and innovate in their practices. However, all these cannot be totally left on schools. In place, there must be a dedicated support system for every school of the school complex/cluster to help it wherever needed.

The NEP clearly says that the idea of a school complex/cluster must be well planned and smoothly executed to achieve good results. It mentions that the School Development Plan (SDP) and SCDP will be the main mechanism to align all stakeholders of the schools together. The SMC and SCMC will keep the SDP and SCDP as basis for oversight of the functioning and direction of the school and will assist in the execution of these plans. The SCDP of each school complex will be endorsed and confirmed by the district administration through its relevant official. Also, necessary resources (financial, human, physical, etc.) will be provided to achieve the SCDPs, both short-term (1-year) and long-term (3-5 years). For better clarity of the work, the apex bodies of the state such as SCERT may share specific norms and frameworks for development of the SDP and SCDP with all schools, which may be revised periodically. All these systemic arrangements are quite important and will take substantial time and energy to develop. In this way, the NEP elaborates several points for execution of the said idea. A few of them have only been discussed in this chapter.

Summing Up

There is no doubt that if this idea of school complex and cluster will be implemented in true sense then the school will function more efficiently in collaboration. The learning of children will be enhanced remarkably due to proper facilities and availability of quality teachers to all learners. However, there are many inherent issues to this idea which needs to be broadly explored and discussed. A take away from the above discussions could be on the focus of creating school complexes/clusters in terms of efficient utility of human resources and the movable infrastructural or pedagogical resources. The idea should be well articulated in its plan and surely discussed with its key implementer in advance. Role of field-based studies and robust research is highly crucial to continuously improve the idea. Therefore, its implementation will lead to the emergence of various new fields of researches related to school education, among them academic leadership, collaborative learning, educational resource management etc. will be prominent. The development of school complexes, their actual functioning, their effect on the progress of the schools including that of the teachers and students, the attitude of the administrators, principals and teachers towards school complexes are some of the issues which will require immediate attention of the researchers.

References

Dittmar, F., Mendelsohn, J. & Ward, V. (2002). *The Cluster System in Namibia.* Raison Publication.

Govt. of India. (1966). *National Development and Education Report (1964-66).* Ministry of Education.

Government of India. 2020. *National Education Policy-2020.* Ministry of Human Resource Development.

McGinn, N. & Welsh, T. (1999). *Decentralization of Education: Why, When, What and How?.* UNESCO Publication.

NCERT. (2017). *National Achievement Survey Report.* National Council of Educational Research and Training.

Singhal, R.P. (1983). *Revitalizing School Complexes in India.* Concept Publishing Company.

Sinha, Jai, B.P. (1981). *The School Complexes–an Unfinished Experiment.* Concept Publishing Company.

8

Indianness in Education: Foundational Key for a Self-Reliant India

Pankaj Arora

The question of 'Indianness' in education, or in other words the question of development of Indian education system has always been a quint essential concern of the educational discourse. 'Indianness' in Indian education remains to be an important aspect, on which most of us often contemplates and wonders why the concern for 'Indianness' is important in Indian education. Why is it being given so much importance? What is the need for it? Is it essential that we get carried away with the question of Indianness or take it as a movement? In today's context, whenever we talk about Indianness in Indian education, author strongly wishes to know how to understand democracy, democratic education, critical pedagogy, educational methods embedded in the Indian context. How to expand it and how these practices can be encouraged in Indian context.

This National Education Policy 2020, is the first education policy of the 21st century, which proposes to give a new shape to the Indian education system in synchronisation with the aspirational goals for 21st century education. At the same time, maintaining the basic essence of India's tradition and cultural values. This policy has been prepared in the light of the rich tradition of ancient and eternal Indian knowledge and thoughts. In Indian thoughts, knowledge, people, tradition, philosophy, and truth has always been considered as one of the highest human goals. In ancient India, the goal of education was not to obtain knowledge for preparation for a worldly life, but to develop pupils with a strong competence of self-realisation and liberation. Indian culture and philosophy have a great influence on the world. This rich heritage of global importance not only needs to be preserved and restored for the future generations, our education system should also contribute substantially to further strengthen in popularising and researching it. It should be enriched, embellished with innovative practices.

The questions related to Indian education often come to author's mind, like any other scholar of education. Many scholars have interpreted 'Indianness' in their own way. This issue has also been very close to his heart and the present chapter is an attempt to understand and explain the same. In this chapter, author has tried to understand 'Indianness in Education' in two ways. First, to

---

Professor, Department of Education[CIE], University of Delhi, Delhi

explain the thoughts of various Indian educationists in the modern context. Secondly, to find the main ideas of western perceptions and modern education in the ambit of Indian education system.

Indianness in Education

Let us begin with a thought-provoking question: What is the meaning of Indianness? In my views, Indianness and the Westerners are two different aspects. 'Indianness' is primarily governed by the inner conscience. Here, I'd like to take a stand. Considering my inner-self, in accordance to my conscience, because I want to be honest with them. When I look at the West, in the global context, I analyse that there is a dominance of the material world. This domination is also seen in their society which has been considered a material world. Is 'Indianness' exist in the curriculum or is it in teaching methods or in research?, this requires a detailed reflection. Ancient experiences have proved that Indianness does not believe in accumulation, but has strong faith and believe in inclusion which connects emotionally. Accumulation means to put together, but 'inclusiveness' is internal, it is spiritual that connects at the ideological level, mental level and interpersonal level.

Pandit Deendayal Upadhyaya had said that the form of democracy in India cannot exist without the feeling of supreme nationality. It means that, the kind of democracy India has adopted, there is a need for a vast and the largest democracy in the world a sense of excellent nationality. Without it, this democracy will not work. At national level, self-reliance and self-independence require a strong economy. Recently, the Prime Minister talked about 'Vocal about Local', in economic terms, and established a founding stone of self-reliant India. In the same way, if we want to awaken national pride which is possible only by a strong educational system. While self-independence is an economic objective, self-reliance is a supreme sentiment, an idea for which an educational system can provide a strong foundation. In my understanding, Indianness connotes India's identity, culture and features that include vedic values and eternal thought. Education should be such that inculcates the essence of service for the nation instead of making it self-centered. It will create a strong connection with the nation, creating feelings such as "This is my nation, I own its ownership, I feel happy and proud to be associated with it". In this context, the education of Indianness is a movement in my understanding, and we should all participate in it and should give it a new stride.

'Indianisation' refers to the re-establishment of Indianness in various spheres of life. Now it is worth noting that we have come back to a position of prestige. That is, the prestige that should have been established naturally, after 73 years of independence; there is still a need to work on it, it needs to be connected. 'Indianness' refers to the idea or sentiment that unites India, which combines the diverse elements of India. Which gives importance to Swadeshi. Swami Vivekananda had said that 'Indianness' is full of spirituality. There are many meanings of spirituality, one of the main meanings being emotional/affective. If Indian education system becomes Indian, then all Indians will consider themselves sons/daughter of Mother India and in such a situation, anti-social elements who work to divide the country in the name of religion, caste, creed, language, etc., will face big challenge and crisis because every educated Indian who will be spiritually connected to Mother India will not become part of those conspiracies. What does 'Indianness' mean? It means – spirit of spirituality, equity, social justice, unity in diversity and aim of *Vasudhaiva Kutumbakam*, these are all world spread thoughts, and above all, 'Indianness' as a main idea in today's context thoroughly discussed by the new education policy. In this policy, in the tradition of knowledge creation, along with Indian knowledge and Indian traditions, cultural values and Indian languages have also been given importance. New education policy has this possibility that in the coming time, we will not remain the followers of western knowledge rather we will be able to joyously celebrate Indian knowledge and can be proud of it.

We can see that for the last nearly 40 years in Indian schools, there has been much discussion about critical pedagogy. The question is whether this critical pedagogy is only in the western form in which it is being presented? Or the way it is explained in our B.Ed. M.Ed. and areas of research? Critical pedagogy is a pedagogy that teaches students, teachers, school and all school members how to analyse and deal with challenges. In such a situation, there is a need to create a platform at the school level that develops critical thinking among students. Now the question arises whether the elements and essence of critical pedagogy can be seen and understood in the Indian context?

Human resources influence the direction and pace of economic and social development of each nation as compared to economic and natural resources. In this context, it is an established truth that education is an important component in the development of human resources and its social development, character development etc. are possible only through education.

In many countries of the world, formal courses of citizenship education and nationality education are integral part of the school curriculum, with the aim of character building of youth and development of nationalism. A compulsory course of nationality and citizenship is introduced in Class IX in many countries like America, England, Australia, France, etc. In the context of India it is unfortunate that even if we try to bring such educational programmes, it will become a matter of struggle and might lead to unresolvable controversy.

In today's context, if we want to make our younger generation the leader of the future, we do not want them to be blind believers rather want to create them as logical and critical thinkers. Students should not become followers of stereotypes but should pursue their point of view by examining them rationally and contribute to the development of nation building. All this will be effectively possible only when we not only focus on discovering the Indian side by following critical pedagogy but also expand our vitas with further research.

Critical Pedagogy in Indian Perspective

Critical pedagogy is considered synonymous with progressivist and innovator. Here, it is important to understand that this concept has not emerged in European countries, its roots can be traced in India from Vedic period. We can visualise it in modern context in B.R. Ambedkar's writing and thoughts. He has given the idea of 'social-justice' to understand and analyse the deprived sections of the society which is no less than the western idea of modern critical pedagogy. We know Babasaheb Ambedkar as a well-known social reformer, these social reforms were started in the 19th century by renowned reformers like Raja Rammohun Roy, Dayanand Saraswati, Mahadev Govind Ranade. All these references are Indian and embedded in Indianness. In the modern context, we talk about democratic education, critical pedagogy and innovative research are clearly visible in the education system of ancient India. Democracy in modern India is not just a principle, it is also not just a resolution, but it is a whole way of life. This important lifestyle should be incorporated in classrooms, schools and curriculums. This idea can be understood in modern as well as in ancient context. An attempt is being made to explain critical pedagogy in the Indian context through the following points:

1. One of the aims of critical pedagogy or democratic pedagogy is to understand, contemplate and to be proud of diversity.
2. Enable students to understand the fundamental rights and fundamental duties (given in the Constitution). Critical pedagogy says that we should adopt a balanced development (sustainable development). In this context, we should help the students to understand the fundamental rights and fundamental duties given in the Indian Constitution and develop respect for them.
3. To educate the younger generation about the importance of democratic culture of India. India, as I said in the beginning, is the largest democracy in the world, so it is very important to build an understanding of the students about democratic culture, and to strengthen democratic identity.
4. To make students inform about the forces that undermined democratic institutions in India for their vote bank politics. Institutions, individuals or groups of individuals who have tried to damage the structure of Indian democracy must be identified. Critical pedagogy and democratic pedagogy play an important role for this.
5. The fifth and last point in this context is that we must prepare the students in such a way that they can relate their feelings/sentiments with Indianness.

The Kothari Commission report came in the year 1964-66 to improve the Indian education system. In independent India, no education commission was larger and comprehensive than the Kothari Commission. The scope of this commission was to review the Indian education system and suggest recommendations for reform. This review was not limited toone level of education, but it was entitled to review the entire Indian education system. The Kothari Commission strongly recommended that character building and personality development – should be the basic objectives of education. Education should be able to generate employment. Education should be a medium of service rather than being considered as an occupation.

In addition to understanding Indianness, some concepts can be taken. For example, feminism and socialism. These concepts are used in teaching and learning in the western countries but in principle mere discussion is held and is less used in practice. While feminism in India is not just a matter of reading and writing and speech alone, it has always been a part of the lifestyle of our society, respect for women in Indian society, the status of farmers and labourers in Indian society can be easily visualised, recognised. Indian society is a very sensitive society. This in itself suggests that these issues are in practice in our daily lives and part of our life system.

If we look at Western critical pedagogy, it only talks about a 'just society' whereas Indian critical pedagogy talks about justice as well as self-freedom. It argues to challenge those problems that permeate the social structure. Critical pedagogy, which is recognised as one of the main pedagogies in today's context, has a much broader foundation in the Indian context. The provisions of democracy, equity, equality, freedom, fraternity and fundamental rights described in our constitution give a comprehensive and vast foundation to Indianness.

I, along with some of my research students, have tried to envision critical pedagogy in the Indian context. In that effort, it was understood that the framework of critical education that we see in the world today has emerged from different times and regions of ancient India itself. Vedic eternal Indian values such as questioning, rationality, dialogue which were the primary practical basis of the Indian education system are the basic foundation of today's critical pedagogy. When I try to understand Vedic education in today's context, I find that there has been a discussion on broad concepts like freedom, which talk of freeing life from the past and future. Such discussions were already there in our Indian literature for centuries and which were also continuously practised.

In these literatures, perfection/completeness/integrity has been talked about not only in the materialistic context but also in the psychological, intellectual and personal context. In the Vedic context, the system of *Gana* and *Parishad*, is the culture of dialogue and discussion among them. It helps to understand that the practice of democratic methods in India has a very long history which is visible to us since Vedic times. I have also written this idea in detail in my book *Democratic Classroom* (2015). In that book I have written a text on Vedic culture and Buddhist culture and explained extensively how the education process used to be democratic in Vedic period.

Initially the knowledge was imparted by associating it with *Shravan*, *Manana* and *Nidhyasana*. All the teaching methods we see in today's context are related to knowledge, understanding and reflection. I strongly believe that *Shravan*, *Manana* and *Nidhyasana* are the Indian references or origin of it. The education that developed in India after the Vedic time had aims of education such as personality, character and intellectual development, which are also discussed by modern evolutionary psychologists.

Evolutionary psychologists have given evolutionary concepts which see personality in terms of increasing physical, intellectual, religious, spiritual, social activity and happiness from the time of Buddhist culture. During Buddha's time the teaching methods were so elaborate that dialogue was given the form of a pedagogy, much importance was given to evidence-based learning.

To understand this in more depth, we will analyse the educational experiments and ideas of five Indian academicians, who have established the question of Indianness in education through their eloquent works.

Indian Educationists

To understand any discussion, mere discussion of concepts is not sufficient, so it is necessary to understand the work of academicians who have done seminal work in this direction to understand Indianness in education. In this sequence, it is necessary to discuss some academicians who gave a new direction to Indian education through their successful experiments/work and made many important changes in Indian education. Ironically many of the works of these academicians have not received much attention, nor have they been noticed, because for a long period of time the centre of our discussions has been Western academicians and their work.

When I take the name of Western scholars, I have no resentment towards them. We must understand that the experiments which succeeded in their particular geographical/social/ cultural environment should not be adopted in Indian education only because they were successful there. It would be more important to test them in the Indian environment, or rather to give more priority to experiments that understand the needs of Indian educational system and provide options to address the challenges of Indian educational world locally. To understand this, it is important to discuss further some Indian academics whose education related experiments are not only done in Indian conditions but also their results show innovative new paths to Indian education.

Gijubhai Badheka (1885–1939)

In this array, first of all I want to discuss the educational experiments of Gijubhai Badheka. Gijubhai wrote many books related to children's lives. The most popular book among them is *Divaswapna*. In this book, he tells an imaginary story of the use of the Montessori method in the education system through a fictional teacher. All his experiments were done 100 to 120 years ago, but if we look carefully, his experiments are equally relevant today. Gijubhai presented a new form of education to us that the purpose of education is not only to teach but also to guide. The aim is not just to take the exam at the end of the year, but to monitor the development with continuous evaluation. Children should learn freely and maintain their curiosity to learn, this is an important goal of education. 'Learning' should be joyful. Gijubhai's name comes first whenever learning and joyful education comes in discussion. This has been explained by Gijubhai based on his experiences and experiments. Gijubhai's ideas are very relevant in the context of modern education, but for some reasons he could not become very famous, neither his thoughts could get space in the research. I think, now we have time and we should add these ideas in the context of Indianness. Gijubhai considers dance, music, sports and excursion all as important components of education. If we want to understand Gijubhai's educational philosophy, then it can be understood with the help of the following points:

1. There is heaven in the happiness of children.
2. Heaven is in the happiness of children, their health and their joy.
3. Heaven is in children's playfulness and their innocence.
4. Heaven is in children's songs and their poems.

The curriculum and education methods of education interwoven around these four elements.

Whenever we hear a very negative view on the condition of Indian education, we should keep in mind the works of people like Gijubhai, who, despite all the difficulties, made very positive experiments in the field of education. The New Education Policy 2020 also talks about making education enjoyable for children. Until the process of learning becomes smooth and joyful, all our experiments in the field of education will be in vain.

Rabindranath Tagore (1861–1941)

Like Gijjubhai, Rabindranath Tagore, whose literature and ideas are well known to us, whose views are the foundation of the famous institution like Visva-Bharati, strongly believed that education is becoming colourless or deviating from the real world like a factory. God has sent us with the qualities of beauty of the world but such activities are being interrupted. Schools are ending our sensitivity. The purpose of education is not competition or blind race of results. Real education is pleasing to the inner self and connecting with nature. The aspect of Tagore's personality that emerges in his creations shows a rebellion against the bookish and artificial environment. Tagore fiercely opposed parrot training. According to him, education should not be for giving instruction but inspiring. Education should not only be a feeling of success, progress and power, but a development of feelings of the heart. Above all, Tagore believed that education should make one feel empathetic, develop a feeling of love and service so that the distinction of caste and colour can be eliminated from the world. Tagore also considered the role of teachers in education as very important. He believed that all the stakeholders in the education system should be given attention. Such thoughts are also incorporated in the National Education Policy 2020.

Indian educationists have been presenting the distinction with critical pedagogy with such beautiful, easy and interesting examples from a long time ago. Tagore's reference becomes necessary when it comes to enable the student to be independent in nature and healthy as he emphasizes in a university curriculum, fine arts, music, dance and other activities such as social work, gardening and student activities should be included so that future social workers and leaders of the society can be prepared. Universities should celebrate different cultures with a lot of enthusiasm. We should sing and share different occasions of different religions. In the new education policy, 2020 the idea of holistic education appears inspired by Tagore's educational ideas.

Mahatma Gandhi (1869–1948)

Gandhi has established the pragmatic principle of John Dewey on ground level reality/real phenomenon and prepared a model of education which became the basis of basic education. In basic education we understood how education can be linked to employment, how education becomes a medium of all round development which considers not only mental and intellectual development but also physical and emotional development. Evolutionary psychologists greatly publicised it but Gandhiji brought his ideas to the ground and associated them with ideas of the mind and soul. Gandhiji strongly believed that education should provide livelihood, ensure culture development and take us towards self-realisation. Education should be a way of merging social and individual goals in our lives. Gandhiji's education has two major elements – the development of human values and use of mother tongue as a medium of instruction.

Critical pedagogy or classes which are full of engagements and discussions make students prepared both physically and mentally towards becoming self-reliant. Mahatma Gandhi has given practical outlook to John Dewey's principles of education, a fundamental form of education and doctrine of learning by experience.

'Basic education' was one of the few experiments in the Indian education system that could not be implemented. In basic education, the reforms that Gandhiji suggested were based on his experiences which were made keeping in mind the conditions of India during those times. Today, after nearly 75 years, the National Policy of Education, 2020 again revolves around the same suggestions which were given by Gandhiji. Whether it is about vocational education in school or education in the mother tongue, the National Education Policy 2020 looks at the provisions of basic education.

Sri Aurobindo (1872–1950)

Sri Aurobindo is one of the few philosophers of our time who has discussed many questions of our life in great detail and depth. There was a balance of all kinds of experiences in the life of Sri Aurobindo, due to which his views on various issues are very pragmatic and in sync with Indian philosophy and thought systems. Sri Aurobindo believed that education is a continuous process from life to death, which aims to bring out the best side/version of human beings.

The basic foundation of Sri Aurobindo's educational philosophy is how to develop this 'superior' aspect of human life? Sri Aurobindo's emphasis was on education in the mother tongue, because he believed that the natural development of the child can be ensured only through his own language (Mother tongue). He believed that five dimensions are very important in education – physical, mental, psychological, spiritual and biological. The development of all these must happen in balanced proportion, if proper development of any one of these aspects is interrupted then it causes problems in life.

Sri Aurobindo did not only gave a philosophical foundation to education but also successfully experimented on Integral Education itself in his life. Many institutions are successfully running in India on his philosophy.

Sri Aurobindo was firmly opposed to division/segregation in education. He believed that students should get all kinds of education like music, craft, arts, etc. It is a happy consonance that Sri Aurobindo's educational philosophy is also reflected in India's new education policy. His ideas of multidisciplinary education and use of mother-language has been given adequate space in the National Education Policy 2020.

J. Krishnamurthy (1895–1986)

J. Krishnamurti says that all round development of learners is the main objective of education. The real purpose of education is to make a person an adult, to move beyond goodness and love. Krishnamurti says that children should take such education which makes them scholars and religious human beings, i.e. the definition of religion should be prepared and decided by children themselves like, what is religion? what is duty? what is the inner self of a religious person? He can identify all of them himself. Krishnamurti also talks about associating education with joyfulness and self-focused activities. The aim of the teaching methods that Krishnamurti wants to promote is to develop a 'how to think' method instead of 'what to think'. J. Krishnamurthy believed that children should be taught how to think and work on thinking skills rather than giving them study material. A major goal of the National Education Policy 2020 is adhering to the process of 'how to think' in place of 'what to think'. It will help children to make decisions for themselves in the future. Also, students and teachers should be considered co-learner; there is a need to eliminate the hierarchy between teacher and students.

J. Krishnamurthy's most influential thing is that he considers education as a matter of dialogue, he says that the prevailing education system has made the learning process extremely difficult which has negatively affected the brain of the children. He believed that we have made our life very complex due to which our behaviour has also become very irrational, the aim of education should be to bring balance and equilibrium in our lives.

Conclusion

Keeping in mind the current situation, it is imperative to understand how these Indian thinkers contributed in the context of critical pedagogy. We all are students of education and are well aware of the types of western ideas that are considered revolutionary in today's context. All the major thinkers discussed in this paper, like Gijubhai, Tagore, Mahatma Gandhi, J. Krishnamurti and Sri Aurobindo, and their thoughts, ideologies and concepts have been discussed to highlight the ideas of Indianness in a critical aspect.

We need further research on understanding more about these thinkers and their contribution in promoting Indianness in education. I am sure a lot of issues can be extracted from such research. It is rather unfortunate to see the way our education system has been following the ideologies of Western pedagogues. We already find the origin of those ideas and concerns in the writings of some of the Indian thinkers. The type of pedagogy we are talking about today, our past Indian thinkers had already worked on it.

In this chapter, I have discussed only five prominent thinkers. Many more such thinkers are still unexplored or less talked about. The subject of Indianness in education is not limited to the Indianness of the textual content, but also incorporates the ideas and practices of thinkers into Indianness.

The inclusion of all these ideas in the Education Policy 2020 represent a respect towards India's rich diversity and culture, as well as the needs of the country in its local and global context. To make the youth of India knowledgeable about their own country and its diverse social, cultural, and technological needs including its incredible art, language and knowledge of its traditions, national pride, self-confidence, enlightenment, mutual cooperation and unity and it is very important to move towards the continuous development and progress of India.

The ancient history of Indian education introduces us with the roots of western education of modern conditions from where these ideologies flourished and achieved standards. Indian pedagogy has been incorporating various types of streams of modern education from the very beginning, whether it is critical pedagogy or evolutionary pedagogy. The modern concepts that we explore in Western thinkers are reflections of all the concepts that we find in Indian education systems and ideas which need to be revisited in a new perspective.

The question of Indianness in education is not a political question but it is basically an educational question, which requires a thoughtful discussion without any prejudice because without Indianisation of education, we cannot create self-reliant India in the field of education.

9

Reading and Writing: A Strong Foundation for Literacy

Usha Sharma

Language is a connector of life, or, we can say that to make new concepts and express those concepts with others can actually be termed as 'living a life' and 'living a language' (use of language). If we look closely, we find that language is scattered and used in every moment of our lives. Right from saying something or listening to someone, reading or writing any message or a letter or an email, language is used everywhere.

In today's technological age, several other mediums, gadgets and techniques for communication have been introduced. Be it WhatsApp, Facebook, Twitter, Instagram or Blogs. In fact, oral mediums such as Radio and Doordarshan are totally dependent on the skills of using a language. Role of a language changes according to our needs. Sometimes we use oral or written forms of language and sometimes in other cases, sign language is used for communication.

Language: Thought and Expression

Language plays a vital role in making our thoughts and expressing them. It is simple to observe and realise that whenever we think of telling or asking something, the thought emerges in a language. This language can be either our mother tongue or any other language which the listener can understand. However, it is observed that we are perceived by the language in which we communicate.

Suppose you have to say to your friend – 'It has been a long time; I have not talked to my aunt in the village. I'm thinking of calling her today!' You say this in the language you were thinking, which means that the thought of meeting your aunt was expressed through a language. In other words, the medium of your thought was through the language you were comfortable with. We can clearly say that language and thoughts are closely connected. It is also important to understand here that we do not always say what we think. There are times when we are thinking something but say something else! However, in this 'something else' the way we think, and the way we express is connected by a language. Suppose, your friend brought a new kurta for you and said, "Look what I've brought for you. Isn't it good!" Now, suppose you liked neither the design of the kurta nor its colour. You thought in your mind – "What a useless

Professor and In-charge, Cell for National Centre for Literacy, NCERT, New Delhi

kurta. This is what he got for me?" However, you cannot reply in such hard terms, so you pretend to be polite and instead say something like this "Hey, what was the need. It's really good!" It is quite evident here that we thought of two different things but chose to speak something which was more appealing and polite. Therefore, it is easy to conclude that language not only acts as a medium of expression of our thoughts but also helps in hiding them. This happens not just with adults, kids also do the same. They tend to use language based on their situations. Thus, language becomes the basis of human life.

On examining the deeper relation of language and thought, it can be said that language is not only the medium for our thoughts; it also works as the producer of them. It plays an important role in organising our thoughts. Different concepts of life are formed with the help of language. It is the language itself that gives meaning to the wide world around us.

Language: Foundational Capabilities

Meaning is implicit in the use of any form of language, whether it is related to understanding while listening or speaking with understanding. It is all about reading or writing with proper understanding. In the absence of meaning, the language is meaningless. When we spend time with children we also realise that before joining school they are already in possession of a wealth of their own native language. They know how to speak in their mother tongue.

Listening and speaking of a language acts as a foundational basis in the formation of concepts and their expression is contemplation. So, read and write. Now, the most important question is: Do the children know how to read and write before coming to school? What are their prior levels in reading and writing before entering the school? Do they have the ability to read and write? You would have realised that there are no definite answers to these questions. Ever wondered why? The answer is, because children who have an environment of reading and writing at their home and the children who get meaningful opportunities to read and write become involved in the process of reading and writing from 'childhood'. These children, after getting adequately acquainted with the acts of reading and writing enter the formal school system. Kindly note, this is 'introduction' to reading and writing and not 'maturity' in reading and writing. This means that children bring with themselves an 'orientation' of reading and writing to the school. Here, the school means pre-primary school wherein children aged three to four years become part of the formal education system. But the question that arises here is- what about those children who do not have any means to write and read formal language? What about those children who do not have a home environment that offers opportunities to read and write in the homes? Such children get involved in the process of reading and writing only after they enter the school. Only after coming to formal school structures they can avail the opportunities to 'start learning' to read and write!

Language: As Subject and a Medium

You would recall that in our childhood days, we used to study more than one language in our school. Even today, the situation is the same as we find that in most of the schools more than one language is being taught. The language could be Hindi, English, Tamil or Khasi. In our schools, language also exists as a medium of instruction. Whenever we study a subject, we read through a language. For instance, to study Mathematics, Science or Social Science, we would use either Hindi or English or Tamil or Malayalam or Khasi language. It is certain that for understanding any subject, any language becomes a medium of instruction. In fact, there are some situations wherein sign language or braille script may also be used as a medium. It is therefore clear that to understand or study a subject, language becomes a necessary medium. One must either possess a strong hold over that language or there should be some sort of skill to read and write in that particular language. Only then we will be able to understand and express our understanding of the concerned subject. If we do not understand the medium, that is, language, we won't be able to understand the subject as well. Similarly, if somehow we have managed to understand the subject but are unable to express it, we will be tagged in the category of 'illiterate' people. Therefore, it is essential to learn to read and write in a language.

Let us now go beyond the world confined to the four walls of school and understand how language exists around us in several written forms such as – in reading newspapers, writing mails, writing and reading letters, day-to-day reading of prices such as of flour, pulses, rice at the ration shop, etc. All these references exhibit certain basic literacy skills which are very important for children to thrive in the real world. Owing to their need, due attention should be given to basic literacy skills from the very early years onwards.

Foundational Literacy: Various Education Commissions and Policies

Like listening and speaking, reading and writing too are some of the basic capabilities associated with language, which are termed as 'Foundational Literacy' in the National Education Policy 2020. The basic question that comes to our mind is why has the term 'foundational literacy' been given so much importance in the National Education Policy 2020? Did earlier policies also discuss the ideas of basic literacy? There has been some discussion on language before independence and after independence, but there has been no specific discussion about foundational literacy or reading and writing of the language in the early years. In fact, if one were to study the report of Dr. Radhakrishnan Commission (1948) carefully, one is bound to come across a mention of promoting foundational literacy at a higher level. This suggestion was made owing to the adverse situations that prevailed during the post-independence times. The Commission had clearly stated in its recommendation that the language of the Indian Union should be developed by embracing words from different sources. It stated that there was a need to give proper place to those words which have made their place in Indian languages from various sources. It suggested that the spelling of words coming from other languages should be fixed corresponding to the vowels already in use in the common Indian languages. In the context of language, an effort should be made so that students at the upper secondary and university levels become capable enough to use three languages– local language, union language and English. Provision of higher education in local languages should also be supported. There should be an option to use the Union language as a medium language. English, as a language, should be taught in schools and universities so as to keep in touch with the knowledge being developed worldwide.

Similarly, several recommendations were made by the Secondary Education Commission (1952) or by the Mudaliar Commission on secondary education. This Commission supports primary education of children in the age group of four or five years and proposes two parts of secondary education at school level. In the context of language, the Secondary Education Commission proposes adopting a two-language formula for teaching-learning. The Commission mentions making mother tongue or a regional language for secondary education and at least two other languages at the level of pre-secondary.

The National Education Commission (1964-66) or the Kothari Commission recommended the use of the regional language as a teaching tool. It also stressed that for development of scientific and technical knowledge it is important that the books and literature are made available in regional languages. The Kothari Commission also emphasised on the mother tongue of the children and said that the appropriate time to learn the three languages should be classes 8-10. Learning in Hindi or English may begin as per the need and relevance. This commission is not, at any stage, in favour of studying four languages. The Commission proposes pre-primary schooling in the period of one to three years and registration in Class I after achieving an age of six years.

The National Education Policy (1968) recommended the development of regional languages, noting that Indian languages and literature are an integral part of the development of education and culture. Regional languages are already recognised as medium of instruction at the primary and secondary levels. It is important that they also become a medium of instruction at university level. The 'Three Language Formula' should be followed at the secondary level, which will have the provision to learn Hindi, English as well as regional languages. Emphasising on the study of English and other international languages, the policy says that knowledge of the world is expanding at a rapid pace, so India should also pay attention to it and strengthen the study of English and other international languages.

The National Education Policy (1986) in Part V emphasised on child growth. It has been clearly stated that "the childcare and pre-education centres will be fully child-centred. There should be a range of activities and games to build the personality of children. Formal reading and writing will not be taught at this stage." (5.3) The policy emphasises three points in addition to primary education– "Universal access, enrolment and all children up to 14 years of age in the field of education preserving and enhancing the standard of education so that all children can meet the level of education needed." (5.5)

Referring to the education policy of 1968 in the field of languages, "it was pointed out that the question of language development was discussed in depth in the education policy of 1968. The basic recommendations of that policy should hardly be reformed, and they are as relevant today as they were before. But the implementation of 1968 policy was not uniform throughout the country. Now this policy will be implemented more actively and purposefully." (8.7)

In the context of books and libraries, it has been said that "Having books available at a low cost is very important for public education. Efforts will be made to make books easily available to all sections of the society. Along with this, steps will be taken to improve the quality of books, develop the habit of reading and encourage creative writing.... The making of appropriate books for children would get special consideration. These will also include textbooks and practice books" (8.8). It also emphasised on a national initiative for the renovation of existing libraries and the construction of new libraries alongside the creation of books. Provisions to be made for library facilities in every educational institution and the level of libraries to be improved.

Learning without Burden (1993) reiterates the recommendation by previous commissions and policies that the mother tongue of a child be the medium of their education. At the same time, it should be ensured that nursery school opening institutions do not persecute children by imposing on them an additional strain of learning in the name of reading-writing and formal mathematics education. Homework should not be given in primary classes. Local and linguistic idioms should be given proper place in language textbooks.

On analysing the recommendations made by various commissions and policies, it can be said that there is no discussion on basic reading and writing of children, but all policies and commissions have laid great emphasis on the mother tongue of the child. At the same time, there is great enthusiasm about making the mother tongue a medium of instruction at various levels of the school. It has also come to the notice that in the initial years, children's reading and writing should not be formalised. If this happens, then it is 'torture' to children in a way. The 1986 National Education Strategy emphasised on children's reading habits and creative writing and it is in this context that different types of quality books and libraries are discussed. Although adherence to the language, trilingual formula has been strongly endorsed in various commissions and policies but in that too, the number, level and nature of the languages that are to be accomplished find a relatively high place. Yet, it is critical that the commission and policies prioritise the study of the child's mother tongue from the point of view of basic literacy and make it the medium of study.

Foundational Literacy and National Education Policy 2020

In the National Education Policy 2020, basic literacy is linked to the capacity to read and write, which basically suggests that children can learn to read and write to an extent where they can use this fundamental ability in life. This ability acts as a foundation in children's ability to use language. The stronger this foundation builds, the more children will be able to use reading and writing in their lives. From the very beginning of their life, children are constantly in the environment of some kind of language(s) and they constantly try to assimilate that language(s). The ability to read and write in languages comes in different contexts of the child's life and has special significance as a medium to read other subjects. Various research findings in the field of language show that children can grow in their ability to read and write from childhood provided there is an environment of reading and writing, opportunities for language use and a lot of children's literature around them. This reading and writing ability is only achievable when the kid has a favourable atmosphere. Due to several reasons, the expected development and achievement of this skill of reading and writing is not being accomplished, towards which the National Education Policy 2020 clearly indicates and various government and non-governmental surveys have also indicated that presently we are dealing with a significant learning issue. At present, a large number of learners in primary school (with an estimated number of more than five crores) have not attained even basic literacy and numeracy. Meaning that such children do not have the capability to read and understand simple text and do basic addition and subtraction with numbers. Given the importance of basic literacy, the recommendations and critical analysis of the recommendations made by the National Education Policy 2020 are as follows –

- *Establishment of National Mission:* Basic literacy has been recommended to be a national campaign; according to which, every child will have to achieve basic literacy by Class III by 2025. For this, work will be done by all the states on many fronts and its progress will be carefully reviewed. Also an action plan will also be prepared with immediate measures and clear objectives defined. It is true that learning a language does not involve learning the language only. It also involves the learning of other concepts. If the basic language skills of the child are strong, they are capable of demonstrating the use of language in learning other subjects as well. Although literacy is primarily concerned with reading and writing, the other two language skills (listening and speaking) help in achieving reading and writing skills. It is also important that national importance should be given to children's learning to read and write and that everyone should make collective efforts in that direction. If children learn to read and write at a particular level, then with this basic skill of language, they can address many situations in their life. Wherever there is a need to read and write, they can use it. The establishment of basic literacy as a national mission will not only give it a direction but will also provide meaningful opportunities for all children across the country to learn to read and write.

- *Filling the vacant posts of teachers:* Teacher is the axis of the entire education system. The vacant teaching posts should therefore be filled immediately, especially in areas where the teacher-children ratio is high and the literacy rate is poor. The teacher-child ratio will be less than 1:30 and the ratio will be less than 1:25 in socio-economically deprived areas. Work will also be done on continuous professional development of teachers. The classroom size inevitably determines the teaching-learning process and the presence of the teacher as well. Keeping this concern at the centre, the National Education Policy is very serious on both the points. There will be many children who are first generation learners or who have come to school for the first time. Parents of such children may not be literate and hence they may not be able to help their children in learning to read and write. With this, the responsibility of school and teacher increases even more, so it is important that the vacant posts of teachers are filled, and the teacher-student ratio is kept appropriate. Ratio of 1:30 seems appropriate, so that the teacher will be able to give personal attention to the child and will help the children to learn to read and write.
- *Placement of foundational literacy in the curriculum:* Special attention will be given to foundational literacy in the curriculum. The foundational literacy development of children will be tracked during the Secondary School Curriculum with a strong, reliable, and consistent evaluation system and particular attention will be given to reading, writing, communicating, and listening simultaneously. The work of organising various activities and restructuring the curriculum of teacher education will be done. It is a notable and commendable point that the National Education Policy supports making the required changes in the structure of school curriculum and teacher education to achieve the goal of basic literacy. There is a need to make such changes in the school curriculum so that children can get opportunities to read and write, learn by doing and special provisions can be made where needed. This is also necessary because India is a diverse country. It is not necessary that one plan or task is useful for everyone. Therefore, states should have the freedom to take necessary steps keeping in mind their local environment. Conceptual understanding of language and basic literacy continues to affect the method and process of teachers, so it is a commendable step to make appropriate changes in the curriculum of teachers' education.
- *Construction of School Preparation Module:* This policy is also concerned for children who have not been able to access ECCE i.e. Early Childhood

Care and Education due to some reasons. These children should not lag behind their peers. The policy recommends a three-month short-term sports-based school preparation module for Class I children. It will consist of various types of activities, practice books etc. for children. Parents will also be assisted in executing this module. While constructing the 'School Preparation Module' recommended by the National Education Policy, it is important to keep in mind that it can shape the activities in accordance with issues related to language learning and pedagogical principles. Also, the socio-cultural environment of the children for whom this 'School Readiness Module' is being designed should be kept in mind. Language is the most important point in this environment. More possibilities can be explored in activities, workbooks, etc.

- *DIKSHA Portal:* Teachers play an important role in children's learning to read and write and the policy discusses the provision of 'Diksha', i.e. 'The Digital Infrastructure for Knowledge Sharing' to make them practise technical knowledge. Diksha will be a platform or portal where a national repository of high-quality resources based on foundational literacy will be made available so that even teachers who are far away can use these resources. Special care will be taken of languages used at these portals. Considering the economic and socio-cultural perspective of India, provision of platforms like 'Diksha' is a commendable move. This will enable teachers (and parents as well) to get quality material that they will not only be able to meet their educational needs but will also be able to support children in learning to read and write. Children and teachers, both would benefit when the special attention is provided to the content available in Indian and local languages on the Diksha portal. This will help in saving time and energy spent in collecting resources. There is no doubt that the availability of national resources would be beneficial for all children and students.
- *Promoting 'Peer Tutoring:* By referring to those researches, National Education Policy emphasises the process of peer tutoring i.e. learning and teaching from their classmates. The policy clearly states that peer tutoring is a voluntary and enjoyable activity in which trained volunteers, both local and non-local, can take part in this national campaign under the supervision of trained teachers. If every literate member of the society commits to teach one student, the policy is confident that it can transform the country's ecosystem and accomplish the campaign's goals. This perception of the National Education Policy indicates that the education of children is the responsibility of all. Although children's learning to read and write demands a certain type of training and understanding, the policy has already made it clear that trained volunteers will be involved in this campaign under

the supervision of trained teachers. This is a positive initiative and will also help the society realise its responsibility. Where there is group engagement, the issue of mother tongue/local language of children can also be discussed and the 'written language' available to children in their local area can be made the foundation.

- *Emphasis on children's literature and library:* Creation of children's literature in all Indian languages and vernacular languages and suggestion to make large quantities of books accessible for students of all levels in school and local libraries, certainly will help in the growth of children's reading culture. The education policy also talks about recommending comprehensive initiatives to ensure availability, access, quality and readership of books in all places, languages, levels and genres through book club, digital library, national book promotion policy, etc. It is a very common notion in the context of learning to read and write for children that children who do not know how to read, who do not recognise a single letter in their language, what will they do with the book? The book is not of any use to them. But in relation to children's literature and basic literacy, this concept is very discouraging, as well as 'fatal'! In fact, being around and constantly in contact with children's literature or books is important for the development of foundational literacy. The more children are exposed to written language, greater are the benefits. Provision of digital libraries is even more important for the availability of books; children can go for the book of their choice.
- *Provision of nutritious breakfast and lunch:* To help children learn, the National Education Policy gives priority to nutrition and health, and therefore the policy also offers morning and afternoon meals for children. In addition, the policy also recommends having dedicated routine health check-ups, vaccinations and making of children's health cards. Research in the field of education suggests that the health of children affects their mental development, so the system of providing nutritious food to children is highly appreciated. Children will be able to perform cognitively better only when they are healthy. It is important to plan nutritious food and breakfast for the children according to the type of community or geographical environment in which they live.

Taking care of almost every aspect of children's lives, the National Education Policy 2020 has not only expanded the children's literacy in terms of basic literacy, but also gave it a meaning. Keeping health at the centre in the context of education of noticeably young children reflects 'vision' of the policy. In order to develop the culture of reading in children, it is laudable to provide books in local languages, children's literature and provision of digital libraries. For language development, it is necessary to see it in totality, make new plans, keep localism at the centre and make various provisions for the recruitment of teachers and their capacity building. The National Education Policy 2020 has opened many new dimensions in this context and has given foundational literacy such an important place in the education system that it is entitled.

Implementation of National Education Policy 2020

As discussed earlier, there are numerous opportunities for reading and writing in our daily lives, such as – reading the newspaper, reading and writing letters, reading the name and number of the shop, reading the price of flour, salt, soap, etc., in the grocery store, making a list of items to be purchased from the market, reading books or children's literature, reading mobile numbers, reading and writing messages on mobile, reading bus numbers and place names, story, poetry, etc., reading the name of the book of one's choice, writing and reading your timetable for self-study, reading the calendar and marking the dates of important tasks etc. All these tasks related to language will be possible only when there is proficiency in reading and writing in language. Basic literacy thus indicates towards this ability to read and write. Now the question arises: what should be done to attain the foundational literacy goals and recommendations mentioned in the National Education Policy? If we think deeply, this task is of utmost importance – providing children meaningful opportunities to read and write! Who will provide this opportunity? Parents or teachers? How will this opportunity be provided? Through books or through classroom studies? In this context, the question also arises: In the early years of children, what is most important in relation to language learning or reading writing? Most important is – To build an accurate and clear conceptual understanding of foundational literacy! If we understand this foundational literacy precisely, then we will also be able to adopt the right approach or methodology for the development of foundational literacy.

In fact, we need to work together on two facades – enhancing classroom processes in school and developing a conceptual understanding of foundational literacy among teachers. That is, to make the correct understanding about foundational literacy in both stages of teacher education – pre-service and in-service teacher education. In this context, it is important to understand that reading and writing are creative processes, and these processes start long before learning about letters. Both processes are related to the 'meaning', although all the skills of language are meaningful but skills without meaning are meaningless. This means that listening, speaking, reading, and writing have meaning or understanding – integral to them. When looking at a picture, it is all about reading, describing, and connecting it to your experiences. In the same way, to draw some lines on paper or on the wall and provide them names or meanings – it is writing only. A 'reading corner' in the classroom or home, where a variety of children's literature or books are accessible to children – helps with foundational literacy! This suggests that children should have opportunities to turn around and talk about their book of choice. Overall, a proper understanding of pedagogy of foundational literacy needs to be developed, for which a variety of capacity-building programmes can be organised! It is also vital for teachers to create materials on print as well as audio-video mode.

It is also important in this context that books should be in the mother tongue/local language/s of the children. Printed and audio books also help in learning to read and write. If traditional literature also gets involved in this, children will be able to associate themselves with books and with its subject matter. Therefore, the stock of books should be within the reach of children. The library should flourish, and children should have the freedom to access books without any barriers. There should be a reading routine in school and home where children can sit with elders (teachers and parents) and read together.

To achieve the goals of foundational literacy, formation of guidelines should be made for the states and in that adequate flexibility is required! This allows all states to implement policies keeping in mind their local context and language. The best method or practice or tasks related to foundational literacy should get a national platform and provision of a portal or digital platform will be required for their dissemination. There should also be foundational literacy guidelines for parents or guardians so that they too can understand the process of learning to read and write properly and can support the expected needs of children.

Paul Freire states that 'reading is not about following only words, but of acquiring their souls.' This statement indicates that reading and writing are related to the process of acquiring meaning. At the same time, he was a promoter of 'word and world' which can be understood as the connection between literacy and learning to read and write. 'Reading a word helps you to understand the world.' The sense of the word here is not only the word itself, but the written language. By reading and understanding the language written in our surroundings, we understand the world around us. Listening and speaking also has a special importance in this. Talking about what you read, what you understood, relating it to your experiences, discussing and writing – all the skills are interrelated with each other. Therefore, the right to foundational literacy will enable children to understand the world and gain a sense of ownership over it.

10

Foundational Numeracy: A Quintessential Ingredient for a Developing Nation

Haneet Gandhi[1] and Mansi Popli[2]

Within the concerns of Mathematicians and Mathematics educators, there is an international consensus that even after years of schooling, a large number of children (or even adults) fail to demonstrate the understanding of basic mathematical concepts and their application in real life situations. Across countries, a large proportion of population functions at low proficiency levels and the root of this gloomy state can be accentuated to a lack in acquiring foundational knowledge of mathematics in the elementary classes. Hence, numeracy skills, on par with literacy skills, are considered as important predictors of subsequent sustenance of any individual. Various government and non-government surveys, such as ASER reports have also been highlighting the low achievements in early mathematical skills. A large population of school children in elementary classes cannot do simple mathematics expected from them. The surveys point to the non-attainment of foundational literacy and numeracy by a large proportion of elementary going students.

It is believed that an early development of mathematical skills leads to higher chances of entering math-intensive fields and opting math-based careers (Orpwood, Schmidt, & Jun, 2012). It is, perhaps, with this perspective that the recent National Education Policy 2020 persuades on establishing strong foundational numeracy in the pre-primary and primary classes. The NEP 2020 clearly states that, "the very highest priority of the education system will be to achieve universal foundational literacy and numeracy in primary school and beyond by 2025. The rest of this Policy will be largely irrelevant for such a large portion of our students if this most basic learning requirement (i.e., reading, writing, and arithmetic at the foundational level) is not first achieved" (p. 8).

Before we proceed to any discussions on NEP 2020 regarding "Foundational Numeracy", it will be wise to take a pause and understand the phrase "Foundational Numeracy" and what makes it so important.

This chapter is dedicated to understanding the term "Foundational Numeracy" and henceforth analysing two major education policies that impacted school education before 2020: National Policy of Education 1986 and National Curriculum Framework, 2005. These two policies have been

[1] Professor, Department of Education [CIE], University of Delhi, Delhi

[2] Research Scholar, Department of Education, University of Delhi, Delhi

analysed to trace back if the premise of foundational numeracy existed in these policies or is it novel to the National Education Policy 2020?

Understanding Foundational Numeracy

Mathematical proficiency has always been a gatekeeper for academic and economic success. It is well known that mathematical skills develop in a cumulative fashion with early skills forming the foundation for the acquisition of later skills. You would also agree, mathematical skills tend to emerge quite early, even before language skills develop. For illustration, an infant develops the spatial skills of holding a milk bottle even when she may not have acquired the skills of speaking.

If the above premise is true and holds an agreement, then we can also build a corollary that differences in early mathematical skills can also be spotted before the formal schooling begins. Many educationists and psychologists hold these differences as predictive of later performances in mathematics (Duncan et al., 2008; Ginsburg, Klein, & Starkey, 1998; Locuniak & Jordan, 2008; Mazzocco & Thompson, 2005). Children who fall behind their peers in early mathematics usually continue to develop at a slower rate (Aunola et al., 2004). And thus, an urgency is to build some basic mathematical skills at the very early stages of the child's development.

The phrase "Foundational Numeracy" can be seen synonymous to "Early Numeracy". Foundational Numeracy refers to developing a sense of handling numbers and basic arithmetic operations like addition and subtraction during the early schooling years. Although there is no clear consensus on the actual meaning of the concept of foundational numeracy, it factors in all the concepts which contribute to handling numbers easily and efficiently.

Some even accord the term foundational numeracy to the presence of certain logical-mathematical skills. This perspective is from the Piagetian view of development of number sense which is a synthesis of conservation of number, classification and seriation. Piaget's (1965) theory on concepts of numbers in young children has dominated psychological research and mathematics education for a long time. His theory has been elaborated by many scholars, each adding more to it. The essence remains in strengthening the concepts that help in developing a number sense.

Tracing the Footprints of 'Foundational Numeracy'

In the Indian education system, the term 'foundational numeracy' first appeared in the National Education Policy 2020; but its need was felt long before. Although the term does not come out in the earlier policies as overly as it did through the NEP 2020, the fact that basic mathematical skills are a must to be acquired by all children unto a certain grade has been mentioned in the earlier policies as well. The tone of expression was, however, subtle and not so emphasising. The concerns related to early numeracy were being realised;

solutions, on the other hand, were left unclear. Let's not go very far in the past. Let's begin with what the National Policy of Education (1986) had to say.

National Policy of Education 1986

Even if one were to study the National Policy of Education 1986 carefully, it is unlikely to find the term 'numeracy' in it. However, you are sure to appreciate the concerns made by the policy on inculcation of basic numerical knowledge at the primary stages. There are two aspects that lead to this conclusion. One, NPE 1986's launching of Minimum Learning Levels at the primary state, and second, is the policy's appeal for achieving maximum literary levels till the eighth five-year plan. The reader must note that in this policy the term 'numeracy' was subsumed under the term 'literacy'.

One of the aims of NPE 1986 was to achieve maximum literacy till the eighth five-year plan. All efforts were directed towards universalising 'basic' education where the learners could be 'literates' if not 'educated'. To promote the mission, there were literacy programmes, where emphasis was laid on development of skills to ensure economic self-reliance and upgraded functional capacities of the learners. Within the phase 'literacy', basic mathematical skills which can be deemed functional for survival were also stated. NPE (1986) stated that to achieve skill-based literacy, the curriculum of mathematics for primary school students must include numbers, four operations and basic geometry.

The Policy also realises the importance of basic mathematical skills for sustenance as it states that these are entry points to the world of the information and communication which are meant to be carried forward to help the citizens enrich their knowledge, acquire skills for improving their functional capability keeping in view the latest developments and for finding solution to their day-to-day problems. In short, basic mathematical knowledge leads to the well-being of a citizen.

Literacy per se is a minimal and imperative entry point to the world of information and communication. It is a basic step towards adult education which is a process of life-long learning. (National Policy of Education 1986, p. 25).

A second aspect of this policy is its marked step towards realising that not all children can attain the high learning goals. Instead of building a society based on ability-based competitions, efforts must be made to ensure all students attain the minimum levels of learning at the end of a grade or a class. The policy therefore identified Minimum Levels of Learning (MLL) for all subjects at the primary level.

MLL have been laid down for the primary stage with the intention of reducing the curriculum load and making it more relevant and functional for those children who have no support for learning at home or outside the school, who are not likely to avail the opportunity of education beyond this stage and who must learn here what is required to sustain them throughout their lives and enable them to function in their world as socially useful and contributing individuals (National Policy of Education 1986, pp. 35-36).

The policy launched Minimum Levels of Learning that must be achieved in one Language (Mother Tongue), Mathematics and Environmental studies for Classes I-V. These MLL served as guidelines for teaching and learning at the primary level as they defined the minimum learning outcomes in the form of competencies that ought to be attained at the end of a particular grade. By laying down the MLLs for primary grades, NPE 1986 announced a child-centric approach for teaching. Teaching got reformed as the focus was on meeting the listed competencies. Defining MLLs gave the mandatory directions for ensuring attainment of certain mathematical competencies at the end of the primary level.

Lest you doubt the claims made above, two caveats of the policy must be highlighted. First, NPE 1986 mentions attainment of basic numerical skills under its 'adult literacy' campaign. The focus of the policy was on attainment of basic numerical sense among the adults. It rained at developing an ability to count and calculate numbers which can help in achieving the literacy level among the older people. Second caveat is related to defining MLLs. The policy only wishes for attainment of certain competencies; it lacks in explicating the real essence of what is meant by number sense. The pedagogical approaches suggested under the MLLs are quite procedural oriented. The policy limits in identifying the basic meaning of numbers, idea of quantification, number sense and geometric thinking.

National Curriculum Framework, 2005

The National Curriculum Framework, 2005 has by far been the only document that recognised the need to define, explicate and elaborate various aspects related to school education. Under the NCF 2005, 21 focus groups were identified and separate documents, explicitly delineating the issues, challenges, concerns and road maps were made. One such dedicated document was the Position Paper on Teaching of Mathematics, 2006.

The position paper on Teaching of Mathematics raised several concerns on the state of mathematics teaching in India. It talked on shifting the focus of teaching from narrow goals dominated by procedural knowhow to higher goals aiming at the 'mathematisation' of the child's thinking. The emphasis was on achieving a clarity of thought, an ability to handle abstractions and an approach to problem solving (NCERT, 2006, pp. 1-2). Children learning mathematics should enjoy the subject rather than fear it. The framework suggested that children should understand the basic structure of mathematics, use abstractions to perceive relationships, visualise patterns, reason out things and argue the truth or falsity of statements. To overcome these challenges, the Position Paper on Teaching of Mathematics (2006) recommended engaging every student with a sense of success, and also offering conceptual challenges to emerging mathematicians.

Let's bring our focus on 'narrow' and 'higher' goals of teaching mathematics. The NCF clearly specified two kinds of aims for school education: a narrow aim, that help learners contribute to the social and economic development, and a higher aim, that helps in developing the inner resources of the growing child.

This calls for a curriculum that is ambitious, coherent and teaches important mathematics. It should be ambitious in the sense that it seeks to achieve the higher aim rather than (only) the narrower aim. (Position Paper on Teaching of Mathematics, 2006, p. 1).

From this statement, one can deduce that the policy points to narrow aim as accumulating basic numerical knowledge related to numbers and number operations, measurement of quantities, fractions, percentages and ratios. Concomitantly, it also cautions that having a functional know-how in these areas must not be taken as the bigger goal of learning mathematics. Doing mathematics in real spirits would encompass possessing the right attitude for problem-solving and approaching them in a systematic manner.

Although this policy also does not specify anything exclusively to 'foundational numeracy', it does recommend a child-centred activity approach to be adopted for teaching basic elementary mathematics to young children. In primary and pre-primary classes, a child must learn with concrete objects to understand the connections between the logical functioning of their everyday lives to that of mathematical thinking. The framework emphasises on inculcating number sense rather than following fixed algorithms to find one answer. It talks about how children must be led to making sense of numbers, use composition and decomposition methods to understand the structure of numbers, play with patterns, measurement and data handling to make a mathematical sense of things around them. These are the key ingredients of numeracy. So, even though the Position Paper on Teaching of Mathematics does not mention the phrase 'foundational numeracy', the document does follow the spirit of it.

Further, the Position Paper emphasises on relating mathematics, at least at the primary level, to the social-cultural milieu of the child. Every child must be encouraged to look out for instances of doing mathematics around his/her surroundings. Family and community to play a key role in helping the young minds identify basic mathematical skills of day-to-day work. An apprenticeship in doing mathematics will not only connect the child to the subject but will also help in reducing the anxiety attached to it. The framework strongly recommends connecting the non-formal ways of doing mathematics to the formal school mathematics. In fact, it recognises the non-formal ways of doing mathematics as strong pillars in reducing the fear of the subject. The primary curriculum should be enriched with a variety of activities, tasks, experiences and anecdotes of mathematics used in everyday dealings.

Accordingly, operations should be introduced contextually which should be followed by the development of language and symbolic notations to help the learners in forming a meaningful link.

For introducing a sense for numbers, the Position Paper iterates that children enter school with a set of intuitive and cultural ideas about numbers and simple operations. There is an emphasis on the development of numbers sense and skills of estimation and approximation instead of solely depending on standard algorithms of addition, subtraction, multiplication and division. It is thus recommended that the teachers at this level must not treat the child as a tabula rasa. They must begin by acknowledging the maths learnt by children from out-of-school contexts. The framework also suggests developing a mastery over logical skills by introducing limited quantities and smaller numbers to prevent an overloading of the child's cognitive capacity.

As a concluding remark, we reinstate – Although in the Position paper of Teaching Mathematics, 2006 there is no explicit mention of the phrase 'foundational numeracy' or 'early numeracy', the recommendations made by the framework are in cognisance to the spirit of promoting a mathematical sense among the primary children. The suggestions made in the framework are elaborate enough to be taken as guidelines for encouraging young minds towards mathematics. The spirit of the policy can be seen in the NCERT's primary textbooks *Math-Magic* wherein a contextualised-conceptualised approach has been adopted. These textbooks illustrate concepts from daily experiences to highlight the interconnections of concepts at primary level. Episodes of people's life have been given to make the books comprehensively context-oriented.

Foundational Numeracy as Espoused in NEP 2020

The recent National Education Policy 2020 is the first document that brings out the phrase 'Foundational Numeracy' in an explicitly highlighting tone. The second chapter of this education policy titled, "*Foundational Literacy and Numeracy: An Urgent and Necessary Prerequisite to Learning*" draws attention to the urgency of promoting basic literacy and mathematical skills from the early stages of a child.

To understand what the policy means by "Foundational Numeracy" we need to first dig out the essence of 'education' that the National Education Policy 2020 conveys. The policy accentuates, "With the quickly changing employment landscape and global ecosystem, it is becoming increasingly critical that children not only learn, but more importantly learn how to learn" (p. 3). The purpose of education, therefore, must be to move towards minimally required content with acumen to learn and think critically. It is imperative to strengthen the abilities to solve problems, be creative and work in a multidisciplinary manner. The policy envisions the citizens of India to be innovative, adaptive and creative to be able to imbibe themselves to varied challenges in life. Such an aim can be achieved through a pedagogy that is driven by tenets of experiential learning, holistic and integrated presentation, inquiry-based, discovery-oriented, learner-centred, discussion-based and flexible outlook.

Particularly for the learning of mathematics, NEP 2020 recognises mathematics and mathematical thinking as indispensable ingredients for the future of India. In future, there will be high stress on the fields involving artificial intelligence, machine learning, and data science. Mathematics and computational thinking will inevitably be seen as ubiquitous subjects.

Thus, mathematics and computational thinking will be given increased emphasis throughout the school years, starting with the foundational stage, through a variety of innovative methods, including the regular use of puzzles and games that make mathematical thinking more enjoyable and engaging. (National Education Policy 2020, pp. 15-16)

One will have to start thinking mathematically from early years onwards. This does not mean increasing the content of mathematics. It means promoting the competencies of logical thinking, computational skills, reasoning, argumentation and decision-making capacities. The policy recognises the need to sow the seeds of mathematical thinking from the foundational stages of a child.

The policy states that the schools in India have laid little curriculum emphasis on foundational numeracy and on mathematical ideas and thinking. The school curriculum moves so quickly for young learners that all the learning in schools quickly becomes rote memorisation. Schools are providing mechanical academic training to the learners and have completely ignored the foundational material essential for learning (p. 15). The policy suggested that the principle of learning must be to provide solid foundation in counting, arithmetic, mathematical and logical thinking, problem-solving and being creative, so that all learning is more enjoyable for learners.

The policy urges for ensuring attainment of "Foundational Numeracy" by the end of primary stage by all students. The policy states that to overcome the learning crisis happening in India, children need to be equipped with the concept of pre-numeracy and pre-literacy which most of the children lack when they enter school. The ability to read and write, and perform basic operations with numbers are the necessary and indispensable prerequisites for all future schooling and lifelong learning. Adequate preparation needs to be done to develop basic numeral skills in early childhood education.

The policy has considered foundational literacy and numeracy as the most basic requirement for the rest of the policy to be relevant. It is estimated that at least five crore students, studying in elementary classes lack the basic ability to carry out addition and subtraction with Indian numerals. Once a student falls behind on foundational numeracy all other areas of mathematics suffer, making it difficult for the learner to catch up later. The nature of the discipline also makes it difficult for the students to understand higher concepts resulting in the fear of mathematics. The fear at times becomes so huge that it becomes a major reason for not attending school or for dropping out altogether.

An urgency to achieve foundational numeracy can be seen in the document as it strongly proposes for the attainment of foundational numeracy. It holds it as an urgent national mission and aims to achieve universal foundational numeracy by 2025. To achieve this aim, it proposes to set up a National Mission on Foundational Literacy and Numeracy by the Ministry of Education. The purpose of this body will be to identify stage-wise targets and goals to be achieved by 2025, closely tracking and monitoring progress of the same and to speed up the entire process.

Thus, to attain foundational numeracy, the policy plans to provide schools with an adequate number of local teachers or those who are familiar with the local languages so that the children can learn in the language they are comfortable with. It also suggests ensuring the pupil-teacher ratio to be under 30:1 so that teachers are able to focus on all the learners and are able to achieve the goal of foundational numeracy. Some other ways for ensuring an early achievement of the target can be one-to-one peer taken as a voluntary and joyful activity under the supervision of trained teachers. The policy recommends that if "every literate member of the community could commit to teaching one student/person on how to read/write numbers, how to perform basic operations, it would change the country's landscape very quickly" (p. 9). All the states and UTs are therefore suggested to establish innovative models to foster peer-tutoring and volunteer activities as well as launch other programmes to support learners to attain foundational numeracy.

The policy has also planned to modify the curriculum of students throughout the preparatory and middle school years. The new curriculum will extensively focus on counting, arithmetic and mathematical thinking with the continuous formative and adaptive assessment to track as well as individualise each student's learning.

The policy also attempts to prepare an initial cadre of high-quality ECCE teachers in Anganwadis by training them through a systematic effort in accordance with the curricular/pedagogical framework to be developed by NCERT.

All the Anganwadis workers who have qualified their 10+2 and above, will be given a 6-month certificate in ECCE, and those with lower educational qualification will be given a one-year diploma covering early numeracy and literacy. (National Education Policy 2020, p. 8).

The curriculum for teacher education and development will be renewed to include the concept of foundational numeracy for both pre-service and in-service teachers. The curriculum will be relevant for the teachers of Grades 1 and 2, and will focus on their preparation of school teaching, ECCE, and multilevel activity-based learning.

Further, a new pattern of assessment has been proposed to strengthen the cause of attainment of foundational numeracy. It is proposed that the students not just be assessed at the end of Grades 10 and 12, but all the students will also be assessed at the end of Grades 3, 5 and 8. At the end of these stages, the students will be assessed for their achievement in core concepts, level of knowledge ascertained by the national and local curricula, along with relevant higher-order skills and application of knowledge in real-life situations. The policy suggests that to track the foundational numeracy and other skills, examinations become necessary for Grade 3 learners "so that corrective measures could be taken at the right time" (pp. 18-19). It has been reported in the policy document that many students drop out of school after Grade 5 or 8 as they find themselves falling behind, and one of the root causes of such a feeling is lack in attaining foundational numeracy and literacy. Thus, monitoring of learning becomes even more essential in the Grade 3 to help learners in continuing education.

Attaining foundational numeracy is incomplete without redesigning the curriculum for teacher education. The policy recommends constant support with continuous professional development to teachers to impart foundational numeracy at all levels. It brings out a focused map of building foundational literacy from the early stages, beginning from Early Childhood Care and Education. "It is envisaged that prior to the age of five every child will move to a 'Preparatory Class' or 'Balavatika' (that is, before Class I), which would have an ECCE-qualified teacher." (pp. 7-8). At this stage, the learning must be based primarily on play-based methods with a focus on developing cognitive, affective and psychomotor abilities with early literacy and numeracy. The policy also acknowledges the large-scale inaccessibility of ECCE. Since a large proportion of children are already far behind the attainment levels, the National Education Policy 2020 suggests an interim 3-month play-based school preparation module for all Grade 1 students. The module will aim to provide foundational numeracy through activities, workbooks around numbers in collaboration with peers and parents.

All the teachers will be expected to participate in at least 50 hours of continuous professional development opportunities every year for their own professional development. These opportunities will cover all the latest pedagogies related to foundational numeracy such as experiential learning, arts-integrated, sports-integrated, and storytelling-based approaches, and also help in doing formative and adaptive assessment on numeracy.

The policy also recommends the creation of a national repository of high-quality resources on foundational numeracy. These resources will be available to teachers on a single platform, Digital Infrastructure for Knowledge Sharing (DIKSHA). To overcome the language barriers while acquiring foundational numeracy technological aids will serve as an important medium.

Some Promises and Certain Misses

As said earlier, the National Education Policy 2020 offers a very promising step as it realises lack of foundational numeracy as one of the reasons for low performance and dropout of children from schools. Building a strong base in numbers will surely help in the retaining the interests of students. The policy needs to be congratulated for the efforts it is proposing at the national and state levels to overcome the impasse created by non-numerical abilities. A focused approach with a targeted timeline does seem to be assuring for the goals to be attained. Enhancing the role of early childhood care and education in developing pre-numeracy will benefit children from disadvantaged socio-economic backgrounds who have not had access to pre-primary education.

Ideologically, the policy indeed offers a hope for a more mathematically-oriented society, however its true essence will unveil only after a plan of action is offered. There are, however, some misses in the policy. First, is the limited way in which the term Foundational Numeracy has been envisaged. A lot of emphasis has been made on building numerical abilities in young children. A true essence of mathematics develops through spatial reasoning, probabilistic thinking, visualisation, estimation and optimisation skills. An acumen to these traits could also have been stated for public attention.

Second observation on the usage of the term "Foundational Numeracy". If one were to study the manner in which the term "Numeracy" is referred to in the world of educators, one would tend to come across a very broad perspective. It not only encompasses basic numerical skills but is also concerned with the adjustment of a person in a mathematically-laden world. We are surrounded with information and data to be interpreted carefully. Numeracy is therefore referred to as a fundamental mathematical acumen required for survival, sustenance and good living. The term is not limited to young children. It shares concerns even with the adults.

The demand of problem-solving skills in all occupations is increasing rapidly and therefore not only our children, our adults should also possess fundamental logico-mathematical knowledge. For survival in the 21st century, one would not only require content-based understanding but also a wisdom to think critically and creativity; embrace innovations; do logical communications; approach situations with flexibility and adaptability; make sensible decisions; and generate optimum solutions. We would need a bunch of mathematical competencies such as reasoning, making logical argumentation, modelling, problem posing and solving, graphical representation, symbolic knowhow and knowledge of tools and technology. All these traits are expected from all age-groups. Thus, along with a mention of 'foundational numeracy', it was expected that the National Education Policy 2020 would also address the lack of "foundational mathematical skills" at the adulthood level as well. Most recommendations are limited to primary stages. The policy hardly mentions the problems faced by adults while dealing with quantification in their everyday life. There is hardly any cognisance to the lack of basic numeracy in adults. In fact, this limitation exists in all policies thus far.

It is wished that in the implementation programme of the new policy of education there will be a plan on building basic logico-mathematical competencies in children as well as in adults. Although some government and non-government organisations are already working in making primary mathematics easy for young children, the efforts are sporadic. Certain government organisations such as Department of Early Education NCERT, Homi Bhabha Centre for Science Education (HBSCE), certain non-government organisations such as Jodo Gyan and Building As Learning Aid (BALA) and some individual efforts such as the youtube videos produced by Gandhi (2020 a, b, c, d, e, f) illustrate the efforts being done in improving the state of mathematical understanding in the country. All such efforts are being done to promote the logico-mathematical understanding among people. It is firmly believed that logico-mathematics is the backbone for a mathematical aptitude which accentuates numeracy skills.

For any country to progress, it is imperative that a logical way of working is established at all levels. Attaining numeracy is therefore a challenge for both adults and children and this needs a lot of attention. Numeracy, in its true sense, is related to a wider application of judgements. The recent National Education Policy 2020 does recognise the need of numeracy in young minds, but it is just hitting the tip of the problem. Underneath, many concerns crawl.

References

Aunola, K., Leskinen, E., Lerkkanen, M., & Nurmi, (2004). Developmental dynamics of Math performance from preschool to Grade 2. *Journal of Educational Psychology*, 96, 699-713.

Department of Education, Ministry of Human Resource Development. (1986). *National Policy on Education.* New Delhi, India: Government of India.

Duncan, G. J., Dowsett, C. J., Claessens, A., Magnuson, K., Huston, A. C., Klebanov, P., et al. (2008). School readiness and later achievement. *Developmental Psychology*, 44(1), 232.

Ginsburg, H. P., Klein, A., & Starchy, P. (1998). The development of children's mathematical thinking: Connecting research with practice. In W. Damon, I. E. Sigel, & A. K. Renninger (Eds.), *Handbook of child psychology*, 5th ed. *Child psychology in practice*, Vol. 4 (pp. 401-476). NJ: John Wiley & Sons Inc.

Gandhi, H. (2020a). Episode 1 : Do you have a mathematical eye ?. https://www.youtube.com/watch?v=NIks0ZLt3oo

Gandhi, H. (2020b). Episode 2 : Eye for Chai. https://www.youtube.com/watch?v=beMCw-e8zPY&t=9s

Gandhi, H. (2020c). Episode 3 : Tale of Tails. https://www.youtube.com/watch?v=Prwwh532Eq0&t=20s

Gandhi, H. (2020d). Episode 4: Maths and Face Masks. https://www.youtube.com/watch?v=xrrjVCbClGk&t=3s

Gandhi, H. (2020e). Episode 5: One, Two... Lace My Shoe. https://www.youtube.com/watch?v=peM5WGJwB5Y

Gandhi, H. (2020f). Episode 6: It's Just a Cakewalk. https://www.youtube.com/watch?v=3gRqDxBt5oQ&t=8s

Gandhi, H. (2020g). Kya aap mien hair vo ganitye nazar. https://www.youtube.com/watch?v=4kwD956Mz7M&t=2s

Locuniak MN, Jordan NC. Using kindergarten number sense to predict calculation fluency in second grade. *Journal of Learning Disabilities.* 2008; 41(5):451-459.

Mazzocco, M.M., Thompson, R.E. Kindergarten predictors of math learning disability. *Learning Disabilities Research & Practice.* 2005; 20(3):142-155.

Ministry of Human Resource Development. (2020). *National Educational Policy 2020.* New Delhi, India: Government of India.

National Council of Educational Research and Training. (2005). National Curriculum Framework. New Delhi: India.

National Council of Educational Research and Training. (2006). National Focus Group on Teaching of Mathematics [Position Paper]. New Delhi: India.

Orpwood, G., Schmidt, B., & Jun, H. (2012). Competing in the 21st century skills race. Ottawa, ON: Canadian Council of Chief Executives.

Piaget, J. (1965). The Child's Conception of Number. New York: Norton.

11

Multidisciplinary Approach to Education: Effective Teaching-Learning Routines

Jyoti Sharma

Learning is an interactive process, vital to the development of human thinking. Learning becomes meaningful when it can be used in practical/realistic situations. Any knowledge that has no visible change in learner's abilities or behaviour cannot be termed as learning. Application of knowledge for the betterment of self or society shall be the ultimate goal of teaching. The teacher is responsible for making students *'learn'* and to prepare individuals who are capable of using formal knowledge acquired in school, for the betterment of self and society. In the existing structure of formal education, knowledge is categorised in the form of different subjects taught by different subject teachers. Teachers are identified by their subject specialisation. The categorization of subjects becomes more and more crude as students' progress from lower grades to higher grades. The progression in complexity of subject matter from the lower grades to the higher grades gradually becomes more abstract and unrealistic for students. Students after passing the school do not find themselves equipped with necessary skills for the job market or for leading a productive future life. The problem of today is a reflection of how the education system has failed to prepare students for future challenges. Classroom is a representation of society. Action taken in the classroom shall target problems present in the society. Education in the modern world cannot be centred only around theoretical knowledge provided through textbooks. It demands education that can serve society by solving complex problems emerging from real life.

Our learners are surrounded with a complex web of societal realities outside the four walls of the classroom. The term 'education' as said by John Dewey is "not just preparation for life, rather life itself". It can be achieved in the true sense only if our teaching-learning practices address these complexities and multifold variations.

"Institutions offering single streams must be phased out, and all universities and colleges must focus on becoming multidisciplinary by 2030", the National Education Policy 2020 proposes. The new education policy aims for "broad-based, flexible learning". 'Multidisciplinary education', a term we have been long exposed to as a part of various policies and advisories over the ages but are yet to be truly integrated in our education framework.

Professor, Cluster Innovation Centre, University of Delhi, Delhi

Let's start with a very simplistic definition of the term and then gradually move towards its complexities in implementation and other challenges.

Multidisciplinary refers to an approach wherein two or more academic disciplines collaborate for a specific purpose. Though a multidisciplinary approach uses the skills and knowledge from more than one academic discipline, the use of knowledge however from different disciplines remains distinct, even though the differences between the disciplines is often quite elusive. We can understand the idea of multidisciplinarity with a simple example of a restaurant where the manager, chef, waiters, cashier commonly work together to provide hospitality services, applying their own set of skills to the task while staying in the ambit of their expertise at an individual level.

Multidisciplinary approach in education is a method of curriculum integration that focuses primarily on the different disciplines and the diverse perspectives they bring to illustrate a topic, theme or issue. A multidisciplinary curriculum similarly, is one in which a common topic is studied from the viewpoint of more than one discipline.

The other approaches to curriculum integration are interdisciplinary and trans-disciplinary. Though interdisciplinary and trans-disciplinary seem very similar to multidisciplinary approach of curriculum integration, yet there is clear difference among the three approaches in terms of aim, planning and content organisation.

In a multidisciplinary approach, the context of knowledge is studied through perspectives of multiple (more than one discipline) disciplines adding breadth to the available knowledge without merging disciplinary boundaries. Learners are encouraged to make meaningful connections across different subject domains.

Interdisciplinary approach brings disciplinary knowledge from different subject domains together to develop a synthesised body of academic knowledge. Interdisciplinary approach harmonises disciplinary boundaries to create new, integrated and holistic understanding of subject matter.

Trans-disciplinary approach transcends disciplinary knowledge from more than one discipline to study a problem/an issue using an inquiry-based approach. It allows working across multiple subject domains and eliminating disciplinary boundaries to create something new and different.

The present chapter explains the essential features of multidisciplinary approach as a method of curriculum organisation and classroom practices. The discussion will enable readers to know about the essentials of multidisciplinary with reference to curriculum design, teaching practices and learning paradigms. It will outline the ways to enhance students' engagement in classroom processes, creating an inquiry-based learning culture in the classroom and making curriculum more inclusive.

Multidisciplinarity as Concept

As defined by IGI Global (n.d:1), Multidisciplinarity refers to cooperation of experts from different scientific disciplines. The definition emphasises integration among different scientific subjects. It is important to highlight that subjects from non-science categories are equally important in defining the scope of multidisciplinarity. Also, the definition does not describe the purpose of cooperation. Any educational activity without a purpose is insignificant. Therefore, it is imperative to outline the purpose and scope of an integrated academic activity seeking collaboration among multiple disciplines.

UNESCO International Bureau of Education (IBE) defines multidisciplinary as an 'approach' to curriculum integration bringing different disciplines together to illustrate a topic, theme or issue from different perspectives. It further explains that in a multidisciplinary curriculum the same topic is studied from perspectives of more than one discipline.

The Stony Brook State University of New York offers degree courses in multidisciplinary studies and describes multidisciplinary studies as a programme that allows students to design a major programme in more than one field of study by drawing on the courses from more than two areas of study.

Doyle and Bozzon (2018) emphasises the role of multidisciplinary teaching to inculcate in students the capacity to think deeply, analyse information, and integrate important ideas to integrate knowledge and tackle the big questions connected to live experiences.

In the present scenario, teaching is confined in silos of subject boundaries leaving students unprepared to make realistic interconnections. The learning is enjoyable and meaningful when students make connections between different subject areas. It is therefore desirable to step out of discrete disciplinary zones and build up co-taught multidisciplinary courses.

The underlying assumption in a multidisciplinary plan of study is that no subject exits as a disconnected field of study. So, in order to understand the underlying structures of knowledge, one needs to see the ways that discrete subjects connect in a larger perspective. The overarching goal of multidisciplinary education is to teach students in a way that shall have relevance in their lives.

Researchers have reinforced the use of more than one discipline to teach or clarify a concept for a better understanding of the topic, theme or the content under study. (Adeyemi, 2010). Adeyemi explains multidisciplinary teaching as a thoughtfully planned activity that connects key concepts and skills from many disciplines into the presentation of a single unit. Multidisciplinary as an approach can be understood with reference to multidisciplinary programme, multidisciplinary task, multidisciplinary person, multidisciplinary teaching and many such reference contexts. Here in the present discussion, we will refer to multidisciplinarity in context of education and multidisciplinary teaching.

Classroom learning experiences for students shall always come to them in an integrated way rather than subject wise divisions of learning. Knowledge of core curriculum in foundation subjects shall be the basic necessity paving way for more advanced learning because basic knowledge of core subjects shall be the starting point for making meaningful connections across subject domains. There is a strong need to make formal education more realistic and connected with everyday life experiences. The shift is needed to bring a multidisciplinary approach in the courses and methodology of teaching. It helps learners to connect different strands of school subjects and prepares them to work on realistic problems by applying knowledge acquired through different subject domains. It makes learners better problem solvers by developing scientific approach and analytical skills, on the other hand, it makes learners more accepting and humanistic.

Till the time we do not break the shackles of the traditional compartmentalisation of disciplines, we cannot truly achieve a holistic education in the true sense of the term.

The National Education Policy 2020 constantly emphasised the need for a multidisciplinary approach to education. While there are many ways of achieving this, let's try to first understand what the term actually implies.

Let's take the example of a History classroom. The teacher has to talk about the Red Fort as a subset of the Mughal architecture. In a traditional classroom, the teacher would present to the learners a historical narrative, a few pictures and historical writings on the same. In a classroom where the teacher inculcates a multidisciplinary approach, he/she will bring forth the learners a wide array of options to explore. The learners will be able to draw connections to various disciplines they study in their other periods. They will be given the scope to explore the dimensions of the structure (mathematics), the chemical composition of the construction material used (science), the various literary works (poems/ plays/ stories/ monologues) written in praise of the monument (English/Hindi), the geographical terrain of the place where the monument is constructed (geography), amongst others. The students will also be sensitised to the need of protecting our heritage and fruitful discussions will take place on how they as a citizen of the country can contribute to the same (value education).

While the above discussed is just one of the many examples we can think of in the context of multidisciplinary approach to education, it is essential to devise effective teaching-learning strategies to be able to truly achieve the above-mentioned. School learning experiences for students shall always come to them as an integrated learning experience rather than subject wise division of content. Learning of core curriculum in all subjects shall be the basic necessity for more advanced learning instead of end in it.

Multidisciplinary teaching is one such method to help learners connect different strands of school subjects. This method of teaching-learning can serve dual purpose. Firstly, it enables learners to work on realistic problems by applying knowledge acquired through different subject domains. Secondly, it also helps learners to work together by developing a sense of learning communities. On one hand, it makes learners better problem solvers by developing a scientific approach and analytical skills, while on the other hand, it makes learners more accepting and humanistic.

To better understand the concept of multidisciplinary teaching, let's look at an example:

Vignette

A Geography teacher was discussing the idea of weather forecast with grade VIII students. The discussion was focused on solving an independent problem on the weather forecast for the next two days.

Now, the problem can be presented to students as a mechanical problem that needed some calculations, which may not make much sense to students unless it is:

- *connected with scientific reasons effecting the weather;*
- *explained using mathematical models for making accurate weather forecast;*
- *discussed with social lives of people in that area;*
- *assessed the far better planning and infrastructure to prevent natural calamities due to changing weather;*
- *reviewed possible economical fall out due to extreme weather conditions;*
- *explored about latest research and instruments that are used in making weather forecast;*
- *analysed projecting the long term effect of changing weather conditions on the ecosystem.*

Another way of teaching Weather Forecast can be a method infused with inquiry-based teaching where learning context studied more holistically using knowledge from multiple disciplines.

The above example highlights the scope of teaching a topic from multiple perspectives and how bringing in diverse subject knowledge makes learning more holistic and far-reaching.

The idea of connecting disciplinary knowledge from several subject areas to solve challenging problems or to create new knowledge was advocated by John Dewey (1859-1952) who introduced the idea through his famous theory of *learning by doing*. His work at University of Chicago's Laboratory school, founded by him in 1916 led to his pedagogical ideas on project-oriented learning. The most outstanding aspect of Dewey's laboratory school was the multi-dimensional approach of teaching, based solely on experimentation and exploration. It was a set-up where learners were given the scope of 'choice' cutting across subject compartmentalisation unlike the contemporary traditional American classrooms of that time.

Developing Dewey's work, William Heard Kilpatrick (1918; 1921) emphasised the role of classroom activities which originate from the experiences of students. For him, acquiring subject-based knowledge was less important than constructing intrinsic connections among different threads of knowledge. In his seminal article, *The Project Method,* Kilpatrick referred to the project as any purposeful experience and education as life itself rather than preparation for later life (1918). He placed the child at the centre of learning where wholehearted purposeful learning experiences are provided in meaningful social contexts rather than drawing boundaries on the basis of subject disciplines.

Kilpatrick categorised four kinds of projects:

1. Projects that result in physical manifestation of an idea such as product development;
2. Projects that aim to fulfill an aesthetic purpose such as enjoying board games;
3. Projects that aim to solve an intellectual problem such as solving parking problem;
4. Projects that aim to master a skill such as learning Excel for data handling.

If we carefully observe all the above-mentioned categorisations, we will see the need of a multidisciplinary scope of learning to be able to achieve either of the goals. Restricting our teaching learning strategies cannot lead to imparting productive skill development in our learners for everyday or future life.

As Project Method propagated by Dewey and Kilpatrick became popular and tried out in various educational institutions and occupational fields (such as business, economics and management), the project method emerged as a powerful scientific technique for various kinds of investigations, reinforcing the idea of more holistic and multidisciplinary education.

Multidisciplinary approach when placed in an educational context can diversify a learning situation into a highly powerful teaching strategy. Multidisciplinary education is a progressive shift that influences all aspects of learning discourse. It is a teaching-learning model that requires a shift from isolated, short and teacher-centric activities to comprehensive and long term, student-centric activity. The learning culture in a multidisciplinary classroom in most cases, are interdisciplinary, collaborative, student-centred, inquiry-based and are formulated on real time problems/issues/contexts. As a pedagogical approach, it requires teachers to know their learners well by collecting information about learning strengths and interests of all students. It also demands a clear shift from traditional classroom culture to progressive classroom culture. This pedagogical approach is strictly based on multidisciplinary context that aims to investigative real time challenges. It is a method of learning that promotes transfer of theoretical knowledge to practical applications through the intermingling nature of various subject ideas.

The need of the hour is to imbibe in our education framework, imbibes Dewey's principles of practical learning and Gandhi's ideology of basic education that emphasises learning through hands-on. This can be achieved only when we foster multidisciplinary teaching methods (project based learning being one of them).

In a multidisciplinary learning environment, we not only impart in our learners the skills to draw logical connections from different disciplines but also make for them the classroom content more relatable to their everyday life. This not only makes them contribute more productively to society but also makes them better understand the complexities and variations surrounding them every day at various levels. Thus it becomes vital to cut through the watertight compartmentalisation of subjects focusing only on academic merit to a more tolerant and flexible framework where 'freedom of choice and exploration' is present.

Let us look at the multiple features of a multidisciplinary approach to learning:

Meaningful themes: Teaching-learning themes shall be meaningful so that students find purpose in doing the tasks and the themes shall emphasise the active construction of knowledge.

Socially responsible themes: Since a multidisciplinary approach is directly aimed towards making learning relevant to the immediate societal context of the learners, the theme shall develop a sense of connection and social responsibility among students. Tasks shall be so designed that students feel themselves as an active member of the society.

Open-ended opportunities: Tasks shall be designed in a way that they give freedom of choice and space to the learners with some components that are open ended and promote creative thinking.

Generic framework for better planning: Multidisciplinary teaching strategies shall have a structured but flexible framework which allows students the time and resources for efficient management and planning.

Scope for reflective thinking: This approach to teaching shall have scope for reflective moments even during the development of the task so that students are able to think critically, creatively and clearly. It must give to learners the opportunity to draw logical connections and to further develop upon both, individually and collectively on the multifold nature of disciplines presented before them.

Let us now sum up from our understanding, the various benefits of a multidisciplinary approach to teaching:

- It leads to developing habits of mind for scientific thinking.
- It creates opportunities for learning in a real time context.
- It helps teachers to develop detailed learning profiles of students, gauge their strengths and weaknesses.
- It enables students to diversify their interests.
- It promotes interdisciplinary approach
- It creates an inclusive culture in the classroom.
- It prepares students for future challenges.
- It helps students to be more realistic and innovative.
- It develops tolerance and collaborative learning among students.

- It minimises direct involvement of the teacher and gives scope to both the teacher and learners to reflect at an individual level with personal preferences.
- It helps students to realise their own potential.
- It helps teachers to take up such learning contexts which are otherwise not possible to carry out in traditional classrooms.
- It extends the scope of a subject beyond the textbook content.

If planned appropriately, a multidisciplinary approach can enrich students with holistic learning experiences that bring a more sustained and long lasting change in their learning behaviour.

Let us look at an example of a multidisciplinary try out plan:

TRYOUT I

Title of the project: Design your Number System
Subjects: Mathematics, History and Social Science
Grade: VIII
Number of students: 5-6
Timeline:6 weeks

Objectives:

Students will be able to:

- trace back the history of Numbers and Number System;
- understand structure of a Number System;
- uniqueness of present Number System;
- appreciate contribution of India in development of Number System;
- define rules to design their own Number System;
- propose road map to implement new Number System;
- convert decimal numbers in binary number system;
- use binary number systems in computer applications.

Learning Opportunities:

Social Science: Students will know the historical significance of development of numbers and number systems. They will be able to understand why conceptualisation of numbers was an important landmark in the evolution of civilisation.

Science: Students will be able to understand what is a system and why we call a set of numbers a Number System. How many systems are there in science?

Language: Students will be able to use language and creative expression to describe and define Number System.

Mathematics: Students will be able to understand the structure of a number system. They will also be able to generalise rules of defining Number Systems. They will be able to know the significance of choosing the right base, place value and need of having a zero.

Computer Science: Students will be able to learn the applications of binary number systems in computer applications.

Creativity: There will be ample scope of creativity. Students can design their own symbols and patterns.

Higher Order Thinking Skills: Project will help students to develop higher order thinking skills such as analysis, generalisation, create and justify.

Real time connection: Students will be able to compare the new number system with existing number systems and will further act as decision-makers to propose implementation plans for bringing in new number systems.

The final outcome of the task can be presented in multiple ways. It can be an opportunity to use most innovative methods for presenting the work. Below are few suggestions:

Students can submit it in the form of a simple project file which includes and can simultaneously present their findings as a group.

They can display it in the form of Theme Wall and can introduce it to the audience. During the interaction, they can answer the questions raised by the audience.

The work can be presented in PowerPoint form using interesting animation and presentation style. Presentation can be followed by a question-answer session.

Students can make interesting videos by using simple freely available software. It will help them to add many additional features that were otherwise not possible in other forms of presentations.

Students can work in groups and two or more groups can be asked to compete by presenting, defending and justifying their 'Number System'.

Students can weave the entire task around an interesting story and then can present it as a small play, which highlights the need of a new number system. Their planning and efforts to make a new number system and finally preparing the community to adopt a new number system.

Evaluating the task

The task can be evaluated against multiple parameters. A detailed learning scale can be developed to do systematic and descriptive evaluation.

TRYOUT II

Title of the project: Cricket Fun
Target concepts: Data Handling, Planning, Estimation, Social Structure, Safety Rules
Target group: Grade: VI
Context: Refer to International Cricket T20 Tournament-2019 timetable. Make a list of teams who participated in the tournament.

Prepare a detailed chart of all the matches played among the teams.
Find out which matches were played on which ground.
Note down the sitting capacity of the ground.

Assume 200 seats were reserved for VVIPs and 500 seats were reserved for VIPs for every match then what fractions of seats were available for the general audience.

Plot the location of matches on a self-designed map. What safety rules organisers of the stadium must have adopted to manage such a large crowd?

Design your dream stadium that can have capacity to accommodate one million audiences. Keep in mind that the stadium shall be equipped with all the latest facilities and have full proof safety protocols.

Objectives:

Students will be able to:

- collect, organise and present data
- work with large numbers
- learn the skills of planning and estimation
- learn about the safety protocols for public events
- learn the basics of architecture
- visualise and create the design of stadium
- justify their choice of design

Learning Opportunities:

Social Science: Students will get opportunity to learn about how games are planned and why games attract large number of people

Science: Students will become familiar with the basics of architecture and scientific principles of safety measures.

Language: Students will be able to use language and creative expression to describe their design.

Mathematics: Students will be able to work with realistic data. They will be able to interpret large data and make estimation and inferences using large data. They will be able to use scaling drawing to draw three dimensional large scale design.

Creativity: There will be ample scope of creativity. Students can make their own design of the stadium. They will be learning the principles of aesthetics and symmetry.

Higher Order Thinking Skills: Project will help students to develop higher order thinking skills such as analysis, infer, create and justify.

Real time connection: Students will be given the opportunity to know the latest trends in technology and design. They shall be asked to search the internet to know about modern architecture designs. They will update themselves with innovations in safety gears and devices.

Presentation

Students can present their work using project files or through power point presentation or making videos or making a three-dimension miniature model of a stadium.

The work can be divided into several parts such as data collection, organisation and presentation; collecting information on what all is required to make large buildings safe; learning about principles of architecture and design. Each subgroup of the project team can be assigned to each component where members work within the group but continuous sharing and learning from each other is the norm, not a choice.

The above discussion helped us to understand how fundamental ideas of discrete academic disciplines overlap basic competencies and how multidisciplinary education can help to develop skills necessary to respond to the challenges of the 21st century.

In the next section, we will discuss the underpinnings of multidisciplinary education as referred to in national education policies.

Kothari commission 1964 recommended transformation of the education system to relate it more closely to the life of the people. It emphasised that there should be an emphasis on the development of science and technology and on the cultivation of moral and social values. The education system should produce young men and women of character who can contribute to national progress. The strong conviction that education is fundamental for national development, initiated the thought process of integrating education with life. Although the idea of multidisciplinary education did not get clear mention, yet it did necessitate the need of more realistic education.

National Education Policy 1968 envisioned education for economic and cultural development, for national integration and for maintaining the socialist pattern of society. To achieve such aims, the policy proposed integration of valued-based education, community service and work experience as part of the main curriculum. The idea of integration furthered spread across practical training in industry to make academic curriculum more experiential.

Education Policy 1986 and its subsequent action plan 1992, envisaged "Education as Fundamental to all round development, both material and spiritual" of students.

Recognising Education in Acculturating Role, the policy emphasised the role of education in building sensitivities and perceptions that contribute to national cohesion, a scientific temper and independence of mind and spirit – thus furthering the goals of socialism, secularism and democracy enshrined in our constitution (NEP 1986).

Though the policy did not specifically mention the role of multidisciplinary education, the underlying philosophy of preparing minds that demonstrate scientific temperament and also possess constitutional values, gives us enough reason to find the scope of multidisciplinary education. The policy greatly emphasised the need of promoting multidisciplinary research culture in higher education institutes. It further suggested setting up rural universities, technical and management institutes. All such institutes require multidisciplinary programmes concentrating on societal problems/development issues or programmes on cutting edge technology for the future. It encouraged offering few multidisciplinary degree courses in rural development, rural management, developmental studies and highly skilled programmes on technology and scientific endeavours.

NEP 1986 recognised the need of integrating vocational course/tertiary level courses in the main curriculum leading to employment. The committee also felt the need to integrate existing courses to create need based technical and management courses.

We can safely say that though Education Policy 1986 did not directly put forth the need for a multidisciplinary approach but it did pave the way for need-based programmes that require expertise of more than one discipline. So, it was a welcome shift from distinct discipline programmes to need-based specific programmes requiring understanding of multiple disciplines.

National Education Policy 2020 recommends the need for a proficient workforce, skilled in multidisciplinary abilities across the sciences, social sciences, and humanities that can respond to the current and future challenges. Multidisciplinary learning experiences shall make learners to be creative and innovative. Such an education demands a pedagogy that is experiential, holistic, integrated, inquiry-driven and learner-centric. It requires a dynamic curriculum building strong foundations in basic disciplines and well integrated with realistic challenges.

The policy mentions the illustrious heritage of the ancient Indian education system that aimed for a life beyond schooling and moving towards complete realisation and liberation of the self and how educational institutes in ancient India created high standards of multidisciplinary teaching and research. It reaffirmed the need and faith in the highest level of multidisciplinary education to create an equitable, inclusive, and plural society as envisaged by our Constitution.

The policy positions multidisciplinarity education across the sciences, social sciences, arts, humanities, and sports as one of the fundamental principles that shall guide the course of education in coming years.

Promoting students to make disciplinary connections, the policy recommends introducing multidisciplinary study in the Secondary Stage comprising four years, building on the subject-oriented learning of the Middle Stage, but with greater depth, greater critical thinking, and greater flexibility of subject choices.

NEP 2020 strongly recommends all colleges and universities becoming multidisciplinary and moving teacher education programmes into multidisciplinary institutes providing high quality content and pedagogical knowledge to future teachers.

The policy envisions moving towards a more holistic multidisciplinary undergraduate education and setting up multidisciplinary universities and colleges, with at least one in or near every district. The higher education system in the country shall symbolise multidisciplinary institutes providing education in all branches of creative human endeavour including vocational subjects, professional subjects and soft skills. It further outlines the aim of multidisciplinary education to develop intellectual, aesthetic and social faculties of students in an integrated manner.

One of the core recommendations of the policy is to set up Multidisciplinary Education and Research Universities (MERU) that will aim to provide flexible curricular structures, rigorous research-based specialisation and multidisciplinary work opportunities.

Conclusion

The experience of multidisciplinary teaching within the existing course combinations will always be more enlightening as compared to the stand-alone versions. It provides scope of flexible learning arrangements enabling students to make spontaneous interconnections of knowledge. It will broaden their understanding that knowledge is not discrete and help them see the larger view of intellectual connections. Content coherence and synergy in teaching are centric to make multidisciplinary approach a reality.

It does not require building new physical infrastructures but it does require a complete overhaul of organisational and academic ecosystems. Curriculum restructuring shall be done carefully by identifying content themes. Content maps shall be designed integrating themes with multiple disciplines. Learning objectives shall focus on developing necessary skill sets and assessment patterns shall also emphasis on analytical thinking, problem-solving, creativity and synthesis of ideas. The teachers' preparedness to carry out multidisciplinary teaching is critical to successfully achieve the desirable goals. The synergy in team teaching, coherence in academic content, flexible assessment practices are essential to make multidisciplinary teaching a reality. At a deeper level, it requires academic maturity, sensitivity to the larger issues and willingness to accept multiple perspectives. Multidisciplinary Education celebrates the academic diversity to be inclusive and realistic.

12

Equity and Inclusion in Higher Education

Navleen Kaur

The theme "Equity and Inclusion in Higher Education" finds place in Chapter 14 of the new National Policy of Education 2020. The National Education Policy 2020 is the first education policy of the 21st century which replaces the thirty-four-year-old National Policy on Education (NPE) 1986 which was modified in 1992. Its vision and mission rests on the five columns of 'Access, Equity, Quality, Affordability and Accountability' for bringing changes from school education to higher education. This policy is united with the Goal 4: Quality Education of Sustainable Development Goals Agenda 2030, where it critiques and restores the country's education system, with its directives and governance, making both school and higher education more comprehensive, pliable and multidisciplinary.

The Discernment

Before we move further it is significant to understand the meaning of the terms *"Equity"*, *"Equality"*, *"Diversity"*, *"Inclusion"* which have been used effusively in this chapter of NEP 2020. *Equality* implies treating everyone the same and giving everyone access to the same opportunities. *Equity* means the quality of being fair and impartial, giving each student the tools s/he precisely needs to succeed. *Equality* focuses on creating the same starting line for everyone whereas *Equity* has the goal of providing everyone with the full range of opportunities and benefits, the same finish line. Meanwhile, equity refers to proportional representation (by race, class, gender, etc.) in those same opportunities. *Equality* is about sameness; it focuses on making sure everyone gets the same thing. *Equity* is about fairness; it ensures that each person gets what the person needs. This distinction is imperative in education, where we find visible gaps in opportunities and outcomes for large number of students. Likewise, *Diversity* means understanding that each individual is unique, and recognising individual differences. These can be of race, ethnicity, gender, sexual orientation, socio-economic status, age, physical abilities, religious beliefs, political beliefs, or other ideologies. What *inclusion* means is actually going beyond the numbers and bringing people to have a common shared valued experience. *Inclusion* means that all people, regardless of their abilities, disabilities, or health care needs, have the right to be respected as valued

---

Professor, Department of Community Education and Disability Studies, Panjab University, Chandigarh

members of their communities, and get the opportunity to participate in different recreational activities. Therefore, *Diversity* refers to the traits and characteristics that make people unique while Inclusion refers to the behaviours and social norms that ensure people feel welcome (Frederickson & Cline 2002).

Largely scholars pronounce education as a bipolar process where in compounding 'the educand' with 'the educator', the learner with the learned, the pupil with the teacher, subsequently affecting the disposition of the learner. The knowledge stemming from the teacher to the pupil connects them in a reciprocated discourse. John Dewey accentuates the sociological aspect of this process where he supplements explanations that 'All education proceeds by the participation of the individual in the social consciousness of the race. All education takes place in and through society. Thus, the three vertices of the triangle of education are– pupil who receives education; the teacher who imparts it; the social milieu or the social environment in which all education is imparted.' The teacher shapes the personality of the child as per the prevailing societal set-up, of which the child is also a significant member. This is thinkable only when the child gets the opportunity of participating in the educational activities. For a just and democratic society, education is a planned inter-action within an institution, developed specially for the purpose, based upon the confidence in the pliability of human nature resultant in the desired change of behaviour of the persons involved. Hence, justifying inclusion.

Inclusion Perspective

Inclusion is a paradigm shift for education systems to include and serve ALL schools, classrooms, and higher education institutions. Students with disabilities or different abilities attend regular schools and classrooms. Every child is an equal participant in the learning process with the support they require to succeed. Inclusion embraces gender, caste, class, family income, ethnicity, perspectives, language, disabilities, sexuality or religion. Focus is on respecting, understanding and taking care of cultural, social and individual diversity; Provision of equal access to quality education; Flexible approaches to teaching and learning at all levels; Bringing about change in curriculum and teaching practices within the school so that different needs of different children can be met; Reducing exclusion, discrimination barriers to learning and participation; Restructuring culture, policies and practices to respond to diversity in ways that value everyone equally. Inclusiveness has to be reflected in the framing of curriculum, teaching the curriculum, training of teachers on the curriculum, assessing and evaluation on the basis of the curriculum. Therefore, modifications have to be made at the Instructional level; Content/Curriculum; Performance Criteria; Assignment Structure; Teachers Training level where emphasis must be given to Multi-Sensory Teaching– Visual, Auditory, Tactile and Kinesthetic. It has attained importance after The Rights of Persons With Disabilities (RPWD) Act 2016 came into force with twenty one disabilities enlisted in it.

Place of Equity and Inclusion in Earlier Policies

India, as one of the oldest civilisations, with a rich cultural heritage, has come a long way after its independence. A land with a population of more than 1,380,004,385 people from 28 states and eight union territories, is an exceptional Indian society with 'Unity in Diversity' observable in its religions, languages and cultures. The country's education system works in tandem with the existing societal set-up with caste hierarchies, economic status, gender relations and cultural diversities deeply impact matters relating to access and equity in education. With the early education system caught up in social inequalities, social prejudices and economic inequalities, provide challenges for national development. Providing educational opportunities to the marginalised groups has been thought out to be a remedy to this ancient discrimination. Numerous efforts have been made by the social reformers and activists in making education accessible and achievable to the fringe groups with mixed success rates. Higher Education finds a place in the Concurrent List of the Indian Constitution, wherein it is a shared responsibility between the Union/Central Government and the State Governments.

In the year 1964-66 Indian Education Commission, popularly known as Kothari Commission was set-up by the Government of India under the Chairmanship of Daulat Singh Kothari, the then Chairman of the University Grants Commission, to scrutinise all facets of the educational set-up in India, and develop guidelines and policies for the advancement of education system in India. The first education policy was introduced in 1968. Since its adoption, the country witnessed a considerable expansion in educational facilities at all levels. This policy contained the decisions of the Central Government mainly based on the recommendations of the Kothari Commission 1964-66. For instance, strenuous efforts were made to implement Article 45 and provide Free and Compulsory Education to all children in the age group of 6-14 years. This policy had proposed for a *National School System*, wherein all students irrespective of caste, creed and sex, would have access to education of a similar quality up to a given level. Further, it envisaged a common educational structure (10+2+3) which was accepted across the country. It also advocated use of mother tongue as a medium of instruction in early school years. Another major call was firming research in the universities. The 1968 policy was not very successful due to factors like a proper programme of action was not framed; shortage of funds; and during this time education was in the State list and the role of the Central Government was almost negligible on implementing this scheme by the States. But the general formulations incorporated in this policy were not translated into a detailed study of implementation. Problems of access, quality, quantity, utility and financial outlay, accumulated over the years, assumed such massive extents that they required to be addressed urgently. Therefore, in 1985 the Government of India announced the formulation of New Education Policy in the Country.

A status paper 'Challenge of Education–A Policy Perspective' was issued by the Ministry of Education, Government of India. This document included a comprehensive appraisal of the existing system of education, ensuing a countrywide debate on bringing educational reforms in the country. Finally, the Education Policy 1986 was approved by the Parliament in May 1986.

During this period India reached a stage in its economic and technical development when a major effort had to be made to derive the maximum benefit from the assets already created, to ensure that the benefits of such development reach all sections of society. It was felt that education is the thoroughfare to reach this goal. To fulfil these aims, the Government of India formulated this policy.

National Policy of Education 1986 made provisions like– Education is the key to our all-round development, material and spiritual; the national system of education envisages common educational structure; a meaningful partnership between the Centre and the States; education for equality. It projected to make all possible efforts to remove disparities and to equalise educational opportunity by attending to the specific needs of the women, scheduled castes and scheduled tribes, the minorities and the handicapped. This policy focussed on modernisation and role of information technology in education. More attention was paid on restructuring the teacher education, early childhood care, women's empowerment and adult literacy. It also accepted autonomy of universities and colleges, something which was resisted in the past. So, 1986 policy comparatively performed better than the previous policy. The reasons were that this policy came after the 42nd amendment in 1976. In this amendment, five subjects were transferred from State to the Concurrent List including Education, Forests, Weights and Measures, Protection of Wild Animals and Birds; and Administration of Justice. With this, the Central Government was able to take a broader responsibility and introduced a number of programmes and schemes like Sarva Shiksha Abhiyan, Mid-Day Meal Scheme, Navodaya Vidyalayas, Kendriya Vidyalayas and use of information technology in education.

In order to implement the provisions of 1986 a Programme of Action (POA) was developed. A review of the 1986 policy was conducted during 1990-92. The Central Advisory Board of Education (CABE) in its 47th meeting held on May 5-6, 1992 considered the report of the committee on policy set-up to make an in-depth study of the report of the committee for review of NPE 1986. While endorsing the policy, it recommended certain modifications in the light of the developments during the last few years and the experience gained in the implementation of the policy. The revised policy was tabled in the Parliament on May 7, 1992. It prioritised universalisation of elementary education, equalisation of educational opportunities, women's education and development, vocationalisation of school education, consolidation of higher education, modernisation of technical education, improvement of quality content and process of education at all levels. It defined the crucial role of universalisation of elementary education by providing equal opportunities to all for the development of their inherent individual potential; prioritising operation blackboard by providing three chalkboards to each school; retention of students at the elementary stage; rural areas given adequate attention in providing quality education through Navodaya Vidyalayas; emphasised on National Open School which gave opportunity to the educationally and socially disadvantaged categories; integrated education for the disabled children; educational concessions to children of armed forces personnel killed or disabled during hostilities; promotion of culture/art/values and innovative programmes, and the like.

Everything changes with time; this is the law of the universe. Our education policies have also evolved with the changing times. What is imperative to be evoked is the previous policies were framed in the environment of that period. The 1968 policy was written in the times when India was emerging as a democracy, hence the policy concentrated on Nation Building with emphasis on Justice, Equality, Liberty and Fraternity. The 1986 policy stressed on individual independence.

The National Education Policy 2020 is the first education policy of the 21st century which replaces the thirty-four-year-old National Policy on Education (NPE) 1986 which was modified in 1992. Now the NEP 2020 ventures towards competitiveness and race for development and economic growth.

National Policy of Education 2020 on Equity and Inclusion in Higher Education

The National Education Policy 2020 is the first education policy of the 21st century which replaces the thirty-four-year-old National Policy on Education (NPE) 1986 which was modified in 1992. NEP 2020 has maintained a balance between the traditions and the interdisciplinary approach. Out of 121 crore population of India, 2.68 crores are disabled i.e. 2.21 % of total population of India. Fifty six per cent (1.5. crores) are disabled males and 44% (1.18 crores) disabled are females. India has a total population of 51% males and 49% of females. Sixty-nine per cent disabled reside in rural areas and 31% in urban areas i.e. 1.86 crore disabled in rural areas and 0.81 crores in urban areas. After the Right to Education Act 2009 came into force India has seen improvement in education especially in education infrastructure and student's enrolment. Increased enrolment in the upper primary level (Class VI-VIII) between 2009–2016 by 19.4 % was seen in the country. The implementation of Government of India schemes of mid-day meal, safety, hygiene and sanitation also facilitated for sustenance of student enrolment in the country. As per the Census of India 2011 report women literacy rate was at 65.5 %; 68.5% were Muslims and 66% in Schedule Caste communities. In spite of these substantial enhancements, Indian education system continues its struggle for equality, equity and inclusion. Receiving quality school education is still a cherished dream for the rural, vulnerable and marginalised groups, and the situation is even more grave in higher education. These groups have higher dropout rates due to a plethora of reasons, ranging from lack of accessibility for tribal communities i.e. geographic, to historical exclusion of communities from the education system for being classified into socio-cultural identities.

National Educational Policy (NEP) 2020 has endeavoured to focus on the factors affecting equality, equity and inclusion in our education system. It identifies barriers that lead to inefficient resource allocations such as small school campuses and causes for lesser participation of the girl child in rural areas, and educational needs of children living in geographically difficult areas, still being unaddressed. For Children with Special Needs (CWSN) or Divyangjan, the policy recommends "creating enabling mechanisms for providing the same opportunities of obtaining quality education as any other child."

NEP 2020 has made a distinct reference of a category of "Socio-Economically Disadvantaged Groups" (SEDGs). These can be largely considered on the basis of Gender Identities, particularly female and transgenders; Socio-Cultural Identities, like Scheduled Castes, Scheduled Tribes, Other Backward Classes, and Minorities; Geographical Identities e.g. students from villages, small towns, and aspirational districts; Disabilities (including learning disabilities); and Socio-Economic Conditions, like migrant communities, low income households, children in vulnerable situations, victims of or children of victims of trafficking, orphans including child beggars in urban areas, and the urban poor. These groups have never been given importance even in the previous education policies. For specially addressing their educational needs, the new policy has clubbed gender identities, socio-cultural identities, geographical identities, disabilities, and socio-economic conditions to create a new social group called SEDGs. Acknowledging their special needs, the policy endorses certain schemes and policies like targeted scholarships, conditional cash transfers to motivate parents to send their children to school, providing bicycles for transport that have worked in the past to increase enrolment, and to create more representation.

New policy proposes the creation of a 'Gender-Inclusion Fund' to create better educational spaces for women and transgender individuals. The fund will be accessible to states to create systems that will help the inclusion of these students. The fund will initiate provisions of sanitation, conditional cash transfers, bicycle distribution schemes, etc. These would enable the states to support and augment effective community-based interventions for female and transgender children to obtain and participate in the education process. The policy is silent on planning to increase the enrolment of transgenders which is proportionately high in the country. Also, it is not expressive to suggest ways to solve discrimination faced by them once inside the educational institutions, which leads to excessively aggravated dropout rates.

The new education policy acknowledges the needs of special needs children and include them into the mainstream of education. It lines-up with the intent of Rights of Persons with Disabilities Act 2016. The policy sets forth to recruit special educators in all school complexes to make sure that teaching is more inclusive and conscious of the needs of children. Persons with benchmark disabilities (means a person with not less than forty per cent of a specified disability as per the RPWD Act 2016) will be allowed to opt for home schooling and would be provided with special educators for acquiring the best of educational facilities. This gives a responsibility to the higher education institutions in training teachers on various aspects of special education, instructional strategies and inclusion. The teachers will be trained to identify learning disabilities in children and help them through remediation, succeed in education and take care of their mental health. It proposes to set up National Assessment Centre, PARAKH, to create equitable systems of assessment for children with learning disabilities, and suggests alternate models for schooling. This is further reinforced in Chapter III, Section 17 of the RPWD Act 2016 which "directs the government and the local authorities to establish adequate number of teacher training institutions; to train and employ teachers, including teachers with disability who are qualified in sign language and Braille and also teachers who are trained in teaching children with intellectual disability; to train professionals and staff to support inclusive education at all levels of school education;...to make suitable modifications in the curriculum and examination system to meet the needs of students with disabilities such as extra time for completion of examination paper, facility of scribe or amanuensis, exemption from second and third language courses; to promote research to improve learning; and any other measures, as may be required." In Chapter VI Special Provisions For Persons With Benchmark Disabilities of the RPWD Act 2016 under "Reservation in higher educational institutions" Section 32 states that "(1) All Government institutions of higher education and other higher education institutions receiving aid from the Government shall reserve not less than five per cent seats for persons with benchmark disabilities. (2) The persons with benchmark disabilities shall be given an upper age relaxation of five years for admission in institutions of higher education." Also Section 34 of the Act states, that every government establishment shall appoint not less than four per cent of the total number of vacancies in the cadre strength in each group of posts meant to be filled with persons with benchmark disabilities within the cadre. In Section 35, under "Incentives to employers in private sector" the Act states that "The appropriate Government and the local authorities shall, within the limit of their economic capacity and development, provide incentives to employer in private sector to ensure that at least five per cent of their work force is composed of persons with benchmark disability." NEP 2020 gives credence to this Act.

The luminary endorsement in NEP 2020 is to Special Educational Zones (SEZs) in the regions with significant population belonging to Socio-Economically Disadvantaged Groups and in self-improving districts. The main resolve is to spread education in the remotest and farthest places in India. This will be done by propelling extra resources and aligning multiple schemes and programmes of Centre and states to transform these areas. This impression holds promise to transform educational access in remote areas of the country like urban downtown with large minority population. The policy is not explicit in defining norms for these zones and how will these be differentiated into urban and rural landscapes.

In a nutshell NEP 2020 specifies the actions to be taken up by the government and the Higher Education Institutions (HEIs) for implementing the policy. The steps to be taken by the Government include allocating funds for education of Socio-Economically Disadvantaged Groups (SEDGs); setting clear targets for increasing Gross Enrolment Ratio (GER) of Socio-Economically Disadvantaged Groups; Augment gender balance in admissions to Higher Education Institutions (HEIs); make HEIs accessible in self-improving districts and Special Education Zones (SEZs); to develop and provide for HEIs that teach in local/Indian languages; provide for financial assistance and scholarships to SEDGs in both public and private HEIs; to organise outreach programmes on opportunities and scholarships in higher education for SEDGs; and support technology tools for better participation and learning outcomes. The Higher Education Institutions (HEIs) will work on easing the costs and fees for pursuing higher education; provide more financial assistance and scholarships; organise outreach on opportunities and scholarships in higher education; make admission processes more inclusive and following the RPWD Act 2016; make curriculum more inclusive as per the needs of the learners and the industry; increase employability potential of higher education programmes; develop more degree courses taught in Indian languages; ensure all buildings and facilities are barrier-free and disabled friendly; develop bridge courses for students that come from disadvantaged educational backgrounds; provide socio-emotional and academic support and mentoring; ensure sensitisation of faculty, counsellor, and students on gender-identity issue and its inclusion in all aspects of the HEI, including curricula; and firmly enforce all no-discrimination and anti-harassment rules.

Summing Up

The new education policy has emphasised the integration of technology in all levels of learning, to enhance learning, assessment, planning and administration, and to improve classroom processes. For this Covid-19 has trained India to adapt to online education resources. It has been very rightly said that "Every society that values social justice and is anxious to improve the lot of the common man and cultivate all available talent must ensure progressive equality of opportunity to all sections of the population. This is the only guarantee for the building up of an egalitarian and human society in which the exploitation of the weak will be minimized". (The Education Commission, GOI, 1966.) Hence, the National Education Policy 2020 intends to provide an inclusive, participatory and holistic approach to education with field experiences, empirical research, stakeholder feedback, as well as lessons learnt from best practices. The stray resemblances are found in previous policies too, but the challenge is to make this policy imaginable and if implemented in the true letter and spirit, will make India outshine in the world.

References

Agarwal, Pawan. 2009. *Indian Higher Education: Envisioning the future.* New Delhi: SAGE Publications India Ltd

Chanana, K. 1993. "Accessing Higher Education–The Dilemma of Schooling: Women, Minorities, Scheduled Castes, and Scheduled Tribes in Contemporary India". In Chitnis, Suma and Philip Altbach (eds). *Higher Education Reforms in India: Experience and Perspectives.* New Delhi: Sage Publications.

Chitnis, S. 1988. Educating the Weaker Sections of Society, in Singh Amrik and Philip Altbach. (eds) *Higher Education in India: The Social Context.* New Delhi: Konark Publishers.

Dash, B.N. 2011. *History of Education in India.* New Delhi: Dominant Publishers and Distributors Pvt. Ltd.

Deshpande, S. and U. Zacharias. 2013. *Beyond Inclusion: The Practice of Equal Access in Indian Higher Education.* India: Routledge.

Dewey, J. 1939. *Democracy and Education: An Introduction to Philosophy of Education.* New York: G.P. Putnam Sons.

Frederickson, N. and T. Cline 2002. *Special Educational Needs inclusion and diversity: a textbook.* Buckingham, Philadelphia: Open University Press.

India, Education and National Development: Report of the Commission (1964-66). New Delhi, Ministry of Education, Government of India, 1966.

National Education Policy 2020, Ministry of Human Resource Development, Government of India, New Delhi.

Sharma, Y.K. 2001. *History and Problems of Education,* Vol. I-II. New Delhi: Kanishka Publishers, Distributors.

The Rights of Persons with Disabilities Act 2016 (RPWD), The Gazette of India, Ministry of Law and Justice, New Delhi.

Tienda, M. 2013. Diversity-Inclusion: Promoting Integration in Higher Education. Educ. Res. 2013 December 24 (9): 467-475. Author Manuscript available on PMC 2015 August.

13

NEP 2020 Recommendations on Vocational Education: A Critical Analysis, and the Way Forward

P.K. Misra

Background

India is termed as a nation of youths nowadays. In comparison to other countries of the world, India has a relative advantage in terms of the distribution of the youth population. It is expected that India will remain younger longer than China and Indonesia, the two other major countries of Asia in terms of population (Ministry of Statistics and Programme Implementation, 2017). Highlighting the share of youths in the Indian society, National Policy for Skill Development and Entrepreneurship 2015 observes,

Today, India is one of the youngest nations in the world with more than 62% of its population in the working-age group (15–59 years), and more than 54% of its total population below 25 years of age. Its population pyramid is expected to bulge across the 15–59 age group over the next decade (Ministry of Skill Development and Entrepreneurship, 2015, p. 2).

These statistics make it clear that India is having a demographic dividend. This demographic trend is expected to last until 2055. Studies show that many Asian economies like Japan, China, and South Korea were able to use this 'demographic dividend' for their economic development. Can India also do it? There are possibilities, but, we have to keep in mind that the demographic dividend automatically does not result in economic gains. To harness the economic potential of the youth bulge, countries need to provide good health, quality education, and decent employment to its entire population (Thakur, 2019).

The message for India is clear. Besides offering quality education and good health services, the government must find ways to offer ample employment or self-employment opportunities to the young workforce of more than 450 million. But, this is easier said than done. Generating productive and paid work opportunities for such a large population is a mammoth challenge. Fortunately, vocational education can play a very useful role to meet this challenge. Before discussing the role of vocational education in preparing the workforce for mid-level vocations, let us understand its purpose and characteristics.

Professor, Chaudhary Charan Singh University, Meerut

Vocational Education: Purpose and Characteristics

Vocational Education (VE) is also termed as Vocational Education and Training (VET), Career and Technical Education (CTE), and Technical Education (TE). These terms are interchangeably used in literature and policies related to vocational education. Vocational education has mainly been seen as a process to prepare people for productive jobs. In simple terms, 'vocational education is learning about a particular trade or job which involves hands-on experience and technical training that sometimes involves apprenticeship' (Misra, 2011, p. 28). Vocational education aims to develop expertise in a particular job or activity, as observed by Cedefop (2009),

Vocational education and training (VET) comprise all more or less organized or structured activities that aim to provide people with the knowledge, skills, and competencies necessary to perform a job or a set of jobs, whether or not they lead to a formal qualification. VET is independent of venue, age, or other characteristics of participants and previous level of qualifications. VET may be job-specific or directed at a broader range of occupations. It may also include elements of general education (p. 18).

While All India Council for Technical Education envisions that vocational education ... prepares learners for jobs that are based in manual or practical activities, traditionally non-academic and totally related to a specific trade, occupation or vocation, hence the term, in which the learner participates (AICTE, 2020).

Based on these discussions, it can be said that vocational education

- Aims to prepare individuals to work in various fields
- Involves various forms of learning i.e. formal, non-formal, and informal
- Can be pursued by any section of the society of any age-group
- Promotes practice-based and vocation-specific qualifications
- Does not involve higher-level academic qualifications.

Based on these discussions, it can be said that contrary to main-stream education that mainly provides theoretical understanding, vocational education teaches those skills that are a must to get entry into or practice a vocation. In continuation of this discussion, it will be obvious to know about the provisions of vocational education as well as the availability of vocational courses.

Vocational Education in India: Provisions and Courses

Vocational education is provided in almost all countries of the world. A review of the literature reveals that there are three popular types of vocational education. Each type caters to different age-groups and aims for different purposes. The three types are:

- *Prevocational Education and Training (PVET):* Aims to prepare young people for transition to a VET programme at the upper secondary level. In India, some schools offer this in classes IX and X in the form of pre-vocational education.

- *Initial Vocational Education and Training (IVET)* : A training that leads to an initial (upper secondary) vocational qualification. IVET is in most cases education and training for young people aged 16–19, but can also be adult education. In India, schools affiliated to different boards offer it at classes XI and XII in the form of vocational education or vocational courses.
- *Continuing Vocational Education and Training (CVET):* This refers to education or training taken after initial education and training or after entry into working life. CVET aims at helping individuals to improve or update their knowledge and skills, to acquire new skills for a career move or retraining, and to support their personal or professional development (Misra, 2011). The institutions like National Institute of Open Schooling (NIOS) and many private institutions offer this type of vocational education in India.

In many countries, especially European countries, the majority of PVET and CVET is provided in an organised and structured manner by public or private institutions and regulated by the public administration. In comparison, the share of the formal schooling sector in PVET and IVET is very less in India. Here, the majority of vocational education is imparted by the private sector in a very informal way. Let us understand it by the example of two young girls, one in Germany and one in India, aiming to be a Carpenter. The paths that both will trade are as follows

- *Popular Vocational Education Route in Germany:* She has to attend a school, where she will learn the knowledge, theories, and practices relevant to the job of a carpenter (usually four days in a week). Simultaneously, she will be admitted to a carpentry firm to have the first-hand experience of the job and will be trained to produce goods in the supervision of a master craftsman (normally two days in a week). This training, which is usually paid, will go for 2-3 years. After completing the education from both the places, she will be awarded a vocational qualification that will allow her to enter the job market. Without this qualification, she will hardly get the job of a carpenter.
- *Popular Vocational Education Route in India:* She will look for an experienced carpenter and request them to help her in learning the job of a carpenter. After getting his consent, she will work with the experienced carpenter (called *ustad, master ji*) for a duration that is not fixed. During this training, she will assist the master in the workplace, and learn by assisting him. She will, usually, not get any money during the initial phase but start getting a meagre amount after gaining some experience. During this training, she will mainly learn practical aspects

but hardly any higher level of theoretical understanding. She will discontinue the training after realising that she had learned enough and look for possibilities in the job market. There is no certification involved in the process and she will get the job merely propagating or demonstrating her skills of carpentry.

This example helps you to realise that vocational education is mainly provided by the unorganised non-formal sector in India. Besides, the formal sector also offers vocational education opportunities for learners. At the school level, vocational education is mainly offered at the senior secondary level (Classes XI and XII). Different School Boards (CBSE, State boards) and NIOS offer various vocational courses for the selection of learners. For example, the Central Board of Secondary Education (CBSE) offers several vocational courses under different vocational streams (CBSE, 2017):

- *Commerce based vocational courses*: Office Secretaryship, Stenography and Computer Application, Accountancy and Auditing, Marketing and Salesmanship, Banking, Retail, Financial Market Management, Business Administration
- *Engineering based vocational courses*: Electrical Technology, Automobile Technology, Civil Engineering, Air Conditioning and Refrigeration Technology, Electronics Technology, Geo Spatial Technology, Foundry, IT Application,
- *Health and Para medical based vocational courses*: Ophthalmic Techniques, Medical Laboratory Techniques, Auxiliary Nursing and Midwifery, X-Ray Technician, Healthcare Sciences, Health and Beauty Studies, Medical Diagnostics
- *Home science based vocational courses*: Fashion Design and Clothing Construction, Textile Design, Design Fundamental, Music Technical Production, Beauty Services
- *Agriculture based vocational courses:* Poultry Farming, Horticulture, Dairying Science and Technology
- *Hospitality and Tourism based vocational courses:* Food Production, Food and Beverage Services, Mass Media Studies and Media Production, Bakery and Confectionery, Front office, Travel and Tourism
- *Other vocational courses:* Transportation System and Logistic Management, Life Insurance, Library and Information Sciences.

Similarly, vocational education is also offered in the higher education sector in the form of Bachelor of Vocational Studies (B.Voc) courses. These courses are offered by universities and colleges included under Sections 2(f) and 12(B) of the University Grants Commission (UGC). The list of B.Voc courses includes Paramedical and Health Administration, Renewable Energy Management, Retail Management, Web Technology and Multimedia, Fashion Technology and Apparel Designing, Industrial

Microbiology, Fashion Designing, Information Technology, and many more (UGC, n.d.).

Irrespective of these offerings at school and higher education levels, the share of the formal education sector (particularly public institutions) in providing vocational education is negligible. Instead of many recommendations and promises of previous policy documents like the Kothari Commission (1964-66), National Policy on Education 1986, Centrally Sponsored Scheme of Vocationalisation of Secondary Education 1988, Programme of Action 1992, and National Knowledge Commission Report 2007 the contribution of the formal sector of education in vocational education is still insignificant. The National Education Policy (NEP) 2020, released by the Ministry of Education, aims to improve this situation and want to make vocational education an integral part of mainstream education in India.

Vocational Education in NEP 2020: Key Recommendations

Vocational education is discussed in NEP under the title 'reimagining vocational education'. This title itself says a lot. From the perspective of a layman, this title means introducing vocational education with new modalities and opportunities to attract the learners. In this quest, the NEP recommends several measures about vocational education. Let us analyse the key recommendations of NEP 2020 about vocational education.

Enrolment in Vocational Education in Formal Education Sector

Since the days of the Kothari Commission (1964-66), India has been dreaming of enrolment of 50% of the students' population at the secondary level in vocational education. Underlining the importance of vocational education, the Commission recommended aiming for 20% of total enrolment at the lower secondary stage and 50% of the total enrolment at the higher secondary stage in the vocational stream. This target, set-up 54 years ago, is still a much-cherished dream as accepted in NEP 2020:

> The 12th Five-Year Plan (2012–2017) estimated that only a very small percentage of the Indian workforce in the age group of 19–24 (less than 5%) received formal vocational education (MHRD, 2020, p. 43).

Comparing this figures (less than 5%) with enrolment in vocational in other countries (USA 52%, Germany 75%, and South Korea 96%), the policy highlights the need to hasten the spread of vocational education in India and diverting at least 50% of learners to it by 2025 through the school and higher education system. The policy also reiterates that the number of students in vocational education will be considered while arriving at the GER targets.

Vertical Mobility to the Takers of Vocational Education

In India, vocational education is mainly offered in the formal sector at Grades 11 and 12 (upper secondary level).But not many students are interested to join the vocational stream at this level due to a lack of opportunities for vertical mobility. Highlighting this dilemma of the learner, NEP 2020 states

> Moreover, students passing out from Grades 11–12 with vocational subjects often did not have well-defined pathways to continue with their chosen vocations in higher education. The admission criteria for general higher education were also not designed to provide openings to students who had vocational education qualifications, leaving them at a disadvantage relative to their compatriots from 'mainstream' or 'academic' education (MHRD, 2020, p. 44).

Accepting this lack of vertical mobility for students from the vocational education stream, the policy states that this issue has been somewhat addressed through National Skills Qualifications Framework (NSQF) 2013. The policy further aims to make enhanced provisions for vertical mobility of students opting for vocational streams.

Image and Status of Vocational Education

Research has proved again and again that vocational education has been accorded a lower place in Indian society. The most probable reason for this situation, emerged from research findings, is considering vocational education as a learning activity for those unable to get admission in mainstream education (Science, Arts, or Commerce) or not serious about studies. This policy has taken note of these observations and summarised that

> Vocational education is perceived to be inferior to mainstream education and meant largely for students who are unable to cope with the latter. This is a perception that affects the choices students make (MHRD, 2020, p. 44).

To overcome this widely prevalent perception regarding vocational education among the masses, the policy aims to re-imagine the policies and practices of offering vocational education to students. To overcome the prevalent biases and social status hierarchy regarding vocational education in society, the policy aims to integrate vocational programmes into mainstream education (both at school and higher education level). Declaring this intent, policy details

> Beginning with vocational exposure at early ages in middle and secondary school, quality vocational education will be integrated smoothly into higher education. It will ensure that every child learns at least one vocation and is exposed to several more. This would lead to emphasising the dignity of labour and importance of various vocations involving /Indian arts and artisanship (MHRD, 2020, p. 44).

New Pathways for Vocational Education

After Independence, vocational education has been seen as an exclusive route for preparing the learners for mid-level occupations. Even in the 1970s, we have an idea of technical schools offering mainly technical education. After the National Policy on Education (NPE) 1986, vocational education was introduced in the different secondary schools but remained a separate stream that had no exchange with so-called 'academic' disciplines. It means one can either be a 'vocational' or 'academic' but not both during studying. The NEP aims to break this boundary between academic and vocational streams:

> The development of vocational capacities will go hand-in-hand with the development of 'academic' or other capacities. Vocational education will be integrated in the educational offerings of all secondary schools in a phased manner over the next decade. Towards this, secondary schools will also collaborate with ITIs, polytechnics, local industry, etc. (MHRD, 2020, p. 44).

In 2013, the University Grants Commission launched a programme named Bachelor of Vocational Studies (B.Voc) for Colleges and Universities across the country. The main purpose of this programme was to attract a segment of higher education students into the vocational stream and offer a vertical mobility opportunity for those who have opted vocational stream at the upper secondary level. Unfortunately, this programme, which is continuing has failed to bring the desired results. To bring amendment in the nature and scope of this programme, it is observed that

> The B.Voc. degrees introduced in 2013 will continue to exist, but vocational courses will also be available to students enrolled in all other Bachelor's degree programmes, including the 4-year multidisciplinary Bachelor's programmes (MHRD, 2020, p. 44).

The policy expects higher education institutions to offer vocational education in partnership with industry and NGOs. And also suggests that higher education institutions (HEIs) will conduct short-term certificate courses in various skills including soft skills. The other notable provision is that HEIs may also choose ODL to offer vocational courses. The policy also focuses on imparting '*Lok Vidya*', i.e., important vocational knowledge developed in India, based vocational courses in educational institutions. As another significant initiative, the policy emphasises on setting up skill labs in the schools and making these a hub for students of different schools to practise different vocational trades.

Integrating Vocational Education in Formal Schooling

As discussed earlier, irrespective of several schemes and initiatives at the level of Central and State governments, vocational education was never integrated into the main scheme of education. It remained an outsider and treated as a watertight compartment reserved for a specific set of students both in the school and higher education sectors. Research tells us that vocational education cannot and will not flourish in this system. The very low enrolment of students in vocational courses in the formal education sector is a testimony to this observation. Keeping a tab on this situation, policy envisions that

> Vocational education will be integrated into all school and higher education institutions in a phased manner over the next decade. Focus areas for vocational education will be chosen based on skills gap analysis and mapping of local opportunities (MHRD, 2020, p. 44).

To convert these intentions into reality, the policy suggests constituting a National Committee for the Integration of Vocational Education (NCIVE). The policy suggests that this committee will have representatives from different ministries, industries, and academia.

Differentiated Models of Vocational Education

In India, there are mainly two types of models to engage with vocational training: (i) join a workplace or individual expert to learn the tricks of the trade, or (ii) join any educational institution (mainly public). The main problem with both these models is that the first one provides practice but lacks theoretical knowledge, and the second one mainly offers theory but hardly any practice. The apprenticeship model of VE that has been seen as a viable model to bridge the divide between theory and practice, and successfully taking place in many countries has hardly been given due weightage in the Indian system. Even in those cases where this model is implemented, it is usually carried by practitioners as an academic engagement rather than picking the threads of chosen vocational trade. From this discussion, it emerges that (i) the most vital component for success of vocational education i.e. real place learning and working is missing in the existing model of vocational education at school as well as higher education level, and (ii) we lack innovative models of vocational education. Appraising this situation, the policy states

> Individual institutions that are early adopters must innovate to find models and practices that work and then share these with other institutions through mechanisms set up by NCIVE, so as to help extend the reach of vocational education. Different models of vocational education, and apprenticeships, will also be experimented by higher education institutions (MHRD, 2020, p. 44).

To promote the interaction between schools and industries, the policy also calls for setting up incubation centres in higher education institutions in partnership with industries.

Recognition of Vocational Education Qualifications

The existing system of vocational education hardly offers any scope to recognise the learning and experiences gained out of the formal education system. Let us understand it with the following example. One boy was enrolled in a school in the automobile course. Due to some family problems, he left school. But, he kept learning the automobile repairing by working in a vehicle maintenance workshop. He learned the job but did not get any certification. He wants to apply for a job in an automobile repairing company but has no certification to show his qualifications. He also cannot take admission elsewhere because he has not completed his prior schooling. The world of vocational education is full of such tragic examples. Taking note of this anomaly, the policy emphasises that

> The National Skills Qualifications Framework will be detailed further for each discipline vocation and profession. This Framework will provide the basis for Recognition of Prior Learning. Through this, dropouts from the formal system will be reintegrated by aligning their practical experience with the relevant level of the Framework. The credit-based Framework will also facilitate mobility across 'general' and vocational education (MHRD, 2020, p. 44).

Many countries in the world need a vocational qualification certification to allow anyone to enter in specific vocations. An attempt in this regard has been made in the National Skills Qualifications Framework. Emphasising on the need to improve the existing provisions, policy states

> .... Indian standards will be aligned with the International Standard Classification of Occupations maintained by the International Labour Organization (MHRD, 2020, para 16.5).

In a nutshell, policy envisions vocational education as a viable means to offer various employment and self-employment opportunities for the young population. To make it happen, policy reflects on different issues and also suggests some measures to increase enrolment in and status of vocational education. This background gives us ample reasons to deliberate upon future possibilities in vocational education.

Implementing the Recommendation of NEP 2020 on Vocational Education: The Way Forward

Before NEP 2020, many recommendations of similar nature have been propagated regarding vocational education by different committees, commissions, and policies as well. But these recommendations did not meet the intent due to lack of proper planning for implementation. Taking a hint from past experiences, proper implementation of recommendations regarding vocational education becomes a must to achieve the intended goals of the policy. We can expect that the government will form an 'expert committee' to chalk out a very clear and focused plan to implement the recommendation of NEP regarding vocational education. The following suggestions may be useful for any such expert committee or task force to move ahead.

Make Workplace Learning an Integral Component of Vocational Education

The vocational courses offered by schools and colleges often lack in terms of practical exposure to the learners. There is a popular joke that 'students of vocational courses learn practical in theory'. Lack of exposure to real work conditions deters the students either to get employment or look for self-employment opportunities. To overcome this situation, a provision of mandatory training/apprenticeship for students of vocational courses for a specified period will be useful. During this period, the students may be asked to prepare a portfolio to showcase his/her activities and learning during training. The provision must also ensure that without completing workplace learning in a real situation, no one will be granted a vocational qualification.

Have Provisions for Seamless Entry in Vocational Education

As discussed earlier, the majority of vocational education takes place in the non-formal sector. This training often provides real-life experiences related to a vocation but lacks theoretical understanding. Those getting vocational training in the non-formal sector hardly get any certification to showcase and prove their vocational skills. Considering this situation, provisions need to be made for certification for such learners. For this purpose, specific schools or institutions may be provided the responsibility of certification of vocational qualifications. This measure will certainly help to identify as well certify vocation-specific skilled workforce from the non-formal sector.

Promote Vocational Courses in Mainstream Education

Irrespective of several efforts and schemes, many parents and students are still not aware of the availability of such vocational courses in the schooling sector. The schools are also not much interested in promoting such courses to the majority of students. They only offer or recommend these courses to those who they think will not survive in mainstream education i.e. arts, science, or commerce. The action plan regarding vocational education must emphasise that every student at the secondary level must take at least one vocational course. The students must also be asked to complete a mandatory apprenticeship/real workplace to complete the course. This measure will be quite helpful to lessen the stigma or overcome the tag of low academic status attached to the vocational courses.

Ensure Vertical Mobility

As accepted by the policy, the lack of vertical mobility is one of the main challenges in the vocational education sector. At present, vocational education is offered at both the school and the higher education sector. But there is hardly any synergy between them. Efforts should be made to offer a continuum for those who would like to carry on with their vocational studies at graduation and post-graduation level. The advanced version of the courses offered at the secondary level must be made available at the higher education level. Besides, the provision of offering higher-level courses in blended mode may also be made. Where, instead of coming to the institution every day, the students will be given the flexibility to attend an institution for a specific number of days and learn rest via online and working in a real workplace.

Conclusion

In India, vocational education is a story of 'much hopes but fewer successes'. Since the Kothari commission, several initiatives and schemes have been initiated to increase the share of vocational education in the formal education sector but did not produce expected results. The unorganised non-formal sector played a significant role to promote vocational education, but the contribution of the formal sector remains negligible so far. There are many reasons to it, such as the liking of Indian society for white-collar jobs, considering vocational education inferior to mainstream education, the reluctance of parents to admit their wards in vocational courses, poor quality of vocation training in the formal education sector, lack of vertical mobility, lack of provisions for recognising non-formal learning, less confidence of employers in pass-outs from the vocational stream, etc. NEP 2020 reflects on some of these issues and envisions that the school and higher education sector will play a more active and sincere role in promoting vocational education. Highlighting the importance of vocational education for India, as a nation of youths, the policy proclaims:

> By 2025, at least 50% of learners through the school and higher education system shall have exposure to vocational education, for which a clear action plan with targets and timelines will be developed. This is in alignment with Sustainable Development Goal 4.4 and will help to realize the full potential of India's demographic dividend (MHRD, 2020, p. 44).

We can hope that a widely discussed, well planned, and robust mechanism will be in place to convert this vision into reality. The intents shown in policy needs to be matched with a suitable action plan to proclaim in days to come that India is a nation that offers 'every youth a vocation of his/her choice to develop as a productive citizen for society'.

References

AICTE. (2020). *Vocational education.* Retrieved from https://www.aicteindia.org/education/vocational-education

CBSE. (2017). *Scheme of studies and list of vocational courses.* Retrieved from https://cbse.nic.in/newsite/Vocational/scheme_of_studies_2017-18_voc.PDF

Cedefop. (2009). *Implications of demographic change for vocational education and training in the EU.* Luxembourg: Office for Official Publications of the European Communities.

MHRD. (2020). *National education policy.* Retrieved from https://www.mhrd.gov.in/sites/upload_files/mhrd/files/NEP_Final_English.pdf

Ministry of Skill Development and Entrepreneurship. (2015). *National policy for skill development and entrepreneurship.* Retrieved from http://www.skilldevelopment.gov.in/assets/images/Skill%20India/National%20Policy%20on%20Skill%20Development%20and%20Entreprenurship%20Final.pdf

Ministry of Statistics and Programme Implementation. (2017). *Youth in India 2017.* New Delhi: Central Statistics Office, Ministry of Statistics and Programme

Implementation. Retrieved from http://mospi.nic.in/sites/default/files/publication_reports/Youth_in_India-2017.pdf

Misra, P. K. (2011). VET teachers in Europe: Policies, practices and challenges. *Journal of Vocational Education & Training, 63*(1), 27-45.

Shivakumar, G. (April 17, 2013). *India is set to become the youngest country by 2020.* The Hindu. Retrieved from https://www.thehindu.com/news/national/india-is-set-to-become-the-youngest-country-by-2020/article4624347.ece

Thakur, A. (July 22, 2019). India enters 37-year period of demographic dividend. *The Economic Times.* Retrieved from https://economictimes.indiatimes.com/news/economy/indicators/india-enters-37-year-period-of-demographic-dividend/articleshow/70324782.cms?utm_source=contentofinterest&utm_medium=text&utm_campaign=cppst

UGC. (n.d.). *Guidelines for introduction of Bachelor of Vocation (B.Voc) programme in universities and colleges under the national skills qualifications framework (NSQF).* Retrieved from https://www.ugc.ac.in/pdfnews/8508026_Guidelines-on-B-Voc_Final.pdf

14

In Pursuits of Strengthening Academic Research

Pranita Gopal

Academic Research: An introduction

Research finds its origin in the French word "recherche" which means that one goes about seeking knowledge. Although there are many definitions of the term research available, in the context of the present chapter, two stand out. The first definition is from the Organisation for Economic Co-operation and Development (OECD) (2015), "Any creative systematic activity undertaken in order to increase the stock of knowledge, including knowledge of man, culture and society, and the use of this knowledge to devise new applications." This definition is extremely useful in understanding how NEP 2020 is envisaging research because it talks about knowledge that blends man, culture and society and more importantly to utilise this to devise new applications. In other words, OECD defines research as a systemic activity that not only fulfils the academic interests of taking knowledge further but also strengthens the societal fabric by helping the society with its applicability. The second definition of interest to us is by Creswell (2008), who says research is "a process of steps used to collect and analyse information to increase our understanding of a topic or issue". It consists of three steps: pose a question, collect data to answer the question, and present an answer to the question." This definition is useful to remember the systematic process required to understand the context of research and deepen our understanding of any topic.

Before we discuss the various facets of academic research within the framework of NEP 2020, it is important to differentiate between academic research and professional research. Academic research aims to focus on issues that are more theoretical in nature and that which adds to the body of knowledge; while professional research aims to focus on problems are more practical– affecting the industry, and in process aid to the body of research for a particular topic mainly for an organisation's interest. Also, findings in academic research are generally disseminated while in professional research findings are generally kept private. Academic research prides on laying the foundation for further research, contemplating and focusing on ideas raised by previous research, while professional research is solely driven by the needs and interest of the organisation that it serves, which is ultimately driven by economics.

Instructional Coach and Educational Consultant, Gurugram

An interesting paper was published in 2003, in the Cornell Hotel and Restaurant Administration Quarterly, by Piccoli and Wagner titled "The Value of Academic Research". The authors in this publication acknowledge *academic research is an endeavour that is qualitatively different from the work of practitioners, consultants, trade-publication writers, and vendors* (Piccoli and Wagner, 2003). The authors while discussing how research informs practice, state, "*academic researchers are required to reflect on the implications of innovations in an effort to distill knowledge that will stand the test of time and be applicable over a wide array of situations*" (Piccoli and Wagner, 2003). In the same paper, authors acknowledge the difference between academic research and professional research based on the subject of inquiry. They also discuss a hallmark of academic research – the rigour of the inquiry process – which differentiates it from professional research. They also share their concern of the side-effect of a rigorous inquiry process – narrowing down of scope, because of a single research report may not seem to have much relevance but if viewed under the lens of the subject discipline it presents a cumulative knowledge mosaic that lays the foundation for further studies and research.

Academic Research before the NEP 2020

In 1986 the last National Policy of Education was formulated. This policy was followed by the Programme of Action six years later in 1992. The National Policy of Education 1986 presented a detailed overview of the status of research in the country. The NPE 1986 laid tremendous stress on helping institutes establish infrastructure for conducting research in various fields –especially in the field of science and technology. But the strength of this policy lies in its detailed identification of main problems encountered by researchers in our higher education institutions. For example, it acknowledges the uneven spread of research effort and research scholars, because of which there is a visible lag in the research thrust within institutions. This problem is compounded by the presence of cumbersome rules and procedural difficulties that dissuade the research efforts of academic institutes.

The document in its part, also discusses how the absence/weak linkage with the industry needs is hampering research in the field of technology as primary inputs needed for technology research are missing. The weak and often missing link between industry and academic research has created a lacuna for highly professional and competent researchers to leave the field of academic research and venture into the field of professional research. Further, discussing the problems plaguing the research ethos of the country, the document cites poor library, inadequate information system, absence of computational and reprographic facilities as endemic problems prevalent in the majority of educational institutions.

With regard to research in the discipline of social science, the document clearly states that the research is generally not related to problems of development, nor are the results of social sciences research disseminated adequately to the policy makers in a form that they could be used in policy formulation. The weak linkage between research and curriculum renewal is also documented in this policy document.

Primafacie one might argue that the present situation is no different from 1986, yet evidence in the form of various policies and Government of India initiatives point to the contrary. As a case in point – let us take a detailed look at one of the recent initiatives of the Government of India.

Atal Innovation Mission: The Atal Innovation Mission (AIM) is Government of India's flagship initiative to promote a culture of innovation and entrepreneurship in the country (from https://aim.gov.in/overview.php). The official website discusses AIM's objective as to develop new programmes and policies for fostering innovation in different sectors of the economy, provide platform and collaboration opportunities for different stakeholders, create awareness and an umbrella structure to oversee the innovation ecosystem of the country.

The five major initiatives taken in the first year of establishment by the Atal Innovation Mission is documented on the website as:

- *Atal Tinkering Labs*–Creating problem solving mindset across schools in India.
- *Atal Incubation Centres*–Fostering world class start-ups and adding a new dimension to the incubator model.
- *Atal New India Challenges*–Fostering product innovations and aligning them to the needs of various sectors/ministries.
- *Mentor India Campaign*–A national Mentor network in collaboration with public sector, corporates and institutions, to support all the initiatives of the mission.
- *Atal Community Innovation Centre*–To stimulate community centric innovation and ideas in the unserved /underserved regions of the country including Tier 2 and Tier 3 cities.
- *Atal Research and Innovation for Small Enterprise (ARISE)*–To stimulate innovation and research in the MSME industry.

Figure 1 depicts how the initiatives of the Atal Innovation Mission create linkages between the industry and the academic institutions – from schools (Atal Tinkering Labs) to research that support the micro, small and medium enterprises (MSME). Such a large-scale initiative that spreads across academic groups (school, college and research) has the ability to plug the many lacunae identified by the National Policy of Education 1986. Like, the Atal initiative helps create a strong link between the industry need and academic research focus; as the initiative lays thrust on MSME – local research institutes and bodies can establish themselves to support local industries and in the same space, local industries can fund research that could augment their knowledge base.

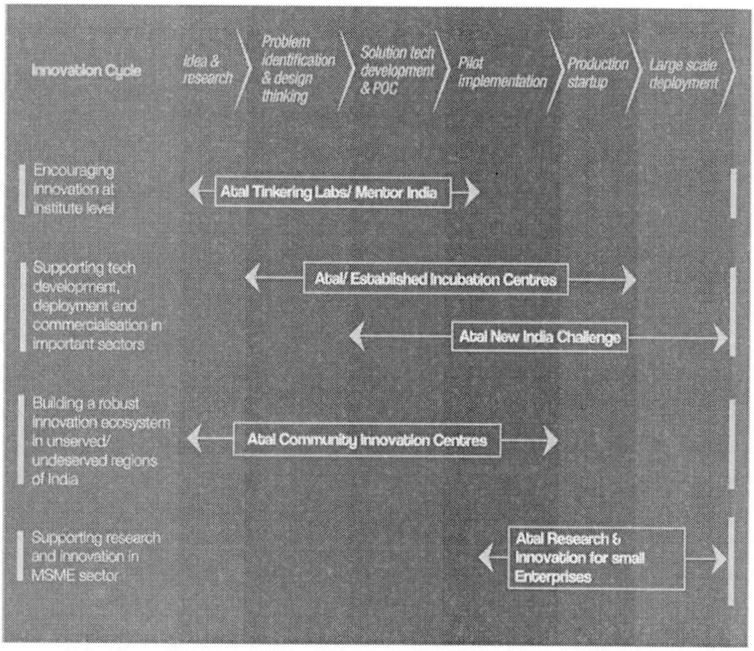

Figure 1. Initiatives of the Atal Innovation Mission mapped to the Innovation Cycle

The Atal Innovation Mission is one example that focuses on giving research its due for the upliftment of the society. Other initiatives like the existence of the API score index for faculty recruitment and career progression, dissuading inbreeding within institutes, close ties with industries in the form of the skill development programmes are some of the ways in which the problems identified in the NPE 1986 have been addressed.

But, those initiatives are not enough. What is needed is a strong focus on bringing research to a grassroot level and establishing a G2G – Grassroot to Global focus.

The G2G focus can sustain itself only and only if it is sustained across the entire curriculum and is able to bring a mindset change within all stakeholders of education. Keeping this focus at its forefront, the National Education Policy 2020 lays its foundation and maps the way forward for the Indian Education System.

Academic Research as Envisaged in NEP 2020

In the Draft Policy Framework of NEP 2020, published by the MHRD, GoI (2019) mentions –

- Levels of Research and Innovation (R&I) investment in India has steadily dropped over the last decade – from 0.84% of GDP in 2008 to around 0.69% in 2014, where it remains today. For the sake of comparison, the document shares the levels of R&I investment as a proportion of GDP in countries like, United States (2.8%), China (2.1%), Israel (4.3%), and South Korea (4.2%). This document suggests that it is evident that all these countries all invest at least three times as much as a proportion of GDP as compared to India.

- The number of researchers per lakh of population is only 15 in India, as compared to 111 in China, 423 in the United States, and 825 in Israel (Government of India, Economic Survey of India 2016-17). Understandably, a low number of researchers translates into a lower number of researches being produced and being used in the country.
- According to the World Intellectual Property Organisation (WIPO) (2019), China made as many as 13,38,503 patent applications, with just 10% being made by non-resident Chinese, the USA made 605,571 patent applications, while India made a mere 45,057, of which over 70% were by non-resident Indians. This alarming statistics substantiates a problem identified by the National Policy of Education 1986– brain-drain; where researchers use the facilities within the country for their initial education and because of the lack of infrastructure and opportunities within the country, they rather go abroad and work. Further, the lower number of patents also indicates the lack of innovative work driven by Indian scientists.
- In terms of publications, India has been doing somewhat better, showing a steady growth in its output and taking India's share of scientific publications from 3.1% in 2009 to 4.4% in 2013.
- A 2018 compilation of Science and Engineering indicators by the US National Science Foundation showed that both the USA and China published at least four times as many articles as India in 2016.

It is obvious that policy framers understood the dismal state of research in India and therefore, in the NEP 2020, a whole chapter has been allocated to research. The chapter titled *Catalysing Quality Academic Research in All Fields through a new National Research Foundation* highlights the following key points:

- It is only through continuous knowledge creation and research has the potential to uplift the society and inspire the nation. Historical tradition of research in various fields needs to be strengthened to lead India to the 21st century with innovation and research.
- A robust ecosystem of research is needed if the nation wishes to progress intellectually, societally, environmentally and technologically. The current investment of 0.69% in research and innovation is not sufficient if India wishes to capitalise on the potential of the knowledge economy.
- It is only through interdisciplinary research that Indians can have access to cleaner air, cleaner drinking water, better energy management, improved transportation, quality education – as most of these problems

are local and their solutions also must be developed locally. Research in the discipline of arts and humanities along with that of science and technology is extremely important for the progress of the nation.

- Higher Educational Institutes need to engage in research and innovations – the policy very correctly explains the cyclic process of better teaching leading to better research and better research leading to better teaching. It also substantiates the need for multidisciplinary university settings.
- With a comprehensive approach to transforming school education, the policy list down various ways, like, *career counselling in schools, multidisciplinary nature of HEIs, emphasis on holistic education, inclusion of research and internships in the undergraduate curriculum, faculty career management systems,* that can help develop the research mindset in the country.
- The policy envisions the establishment of the National Research Foundation with the *goal of providing merit-based but equitable peer-reviewed research funding* to individuals and universities. The policy lists down the following activities of the National Research Foundation:
    - *fund competitive, peer-reviewed grant proposals of all types and across all disciplines;*
    - *seed, grow, and facilitate research at academic institutions, particularly at universities and colleges where research is currently in a nascent stage, through mentoring of such institutions;*
    - *act as a liaison between researchers and relevant branches of government as well as industry, so that research scholars are constantly made aware of the most urgent national research issues, and so that policymakers are constantly made aware of the latest research breakthroughs; so as to allow breakthroughs to be optimally brought into policy and/or implementation; and*
    - *recognise outstanding research and progress*
- The policy also assures that the institutions which currently fund research such as the Department of Science and Technology (DST), Department of Atomic Energy (DAE), Department of Biotechnology (DBT), Indian Council of Agriculture Research (ICAR), Indian Council of Medical Research (ICMR), Indian Council of Historical Research (ICHR), and University Grants Commission (UGC), will continue to independently fund research according to their priorities and needs.

The key ideas that the NEP 2020 brings forth with regard to research are:

1. Establishment of the National Research Foundation.
2. Establishment of a peer-reviewed process for research funding.
3. Strengthening interdisciplinary and multidisciplinary research.

The next section of the chapter deals with the suggestive roadmap for strengthening quality academic research in the country.

Roadmap for Strengthening Quality Academic Research in India

As we have seen, the National Education Policy of 2020 and the National Policy of Education 1986 have identified lack of funding and lack of infrastructure as few of the major hurdles in academic research. In that direction, the suggestive National Research Foundation – similar to the National Science Foundation of the US is a welcome step. The NSF prides itself as funding research of nearly 236 Nobel Prize winners through its various research grants. These researchers were funded by the NSF grant at various stages of their research work (and not necessarily the research that won them the Nobel). Therefore, if India wishes to reap the benefits of becoming a knowledge society and capitalise on its demographic dividend, quality academic research needs to be strengthened. The following are the suggestions that can pave the way for implementing the NEP 2020:

- *National Research Foundation*: The then Finance Minister, Ms Nirmala Sitharaman, in her budget speech as documented by Sheriff (2019) in the *Indian Express* clarified that *it* (the National Research Foundation) *will ensure that the overall research ecosystem is strengthened with a focus on identifying thrust areas relevant to our national priorities and towards basic Science, without duplication of efforts and expenditure.* The research funding landscape in the country is fragmented. This fragmentation has led to research that is duplicated – of efforts and resources. The fragmented ecosystem has also forced limited interaction amongst stakeholders of various research agencies. Therefore, the National Research Foundation needs to create a robust system so that there is transparency within the funding processes. It is in this regard, unless the multiple funding agencies, like, Department of Science and Technology (DST), Department of Atomic Energy (DAE), Department of Biotechnology (DBT), Indian Council of Agriculture Research (ICAR), Indian Council of Medical Research (ICMR), Indian Council of Historical Research (ICHR), University Grants Commission (UGC), Indian Council of Social Science Research (ICSSR) are not transparent about their funding status, it would be difficult to capitalise on the funding opportunities. This transparency of research funding should be reflected on the website of the institute along with the information regarding the Principal Investigator and the budget that has been approved. This information would also help reduce redundancy – a necessity for a country like India, where there is a limited budget but multiple avenues of expense.

  Another suggestion that has emerged from academicians working in premier research institutes of the country is regarding the disbursement of funds. The NRF should ensure, irrespective of the funding agency, once a proposal is accepted, the funds are disbursed within 30 days according to the terms of reference planned by each funding institute.

- *CSR Funding into NRF*: The National Education Policy 2020 discusses the benefits of having strong ties with the industry to propel the growth of the nation and create a cohesive educational system. It is in this regard, the NEP 2020 has laid a lot of emphasis on Vocational Education. Tapping into the industry links for creating an industry-ready workforce could be a game-changer for the Indian education system. In the same manner, allowing CSR funding directly into the NRF would ensure a close-knit relationship between academia and industry. CSR funding into NRF could be a win-win situation as industries could benefit from the unbiased rigour of academic research while the academic institutes will get an opportunity to work closely with cut-edge research and in demand technologies. A way to encourage CSR funding into NRF would be giving additional benefits to the organisations engaging in CSR funding.
- *Peer Evaluation of Research Proposals*: Roberts and Shambrook (2012) call peer review as "essential to academic quality, fair and equitable, and one of the most rigorous and prestigious forms of scholarly accomplishment." Mayden (2012) and Avin (2019) go even further and call it the 'gold-standard' for evaluating merit of research especially with regard to research funding (Demicheli *et al*, 2007). It is also pertinent to mention Guthrie (2017) who discusses how work subjected to peer-review is a weak predictor of future success. In fact, according to Towne, Fletcher, and Wise (2004) "the peer review process, no matter how well designed, is only as effective as the people involved". And this is the crux of the matter. Majority of research that is available with regard to peer review limits itself on focusing on the outcomes in terms of the funding decisions, and not about the processes involved in creating a system for peer review. There is another area that begs consideration –the practice of peer-review of research funding is common in the Science domain but it does not have a well-documented journey in the discipline of Social Sciences. Therefore, in the programme of action for the NEP 2020, focus needs to be laid on how the peer review of research proposals would proceed for all domains. A one fit formula will not be suitable.

  Within the area of Peer evaluation of research proposals there are few other aspects that need attention:
- *Skill development of peers to undertake the process of peer review of research proposals*: Steiner Davis MLE (2020) in their detailed article discuss how majority of the participants in the research considered training instructions from funding agencies and academic training as the least useful ways to improve panellists' competencies to review research proposals; instead, the participants of the research described skills like listening to panellists make arguments, sharing thoughts during discussions, serving as a peer reviewer for publications, receiving mentorship for colleagues and mentoring others as more useful skills

that help in strengthening the peer-review process of research proposals. Although Steiner Davis MLE (2020) admit this research was limited in scope, yet it warrants attention because the pool of peer reviewers benefit more from academic interactions rather than training. The present pandemic of 2020 has also reduced the need for people to have face-to-face interactions wherever coordination amongst stakeholders is difficult. Online environments cannot be a substitute for face-to-face interaction, but they can facilitate interaction by breaking the boundaries of time and distance.

- *Need for reviewers to have a high moral and ethical code of conduct*: The provision within the funding programme should be such that whenever there is a conflict of interest, members must be able to recuse themselves. The conflict of interest need not be limited to only family relationships but could also extend to institutional colleges and colleagues thereby ensuring complete transparency and meritocracy within the system.
- *Open viewing of proposal defense*: In order to strengthen the area of research, it is also suggested that research defense seminars be conducted from time to time. The research defense seminars could be like the Ph.D defense seminars where the rigour of the academic inquiry process is upheld and all participants benefit from the researcher. This open viewing will also help foster collaboration amongst researchers. It can also lead the way for industries to glimpse into the academic world.

So how does the NEP 2020 act as a Catalysis for Quality Academic Research?

In the chapter so far we have seen the difference between academic research and professional research. We then witnessed the problems faced by researchers as discussed in the last educational policy – almost 30 years back; but we have also seen an in-depth example of one of the many initiatives that the government has taken to move from global to a grassroot level utility. As we conclude the chapter, let us understand the relevance of the word "catalysis" in conjunction with quality academic research and the National Education Policy 2020.

Catalysis is borrowed from chemistry. A catalysis in a reaction is something that accelerates the reaction, but is not consumed in the process instead is available to repeated re-use. So how does the NEP 2020 act as a catalysis for quality academic research? Let us look at four major catalysts:

- *Introduction of vocational education during school years* –Vocational education not only helps students gain financial and skill competencies but also helps students see the interplay of knowledge that is learnt in theory classes within the practical framework. Like when students learn how to calculate the area of a quadrilateral in class, they are able to directly apply this knowledge while designing a table in their carpentry vocational education classes. In the same manner, when they learn about balanced food in their science classes they are able to plan better meals in their home science or baking vocational courses. This visibility of correlation between theory and praxis from a very young age, makes students aware, critical and curious – all hallmarks of a good researcher. By formalising the introduction and paving the road for its implementation within the school education, vocational education becomes the first catalyst that supports the overarching aim of NEP 2020 of helping India become a skill based nation.

- *Breaking silos of disciplines*: Interdisciplinary education with a thrust on application-based education can help students become productive citizens of the country and this is well substantiated in research. Developed nations across the world have laid a lot of focus on interdisciplinary curriculum. NEP 2020 aims to help students either gain domain specific knowledge based on their interest or allows them to gain domain general knowledge based on the curricular framework.

  By allowing multiple entry and exit points within its structure, the NEP 2020, allows young adults and researchers to either continue pursuing their area of interest in their education or re-enter the education system to finish their education. Therefore, bringing the focus on an interdisciplinary approach to education becomes a second catalyst for quality research because it allows students to approach a problem from multiple angles – laying the foundation for a knowledge based economy.
- *CSR funding*: By allowing CSR funding within the education system, the NEP 2020 creates provisions for industries to fund students (and their research) that would augment their own organisational goals and needs thereby creating a strong industry linked education system that supports employability and youth participation.
- *Establishment of the National Research Foundation*: Since, not all industries and areas can be funded via CSR initiatives, the establishment of the National Research Foundation is a huge boon. As social scientists, we understand and acknowledge policy framers need society based data points to make informed decisions regarding various social policies, the country needs to preserve its rich cultural heritage and its vast biodiversity. These umbrella activities cannot be left to the CSR initiatives and therefore, the NRF funding capability will assist researchers. The absence of this provision would have created a country that was solely driven by economics rather than values, traditions, mores and cultural heritage. But, with this provision, the Government of India, can not only sustain research needed for the society but also study the impact of how industries are shaping the society.

It, therefore, can be said National Education Policy 2020 with its postulates of bringing changes from early childhood education to interdisciplinary school education to inclusion of vocational education and establishing of an academic credit bank, provides the next generation of Indians with opportunities to focus on areas of interest that are India-centric and in the process make India self-reliant, modern and prosperous.

References

Avin, S. (2019). Mavericks and Lotteries. *Studies in History and Philosophy of Science Part A* 2019; 76: 13–23. doi: https://doi.org/10.1016/j.shpsa.2018.11.006

Creswell, J.W. (2008). *Educational Research: Planning, Conducting, and Evaluating Quantitative and Qualitative Research.* Upper Saddle River, NJ: Pearson Education, Inc.

Demicheli, V., Di Pietrantonj, C. (2007). Peer Review for Improving the Quality of Grant Applications. *Cochrane Database System Review* Apr 18;(2).

European Commission (2017). *The Economic Rationale for Public R&I Funding and its Impact.* Brussels. Brussels: European Commission DOI: 10.2777/047015 Accessed from: http://bookshop.europa.eu/en/the-economic-rationale-for-public-r-i-funding-and-its- impact-pbKI0117050/ Accessed on 10 Sept 2020.

Government of India (2017) *Economic Survey of India 2016-17.* Accessed from https://www.indiabudget.gov.in/budget2017-2018/es2016-17/echapter_vol2.pdf – Accessed on 10 Sept 2020. New Delhi.

Government of India (2019), *Draft National Education Policy 2019.* Accessed from https://www.mhrd.gov.in/sites/upload_files/mhrd/files/Draft_NEP_2019_EN_Revised.pdf. Accessed on 10 Sept 2020.

Guthrie, S., Ghiga, I., Wooding, S. (2017). What Do We Know About Grant Peer Review in the Health Sciences. *F1000 Research* 6: 1335.

Mayden, K.D. (2012). Peer Review: Publication's Gold Standard. *Journal of the Advanced Practitioner in Oncology* 3(2): 117–22.

OECD (2015). *Frascati Manual. The Measurement of Scientific, Technological and Innovation Activities.* doi:10.1787/9789264239012-en.

Piccoli, Gabriele, and Erica L. Wagner (2003)."The value of academic research: in addition to its intrinsic value, information-system research builds insights for practitioners one step at a time." *Cornell Hotel & Restaurant Administration Quarterly,* vol. 44, no. 2, Apr. p. 29. Gale Academic OneFile, Accessed 10 Sept. 2020.

Roberts TJ, Shambrook J. (2012) Academic Excellence: A Commentary and Reflections on the Inherent Value of Peer Review. *Journal of Research Administration* Apr; 43(1): 33–38

Sherrif, M.K (2019). *More on HRD ministry slate, govt. looks to create world-class institutes, promote research, Indian Express* dated: July 6, 2019, Accessed from https://indianexpress.com/article/business/budget/union-budget-2019-more-on-hrd-ministry-slate-govt-looks-to-create-world-class-institutes-promote-research-5817912/ - Accessed on 10 Sept 2020

Steiner Davis MLE, Conner, T.R., Miller-Bains, K, Shapard, L. (2020). What makes an effective grants peer reviewer? An exploratory study of the necessary skills. *PLoS ONE* 15(5)

WIPO (2019). *World Intellectual Property Indicators 2019. Geneva: World Intellectual Property Organization.* Accessed from: https://www.wipo.int/edocs/pubdocs/en/wipo_pub_941_2019.pdf.Accessed on 10 Sept 2020.

15

Genesis, Current Status and Future of Regulations in Higher Education In India

Anjali Bajpai

Higher education plays a distinct role in the progress of a nation as the socio-economic development to a large extent depends upon the capacity of humans to convert information into knowledge. Powar (2002) mentions that the World Bank in its document 'Higher Education– the lessons of experience' states "Higher Education is of paramount importance for economic and social development. Institutions for higher education have the main responsibility for equipping individuals with advanced knowledge and skills required for positions of responsibility in government, business and profession". The moot point here is that higher education is essential for adequately qualified manpower without which national development is not possible. Indian higher education is one of the largest systems of higher education in the world next only to the USA and China. In the past few years, we have gone for a very large scale massification in higher education. Today, India has over 900 universities (both central and state) and over 40, 000 colleges. It has always been accepted that higher education has a critical contribution to sustainable livelihoods and economic development of a nation. As the Draft of NEP 2020 (which was released in 2019) states "managing such a large system has inherent challenges which we have been trying to handle, some successfully and others not so successfully. The challenge has been of greater value to our pursuit of access equity and reasonable cost per student in public institutions'. The mechanism of regulation has its roots to the inception of the present Higher Education system itself.

Genesis of regulations in Higher Education System in India

The higher education system in India had a unique and arguably glorious past. In ancient times it was mostly individualistic, with the guru having his own specialisation and ashram. The standards and norms were his own and he looked after his own Gurukuls. This later paved the way to some of the most renowned universities of late B.C. and early A.D. era. We had Nalanda, Taxila, Vikramshila, Ujjain, Kashi as seats of learning where renowned international scholars visited and studied. The academicians and scholars had their own say in governance though the patronage was provided by the kingdoms. In the

Professor, Faculty of Education, Banaras Hindu University, Varanasi

medieval times there existed a dual system –in one scholars had their own rules, and in other the ruling class provided patronage to institutions which promoted skill and manpower for replenishment of the troops and courtiers. In eighteen century, gradually, this was taken over by British system of education. The first initiative to regularise was taken by Warren Hastings in 1781 to establish the Calcutta Madarsa. Then the Woods Dispatch 1854 entrusted the government with the responsibility of creating a properly articulated system of education from the primary school to the higher level. It resulted in the establishment of universities at Presidency Towns which replicated the models of London University. The purpose of these universities was conferring degrees upon those who would come from any of the affiliated institutions after passing some required examinations. This led to a new system of education in Indian subcontinent in line with the manifestations of the Britishers, who were ruling the entire country. The Universities at Calcutta, Madras and Bombay were established in 1857, Lahore Punjab University 1882 and Allahabad University in 1885. The commission of 1882 promoted rapid expansion of higher education as the number of colleges increased from 68 in 1882 to 192 by the year 1902. The University Commission of 1902 by the government gave the recommendations as stated in Universities Act of 1904. In this, conditions of affiliations to a university were clearly laid down which had to be followed diligently. This seemed like another attempt of Lord Curzon to throttle higher education in India. The Government resolution on Education policy 1913 supported establishment of more colleges and universities. As a result, BHU (1916), Mysore University (1916), Osmania University (1918), AMU(1920) and University of Lucknow (1920) came into existence along with the five Vidyapeeths. Establishment of these institutions were the efforts of Indian nationalists in response to the British model for India.

The Calcutta University Commission 1916, which was reported in 1919, advocated for 3-year degree courses and talked of Calcutta as a real teaching University. The Intermediate classes from university were to be transferred to secondary institutions and it recommended a Board of Secondary Education. Soon after, in a conference of Indian Universities in 1924 an Advisory Board–Inter University Board was established. Simultaneously, the "Sargent plan" prepared by the Central Advisory Board in 1944 for post-war educational development made the proposal for establishing the University Grants Commission.

Higher Education Regulation since Independence

After Independence, a most significant action of the Government of India in the field of education was the appointment of a University Commission in 1948 under the Chairmanship of Dr. S. Radhakrishnan, a renowned educationist and a famous Vice-Chancellor of Banaras Hindu University. Many questions were raised on setting up this commission, following a top-down approach was one; and second, was deviation from the concern of eradication of mass illiteracy. The Commission itself gave an explanation to these by stating that it was largely conceptualised to realise the dreams of Indian leaders for industrialisation of the country, it is essential to review and plan for establishing colleges, particularly professional colleges. This document, in fact, has guided the development of higher education in the country since Independence.

The Radhakrishnan Commission suggested following recommendations in regard to higher education:

- The aims and objectives of university education and research in India,
- The changes considered necessary and desirable in the constitution, control functions and jurisdiction of university in India and their relation with Government, Central and Provincial,
- The finance of Universities such as maintenance of the highest standards of teaching and examination in the colleges and universities,
- The qualifications and conditions of service, salaries, privileges and functions of teachers,
- University education be placed on the concurrent list of the Constitution.

The concern of the Central Government with the universities should be with regard to finance, coordination of facilities in special subjects, adoption of national policies, ensuring minimum standards of efficient administration and liaison between universities and national research laboratories and scientific surveys, etc.The University Grants Commission as a body be established for allocating grants.

The Kothari Commission set up in 1966 for formulating a national system for education talked of standard institutions, autonomy and governance and also about the role of UGC.The most important reform in higher education suggested by the commission was the development of some 'major universities' wherein first class post-graduate work and research would be possible and whose standards, work and research would be comparable to the best institutions of their type in any part of the world. The UGC should select, as soon as possible, from amongst the existing universities, about six universities (including one of the IIT's and one Agricultural University) for development as major universities.

University Autonomy: The universities will have autonomy in the selection of students, appointment and promotion of teachers, determination of courses of study, methods of teaching and selection of areas and problems of research.

Role and Appointment of the Vice-Chancellors: The Vice-Chancellors should, as a rule, be a distinguished educationist or eminent scholar with adequate administrative experience. The term of office of the Vice-Chancellor should be five years and he should not be appointed for more than two terms in the same university. All posts of Vice-Chancellors should be whole time and carry a salary. The retirement age for the Vice-Chancellors should be 65 years.

The Inter-University Board: All statutory or deemed universities should become members of the I.U.B. automatically. The degree or diplomas granted by a statutory or deemed university in India should receive automatic recognition from all other statutory or deemed universities.

The University Grants Commission: All higher education should be regarded as an integrated whole and the UGC should eventually represent the entire spectrum of higher education. The UGC should consist of 12 to 15 members; not more than one-third should be officials of the government and at least one-third from the universities. The responsibility of coordinating standards should continue to vest in one body, viz., the UGC. State UGC's should not, therefore, be created. The visiting committees appointed by the UGC should visit each university every three years and work in greater detail and depth.

Some measures for improvement of functioning of University Grants Commission as suggested by National Education Policy 1968 are thus:

- UGC type organisations should be set up for dealing with technical, agricultural and medicinal education.
- For the purpose of coordination there should be certain overlapping membership between the UGC and the UGC type organisations.
- It will be advisable for the UGC to adopt a practice of working through a number of standing committees set up to deal with important responsibilities entrusted to it.
- It is essential that UGC should inspect the universities more frequently and more intensely.

The National Policy of Education 1986 enjoined that urgent steps need be taken for protecting the system of higher education from degradation. In view of the mixed experiences with the system of affiliation, autonomous colleges should be helped to develop in large numbers until the affiliating system is replaced by a free and more creative association of universities with the colleges. Similarly, the creation of autonomous departments within universities on a selective basis would be encouraged. Autonomy and freedom should be accompanied with accountability. Courses and programmes should be redesigned to meet the demands of specialisations. Special emphasis would be laid on linguistic competence and increasing flexibility in the combination of courses.

State level planning and coordination of higher education would be done through councils of Higher Education. The UGC and these Councils could develop coordinative methods to keep a watch on standards. Provision to be made for minimum facilities and admission will be regulated according to capacity. A major effort be directed towards the transformation of teaching methods. Audio visual aids and electronic equipment to be introduced; development of science and technology curricula and material, research, and teacher orientation to receive attention. The preparation of teachers at the beginning of the service as well as continuing education during service is required. Teachers' performance should be systematically assessed. All posts will be filled on the basis of merit. Suitable mechanisms will be set up by the UGC for coordinating research in the universities, particularly in the thrust areas of science and technology, with research undertaken by the other agencies. These considerations over the years have given us an overlapping system of regulations, accreditations and monitoring.

Present Regulatory Bodies

UGC: The University Grants Commission (UGC) was formally inaugurated by late Shri Maulana Abul Kalam Azad, the then Minister of Education, Natural Resources and Scientific Research on 28 December 1953. The UGC, however, was formally established only in November 1956 as a statutory body of the Government of India through an Act of Parliament for the coordination, determination and maintenance of standards of university education in India. The UGC has the unique distinction of being the only grant-giving agency in the country which has been vested with two responsibilities: that of providing funds and that of coordination, determination and maintenance of standards in institutions of higher education.

The UGC's mandate includes: Promoting and coordinating university education; Determining and maintaining standards of teaching, examination and research in universities; Framing regulations on minimum standards of education; Monitoring developments in the field of collegiate and university education; Disbursing grants to the universities and colleges; Serving as a vital link between the Union and state governments and institutions of higher learning; Advising the Central and State governments on the measures necessary for improvement of university education.

NAAC: The National Assessment and Accreditation Council (NAAC) was established in 1994 as an autonomous institution of the University Grants Commission (UGC) with its Head Quarter in Bengaluru. NAAC conducts assessment and accreditation of Higher Educational Institutions (HEI) such as colleges, universities or other recognised institutions to derive an understanding of the 'Quality Status' of the institution. NAAC evaluates the institutions for its conformance to the standards of quality in terms of its performance related to the educational processes and outcomes, curriculum coverage, teaching-learning processes, faculty, research, infrastructure, learning resources, organisation, governance, financial well being and student services. Work with vision to make quality the defining element of higher education in India through a combination of self and external quality evaluation, promotion and sustenance initiatives.

AICTE: All India Council for Technical Education (AICTE) was set up in November 1945 as a national-level apex advisory body to conduct a survey on the facilities available for technical education and to promote development in the country in a coordinated and integrated manner. And to ensure the same, as stipulated in the National Policy of Education (1986), AICTE was vested with:

- Statutory authority for planning, formulation, and maintenance of norms and standards
- Quality assurance through accreditation
- Funding in priority areas, monitoring, and evaluation
- Maintaining parity of certification and awards
- The management of technical education in the country.

MCI: The Medical Council of India was established in 1934 under the Indian Medical Council Act, 1933, now repealed, with the main function of establishing uniform standards of higher qualifications in medicine and recognition of medical qualifications in India and abroad. The number of medical colleges had increased steadily during the years after Independence. It was felt that the provisions of Indian Medical Council Act were not adequate to meet with the challenges posed by the very fast development and the progress of medical education in the country. As a result, in 1956, the old Act was repealed and a new one was enacted. This was further modified in 1964, 1993 and 2001.

The objectives of the Council are as follows:

- Maintenance of uniform standards of medical education, both undergraduate and postgraduate.
- Recommendation for recognition/derecognition of medical qualifications of medical institutions of India or foreign countries.
- Permanent registration/provisional registration of doctors with recognised medical qualifications.
- Reciprocity with foreign countries in the matter of mutual recognition of medical qualifications.

BCI: The Bar Council of India is a statutory body created by Parliament to regulate and represent the Indian bar. BCI performs the regulatory function by prescribing standards of professional conduct and etiquette and by exercising disciplinary jurisdiction over the bar. It also sets standards for legal education and grants recognition to Universities whose degree in law will serve as qualification for enrolment as an advocate. In addition, BCI performs certain representative functions by protecting the rights, privileges and interests of advocates and through the creation of funds for providing financial assistance to organise welfare schemes for them. The Bar Council of India was established by Parliament under the Advocates Act, 1961. Approximately 12 statutory functions under Section 7 cover the Bar Council's regulatory and representative mandate for the legal profession and legal education in India.

VCI: Veterinary Council of India (VCI) is a statutory body which regulates veterinary practice in India. Established under the Ministry of

Agriculture of the Government of India in 1984, and based in New Delhi, the council is governed by the Indian Veterinary Council Act, 1984. The first members were nominated in 1989. The first elections to the council took place in 1999. It derives its funding from grants-in-aid from the Department of Animal Husbandry and Dairy of the Ministry of Agriculture. The Veterinary Council worked with nine objectives as:

- To prepare and maintain the Indian Veterinary Practitioners' Register containing the names of all persons who possess the recognised veterinary qualifications and who are for the time being enrolled on a State Veterinary Register of the State to which Indian Veterinary Council Act extends.
- To lay down minimum standards of veterinary education required for granting recognised veterinary qualifications by veterinary institutions.
- To recommend recognition or withdrawal of recognition of veterinary qualifications granted by veterinary institutions in India.
- To lay down the standards of professional conduct, etiquette and code of ethics to be observed by veterinary practitioners
- To negotiate with institutions located in other countries imparting training in veterinary education for recognition of their qualifications on reciprocal basis.
- To regulate veterinary practice in the country.
- To advise the Central and the State Governments on all regulatory matters concerning veterinary practice and education.
- To frame regulations.
- To implement the provisions of the Act, and Rules and Regulations framed thereunder.

NCTE: The National Council for Teacher Education, in its previous status since 1973, was an advisory body for the Central and State Governments on all matters pertaining to teacher education, with its Secretariat in the Department of Teacher Education of the National Council of Educational Research and Training (NCERT). The National Council for Teacher Education as a statutory body came into existence in pursuance of the National Council for Teacher Education Act, 1993 (No. 73 of 1993) on 17 August 1995. The main objective of the NCTE is to achieve planned and coordinated development of the teacher education system throughout the country, the regulation and proper maintenance of Norms and Standards in the teacher education system and for matters connected therewith. The mandate given to the NCTE is very broad and covers the whole gamut of teacher education programmes including research and training of persons for equipping them to teach at pre-primary, primary, secondary and senior secondary stages in schools, and non-formal education, part-time education, adult education and distance (correspondence) education courses. It shall be the duty of the Council to take all such steps as it may think fit for ensuring planned and coordinated development of teacher education for the determination and maintenance of standards for teacher education and for the purposes of performing its functions under its Act.

In addition to the above mentioned, we also have the Pharmacy Council of India (PCI), Indian Nursing Council (INC), Dentist Council of India (DCI), Central Council of Indian Medicine (CCIM) and Rehabilitation Council of India (RCI). All these bodies have an overlapping role along with the UGC. The NEP 2020 has taken cognisance of these large numbers of organisations and tried to suggest a 'light but tight' regulatory mechanism.

NEP 2020 mentions Transformation of the Regulatory System of Higher Education in following ways in its Section 18:

- Regulation of higher education has been too heavy-handed for decades; too much has been attempted to be regulated with too little effect. The mechanistic and disempowering nature of the regulatory system has been rife with very basic problems, such as heavy concentrations of power within a few bodies, conflicts of interest among these bodies, a resulting lack of accountability. The regulatory system is in need of a complete overhaul in order to re-energise the higher education sector and enable it to thrive.
- To address the above-mentioned issues, the regulatory system of higher education will ensure that the distinct functions of regulation, accreditation, funding, and academic standard setting will be performed by distinct, independent, and empowered bodies. This is considered essential to create checks-and-balances in the system, minimise conflicts of interest, and eliminate concentrations of power. To ensure that the four institutional structures carrying out these four essential functions work independently yet at the same time and work in synergy towards common goals. These four structures will be set up as four independent verticals within one umbrella institution, the Higher Education Commission of India (HECI).
- The first vertical of HECI will be the National Higher Education Regulatory Council (NHERC). It will function as the common, single point regulator for the higher education sector including teacher education and excluding medical and legal education, thus eliminating the duplication and disjunction of regulatory efforts by the multiple regulatory agencies that exist at the current time. It will require a relook and repealing of existing Acts and restructuring of various existing regulatory bodies to enable this single point regulation. NHERC will be set up to regulate in a 'light but tight' and facilitative manner, meaning that a few important matters particularly financial probity, good governance, and the full online and offline public self-disclosure of all finances, audits, procedures, infrastructure, faculty/ staff, courses, and educational outcomes will be very effectively

regulated. This information will have to be made available and kept updated and accurate by all higher education institutions on a public website maintained by NHERC and on the institutions' websites. Any complaints or grievances from stakeholders and others arising out of the information placed in public domain shall be adjudicated by NHERC. Feedback from randomly selected students including differently-abled students at each HEI will be solicited online to ensure valuable input at regular intervals.

- The primary mechanism to enable such regulation will be accreditation. The second vertical of HECI will, therefore, be a 'meta-accrediting body', called the National Accreditation Council (NAC). Accreditation of institutions will be based primarily on basic norms, public self-disclosure, good governance, and outcomes, and it will be carried out by an independent ecosystem of accrediting institutions supervised and overseen by NAC. The task to function as a recognised accreditor shall be awarded to an appropriate number of institutions by NAC. In the short term, a robust system of graded accreditation shall be established, which will specify phased benchmarks for all HEIs to achieve set levels of quality, self-governance, and autonomy. In turn, all HEIs will aim, through their Institutional Development Plans (IDPs), to attain the highest level of accreditation over the next 15 years, and thereby eventually aim to function as self-governing degree-granting institutions/ clusters. In the long run, accreditation will become a binary process, as per the extant global practice.
- The third vertical of HECI will be the Higher Education Grants Council (HEGC), which will carry out funding and financing of higher education based on transparent criteria, including the IDPs prepared by the institutions and the progress made on their implementation. HEGC will be entrusted with the disbursement of scholarships and developmental funds for launching new focus areas and expanding quality programme offerings at HEIs across disciplines and fields.
- The fourth vertical of HECI will be the General Education Council (GEC), which will frame expected learning outcomes for higher education programmes, also referred to as 'graduate attributes'. A National Higher Education Qualification Framework (NHEQF) will be formulated by the GEC and it shall be in sync with the National Skills Qualifications Framework (NSQF) to ease the integration of vocational education into higher education. Higher education qualifications leading to a degree/ diploma/certificate shall be described by the NHEQF in terms of such learning outcomes. In addition, the GEC shall set up facilitative norms for issues, such as credit transfer, equivalence, etc., through the NHEQF. The GEC will be mandated to identify specific

skills that students must acquire during their academic programmes, with the aim of preparing well-rounded learners with 21st century skills.

- The professional councils, such as the Indian Council for Agricultural Research (ICAR), Veterinary Council of India (VCI), National Council for Teacher Education (NCTE), Council of Architecture (CoA), National Council for Vocational Education and Training (NCVET) etc., will act as Professional Standard Setting Bodies (PSSBs). They will play a key role in the higher education system and will be invited to be members of the GEC. These bodies, after restructuring as PSSBs, will continue to draw the curricula, lay down academic standards and coordinate between teaching, research and extension of their domain/discipline, as members of the GEC. As members of the GEC, they would help in specifying the curriculum framework, within which HEIs may prepare their own curricula. Thus, PSSBs would also set the standards or expectations in particular fields of learning and practice while having no regulatory role. All HEIs will decide how their educational programmes respond to these standards, among other considerations, and would also be able to reach out for support from these standard-setting bodies or PSSBs, if needed.
- Such a system architecture will ensure the principle of functional separation by eliminating conflicts of interests between different roles. It will also aim to empower HEIs, while ensuring that the few key essential matters are given due attention. Responsibility and accountability shall devolve to the HEIs concomitantly. No distinction in such expectations shall be made between public and private HEIs.
- Such a transformation will require existing structures and institutions to reinvent themselves and undergo an evolution of sorts. The separation of functions would mean that each vertical within HECI would take on a new, single role which is relevant, meaningful, and important in the new regulatory scheme.
- The functioning of all the independent verticals for Regulation (NHERC), Accreditation (NAC), Funding (HEGC), Academic Standard Setting (GEC) and the overarching autonomous umbrella body (HECI) itself will be based on transparent public disclosure, and use technology extensively to reduce human interface to ensure efficiency and transparency in their work. The underlying principle will be that of a faceless and transparent regulatory intervention using technology. Strict compliance measures with stringent action, including penalties for false disclosure of mandated information, will be ensured so that Higher Education Institutions are conforming to the basic minimum norms and standards. HECI itself will be resolving disputes among the four verticals. Each vertical in HECI will be an independent body consisting of persons having high expertise in the relevant areas along

with integrity, commitment, and a demonstrated track record of public service. HECI itself will be a small, independent body of eminent public-spirited experts in higher education, which will oversee and monitor the integrity and effective functioning of HECI. Suitable mechanisms will be created within HECI to carry out its functions, including adjudication.

- Setting up new quality HEIs will also be made far easier by the regulatory regime, while ensuring with great effectiveness that these are set up with the spirit of public service and with due financial backing for long-term stability. HEIs performing exceptionally well will be helped by Central and State governments to expand their institutions, and thereby attain larger numbers of students and faculty as well as disciplines and programmes. Public Philanthropic Partnership models for HEIs may also be piloted with the aim to further expand access to high-quality higher education.

Curbing Commercialisation of Education

The key priority of the regulatory system will be to combat and stop the commercialisation of higher education. All education institutions will be held to similar standards of audit and disclosure as a 'not for profit' entity. Surpluses, if any, will be reinvested in the educational sector. There will be transparent public disclosure of all these financial matters with recourse to grievance-handling mechanisms to the general public. The accreditation system developed by NAC will provide a complementary check and NHERC will consider this as one of the key dimensions of its regulatory objective. All HEIs – public and private – shall be treated on par within this regulatory regime. The regulatory regime shall encourage private philanthropic efforts in education. There will be common national guidelines for all legislative Acts that will form private HEIs. These common guidelines will cover Good Governance, Financial Stability and Security, Educational Outcomes, and Transparency of Disclosures.

Private HEIs having a philanthropic and public-spirited intent will be encouraged through a progressive regime of fees determination. Transparent mechanisms for fixing fees with an upper limit, for different types of institutions depending on their accreditation, will be developed so that individual institutions are not adversely affected. This will empower private HEIs to set fees for their programmes independently, though within the laid-out norms and the broad applicable regulatory mechanism. Private HEIs will be encouraged to offer free ships and scholarships in significant numbers to their students. All fees and charges set by private HEIs will be transparently and fully disclosed, and there shall be no arbitrary increases in these fees/charges during the period of enrolment of any student. This fee determining mechanism will ensure reasonable recovery of cost while ensuring that HEIs discharge their social obligations.

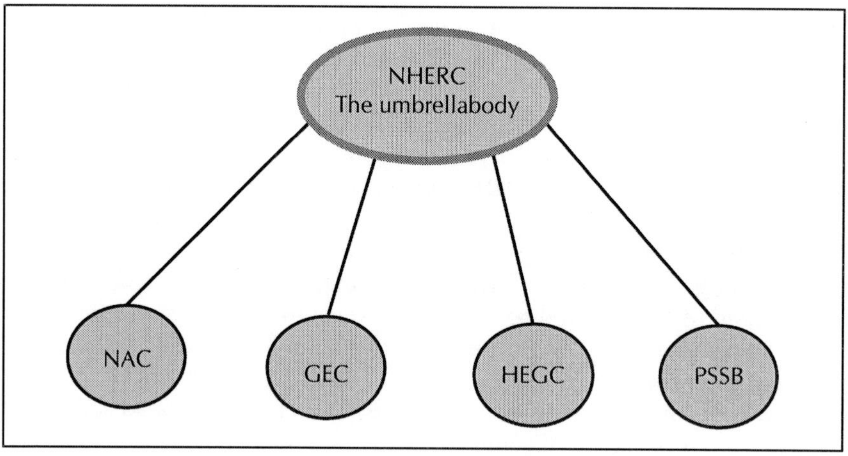

Figure Showing the Regulatory Structure as proposed by NEP 2020

The Way Ahead

The regulatory system should be such that setting up of HEIs is easier and they are set up with the spirit of public service with due financial backing for long term stability. The DNEP 2019

clearly points out that the responsibility of each institution within the new regulatory architecture will be clearly delineated. The existing acts will be modified as necessary to provide an enabling framework. They all will also be collectively held together for quality educational outcomes in the country. Each body may be governed by an Independent Board (IB) consisting of people with expertise in the relevant area, integrity, commitment and a demonstrated track record of public service. The IBs of all may be constituted by a Rashtriya Shiksha Ayog– RSA. These bodies will be accountable to RSA through their IB.

The programme of implementation should be that first the apex body NHERC should be set up. This should within six months plan out the details of the reorganisation of the various bodies. The plan should have the details of –roles of body, mechanism and process of functioning, authority and responsibility, and accountability. Further an apex body should review and monitor the timelines for the restructuring.

The policy has come up with a very innovative system of restructuring, to work it out effectively will require a lot of will, insight and wisdom. All good intentions wither away if not put into action rightly which is the major apprehension with this new structure. We tend to modify things in such a way that only the names change and the things remain the same. With more number of bodies the system might become more entangled instead of simplification. The spirit of the reforms should be considered and we must evolve a new system of regularisation of higher education.

References

Mohanty, J. (1992). *Higher Education: Current Issues in Education.* Cosmo Publication, New Delhi.

Power, K.B. (2002).*Indian Higher Education: A conglomerate of Concepts, Facts and Practices,* Concept Publishing Company, New Delhi. ISBN:81-7022-940-5

UGC.(n.d). *Genesis of University Grants Commission (UGC).* Retrieved September 2020, from https://www.ugc.ac.in/page/Genesis.aspx

NAAC. (n.d.). About us/ mission and vision *of National Assessment and Accreditation Council (NAAC).* Retrieved on September 18, 2020, from http://naac.gov.in/index.php/about-us#vision

AICTE. (n.d.). About us/ history *of All India Council for Technical Education (AICTE).* Retrieved on September 18, 2020, from https://www.aicte-india.org/about-us/history

MCI. (n.d.). *About MCI/Introduction of Medical Council of India (MCI).* Retrieved on September 18, 2020, from https://www.mciindia.org/CMS/about-mci/introduction

BCI. (n.d.).*About/about the Bar Council of India (BCI).* Retrieved on September 18, 2020, from http://www.barcouncilofindia.org/about/about-the-bar-council-of-india

VCI. (n.d.). *About Veterinary Council of India (VCI).* Retrieved on September 18, 2020, from http://dahd.nic.in/veterinary-council-india

NCTE. (n.d.) About National council of Teacher Education (NCTE). Retrieved on September 18, 2020, from https://ncte.gov.in/Website/about.aspx

NEP. (2020). *National Education Policy-2020.* Ministry of Education. Retrieved from https://www.mhrd.gov.in/sites/upload_files/mhrd/files/NEP_Final_English_0.pdf

DNEP (2019) Draft National Education Policy-2019, MHRD, New Delhi

16

Structure and Paradigm of Indian Higher Education System

Geetika Datta

Higher Education is defined as the education, which is obtained after completing 12 years of schooling or equivalent and is of the duration of at least nine months (full time) or after completing 10 years of schooling and is of the duration of at least three years. The education may be of the nature of General, Vocational, Professional or Technical education (AISHE 2018-19). The Indian higher education system is a large system and has seen exponential growth in the last couple of decades in terms of student enrolments as well as in the number of Higher Education Institutions (HEIs). It is second only to China in the post-secondary sector (Nawani, 2019). Though the modern higher education has been largely based on the British model, it inherited the oriental culture, where learning takes place for its own sake, without reference to economic or other external factors (Agarwal, 2010); there have been concerted efforts to break from the British system to a more indigenous system as envisaged by different Policies since 1948.

Structure of Indian Higher Education System

At present, there are following configuration of HEIs are operating in the country:

1. *University/University Level Institutions* – which have degree-granting powers operating under the guidance of UGC.
2. *Colleges/Institutions* – they are institutions which are either affiliated to a University, or are a constituent part of a university, or are given autonomous status as per UGC norms.
3. *Stand-alone Institutions* – institutions which are not affiliated/recognised with University and they are outside the purview of Universities and colleges. They run Diploma level programmes and they require recognition from a Statutory Body.

According to AISHE 2018-19, India's Higher Education (HE) system is divided into the following types of degree awarding institutions:

Principal, Bhavan's Leelavati Munshi College of Education, Bharatiya Vidya Bhavan, New Delhi

1. *Central University:* A University established or incorporated by a Central Act
2. *Deemed University:* A high performing institute which has been so declared by the Central Government under Section 3 of UGC Act, 1956. Deemed universities can be Government or Private (Govt. Aided or Unaided).
3. *Institute of National Eminence:* Institutions established by Act of Parliament and declared as Institutions of National Importance such as IITs (Indian Institute of Technology) and NIT (National Institute of Technology).
4. *State University:* A University established or incorporated by a Provincial Act or by a State Act. State universities may be public or private.
5. *Institute Under State Legislature Act:* An Institution established or incorporated by a State Legislature Act. There are five such Universities: Nizam's Institute of Medical Sciences, Hyderabad; Sri Venkateswara Institute of Medical Sciences, Tirupati; Sher-e-Kashmir Institute of Medical Sciences, Srinagar; Indira Gandhi Institute of Medical Sciences, Patna; Sanjay Gandhi Post Graduate Institute of Medical Sciences, Lucknow.
6. *Other Institute:* An Institution not falling in any of the above categories but established through State/ Central Act and are empowered to award degrees e.g. National Institute of Fashion Technology established through an Act of Parliament.

Levels of Programmes

At present our higher education system offers the following level of Programmes: Under-graduate, Post-graduate, M.Phil., Ph.D., Post-graduate Diploma, Diploma, Certificate, Integrated or dual degrees which can be pursued via Regular/ Formal Mode in either State funded institutions or self-financing institutions and Distance/ Correspondence mode i.e. the distance education mode.

Perspectives in Earlier Policies

History of Higher education in India goes back to the ancient Vedic period which was characterised by Brahmanical and Buddhist systems of education. With the coming of Britishers, a marked differentiation happened in indigenous higher education, which created a class of 'educated' which predominantly served the interests of British rulers; created a class of urban 'elite'. The system was instrumental in creating a huge divide between the urban and rural, men and women, English-speaking and non-English speaking class. It would have been almost impossible to find a rural scheduled caste or scheduled tribe woman studying in a college and there were serious inequalities in the colonial system of higher education (Choudhary, 2008). The need for restructuring the higher education system of the country was felt even before independence, therefore, in order to align the national goals enshrined in the Indian Constitution with the education system, the University Education Commission, under the chairmanship of Dr S. Radhakrishnan was set up, which in its report in 1949 had recommended that the higher education must be placed in the Concurrent List so that minimum standards of university education may be ensured. The Commission envisaged leadership roles for universities. They have to provide leadership in politics and administration, the professions, industry and commerce. They have to meet the increasing demand for every type of higher education, literacy and scientific, technical and professional (knowledge). They must enable the country to attain, in as short a time as possible, freedom from disease and ignorance, by the application and development of scientific and technical knowledge (University Education Commission, 1950). The commission also recommended focusing on research and doing away with 'extreme specialisation' and development of various professional education programmes like medicine, law, agriculture, education, technology etc. As per the recommendation of the Commission, University Grants Commission was set up for coordination and development of the higher education system in India. Most of the recommendations of the commission were accepted; however, it was not until 1976, via the 42nd amendment of the Constitution that university education was placed in the Concurrent List.

One of the most important landmark in Indian education scenario was the Kothari Commission (1964-66), under the chairmanship of Dr. D.S. Kothari, the then Chairperson of UGC, which examined all the critical aspects of education across levels comprehensively; and the report submitted by it became the basis of the first National Policy on Education, 1968. The Commission stressed on the importance of higher education as the most important vehicle for social and economic development of a country; and therefore recommended that a minimum of 6% of Gross National Product must be allocated for education. The report advocated a flexible system of education, a common system for boys and girls, emphasis on science, mathematics, agriculture and allied sciences, work experience, high levels of teaching and research along with focus on Indian values and culture. The Commission also recommended restructuring of courses at the undergraduate level and expansion of higher education to meet the manpower requirements of the country and overall improvement of university education and administration. The commission also stressed on upliftment of women education.

A comprehensive appraisal of the then existing educational scenario was done in 1985 after a process of country wide debate and understanding of the shortcomings in the non-implementation of the recommendations of the Kothari Commission, the National Policy on Education (NPE) 1986, a very comprehensive document, was put in place; which acknowledged the role of education as a unique investment in the present and future (Agarwal, 2010). As regards higher education, the documentation informing the policy expressed great concern regarding the conditions of the colleges and universities so the policy emphasised on consolidation and expansion of facilities. In fact, this policy indicated a major thrust in higher education incorporating expansion of higher education, improvement of the quality of higher education and increased relevance and job orientation in higher education (Mukhopadhyay, 1999 in Choudary, 2008). The policy laid adequate focus on the issues of equality, Women education, Education of Scheduled Castes and Scheduled Tribes and other backward sections of Indian society. NPE 1986 was supplemented with a Programme of Action (PoA) in 1992 which focused on national progress, advances in science and technology, cultivation of moral values and linking education with real life.

Another important landmark in the history of Indian higher education journey is the constitution of a high-level advisory body to the Prime Minister of India, National Knowledge Commission (NKC) in 2005 with the objective of transforming India into a knowledge society under the Chairmanship of Mr Sam Pitroda. The Commission undertook to prepare a blueprint for reform of our knowledge related institutions and infrastructure which would enable India to meet the challenges of the future. The Commission submitted around 300 recommendations on 27 focus areas. Some important recommendation are: creating more universities, changing the regulatory mechanism for higher education, i.e. shift from over-regulated but under-governed system, establishment of Independent Regulatory Authority for Higher Education (IRAHE), increase in the government spending on education as 6% of GDP and on higher education, minimum 1.5% of GDP, establishment of 50 National Universities, reforms to increase the quality of teaching, restructuring of undergraduate colleges, addressing issues of quality and access, focus on quality research and overall administration of Institutions of Higher Education.

Thus, we can see that various commissions and policies have tried to highlight various issues concerned with Indian Higher Education system and have come up with relevant pointers for improvising the system, however as conveyed in the words of Altbach (1993) "the complexity of the social context in which higher education exists (in India) very likely makes systematic reforms impossible" stand relevant even today. The new National Education Policy 2020 attempts to redesign the entire educational scenario and bring more Indianness to our education system across levels with the aim to bring our country on the world knowledge map.

Present Status

Indian Higher Education system is one of the world's largest systems and considering the country's demography and recommendations of NEP 2020, it is expected to expand even further. Higher education has moved from the governmental peripheral interest to a key agenda. Itis now perceived as the most important factor in establishing the country as a knowledge economy. Higher education in India has seen an exponential and impressive growth since its independence in 1947. Overall the number of universities has increased from 28 in 1950 to 993 universities in 2019. The following table gives a glimpse of the growth in the field over the years:

Table 1. Capacity Expansion in Higher Education

Parameters	*1950–51*	*1960–61*	*1970–71*	*1980–81*	*1990–91*	*2000–2001*	*2018–19*
1 No of universities/ university level institutions	28	45	93	123	184	266	993
2 Colleges	578	1819	3227	4738	5748	11,146	39,931 colleges +10,725 stand alone institutions
4 Faculty (in thousands)	24	62	190	244	271	395	14,16,299
5 Students enrolled (in thousands)	174	557	1956	2752	4925	8399	37.399388 million

Source: Agarwal, 2010, Choudhary, 2008 and AISHE, 2018–19.

Expand of Higher Education: As we can see in the table, Indian higher education system has seen an impressive institutional growth since 2000; which has largely happened because of increase in demand for higher education, opening up of the economy since 1991 and the consequent increase in the participation of the private sector in higher education, especially in the field of professional and technical education. At present, as per AISHE 2018-19 report, the system comprises 993 universities, 39,931 colleges and 10,725 stand-alone institutions. There are 47 Central Universities, including one Open University, 127 Institutions of National Eminence, 371 State Public Universities, 5 Institutions under the State Legislative Act, 14 State Open Universities, 305 State Private Universities, 34 Deemed Universities (Government), 10 Deemed Universities (Government aided) and 80 Private Deemed Universities. Of these universities, 110 are Dual mode Universities which offer education through distance as well as regular mode.

In terms of Gross Enrolment Ratio (GER), Economist Martin Trow classified higher education systems worldwide according to their enrolments: 'elite', 'mass' and 'universal' states when the GER ratio is 'less than 15%, between 15 and 50% and more than 50% respectively' (Agarwal, 2010). In this regard, India has made remarkable improvement in the Gross Enrolment Ratio (GER);

higher education which was an 'elite' phenomenon even in the year 2005 (at 11%) grew to 'mass' status at present with GER of 26.3% in 2018-19 (AISHE Report, 2019) which is calculated for 18-23 years of age group. GER for males is 26.3% and for females is 26.4% which is a commendable feat. The policy aims for 'universal' GER for higher education.

College Density, which is defined as the number of colleges per lakh eligible population in the age group of 18-23 years, according to AISHE data is on an average is 28. However, there is a huge diversity state-wise, with as low as 07 in Bihar and 53 in Karnataka.

Social Category wise distribution: According to AISHE data, out of total enrolments, 51.36% are male and 48.64% of the total enrolments are female. Enrolments for Scheduled Castes (SC) is 14.89% and for Scheduled Tribes (ST) is a mere 5.53%. Distribution among male and females and between SC and ST is similar to the national average. Proportion of Other Backward Castes (OBC) is 36.34% out of which 50.83% are males. Among Minority category, 5.23% of the students belong to the Muslim minority and 2.32% are from other minority communities. The data also shows that a total of 85,877 students belong to the Persons with Disability (PWD) category. There is a disparity between male and female distribution among PWD with 48,212 males and 37,665 females. There is no data on the third gender, which is one of the most excluded classes historically, educationally, financially and socially.

Gender Distribution: Overall GER for males is 26.3% and for females is 26.4% which is a commendable feat. In 1950-51 there were only 43 women enrolled in university courses but by 1976-77 they represented 25.8% of the total enrolment for higher education (Choudhary, 2008). But a closer look at total distribution conveys that the ratio of male is greater than female at almost every level except at Post graduate, M.Phil. and certificate level as shown in the following figure. It is also seen that this disparity is spread across all states with only a few exceptions. Though India has come a long way, it is seen that major expansion which is happening in higher education is happening on account of expansion of the private sector; the social and financial dynamics may play a detrimental role for females in the long run.

Growth of Private Sector: Economic reforms of Liberalisation, Privatisation and Globalisation in the 1990s have brought about a kind of revolution in the field of Higher Education. In the periods preceding this phenomenon, opportunities for higher education were severely constrained owing to huge demand and lack of HEIs. Entry of self-financing institutions was and is the need of the hour since 'private higher education provides stark solutions to the dilemma of how to keep expanding access while not expanding public budgets (Levy, 2008 in Agarwal, 2010). The NPE 1986 did not refer to private higher education, however, the two committees that reviewed the policy realised that public spending on higher education is grossly inadequate and a self-financing programme might be a viable solution. This gave legitimacy to full

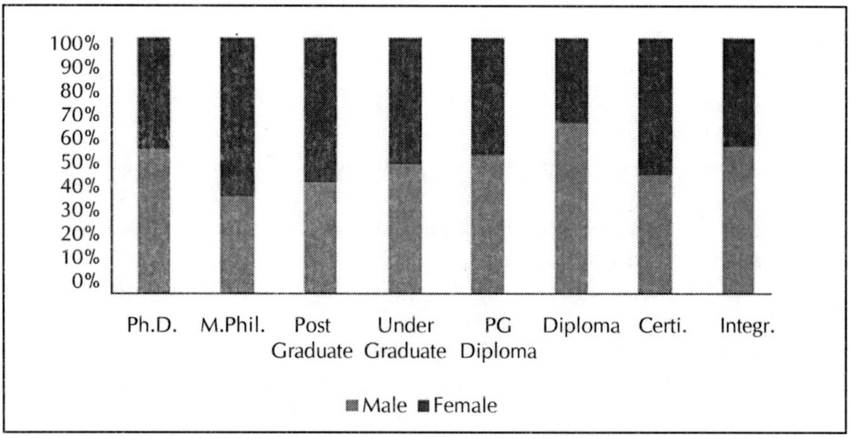

Figure 1. Gender Distribution at various levels (AISHE, 2018-19)

cost recovery from the students particularly in the fields for which parents and the students are willing to pay (Agarwal, 2010). The Planning Commission and National Knowledge Commission also favoured private higher education. At present, there are 385 universities privately managed which comes to around 38% of the total universities. Among colleges, a huge proportion (77.8%) are privately managed, 64.3% are private-unaided and 13.5% are private-aided. Out of total colleges, 34.8% are single programme colleges, out of which 83.1 are privately managed and 38.1% are B.Ed. colleges.

Despite of major achievements Indian Higher Education system faces serious problems which have been highlighted and given due cognizance by the recently announced NEP 2020, which are shown in the Figure 2 below:

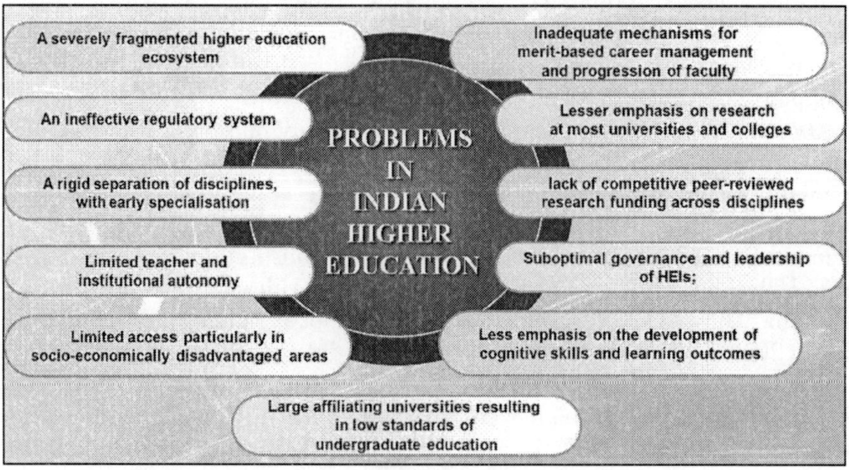

Figure 2. Problems in Indian Higher Education (NEP 2020)

Suggestions Given by National Education Policy 2020

The National Education Policy 2020 has presented a new and forward looking vision for Indian Higher Education System giving a complete overhaul and re-energising of higher education with equity and inclusion, in order to overcome the problems associated with the higher education system. It recognises the role of higher education in inculcation of values at the individual as well as at societal level as upholded in the Constitution, "a democratic, just, socially conscious, cultured and humane nation upholding liberty, equality, fraternity, and justice for all". The Policy endeavours to realise the following Aims and Goals of Indian Higher Education System:

Important Recommendations of NEP 2020

The Policy has given the following recommendations in order to bring about a complete overhauling and re-energising of the higher education system with the objective to overcome the major problems plaguing the system (as mentioned in preceding content):

a) Moving towards a higher educational system consisting of large, multidisciplinary universities and colleges, with at least one in or near every district, and with more HEIs across India that offer medium of instruction or programmes in local/Indian languages;
b) Moving towards a more multidisciplinary undergraduate education;
c) Moving towards faculty and institutional autonomy;
d) Revamping curriculum, pedagogy, assessment, and student support for enhanced student experiences;

Figure 3. Aims of NEP 2020 (w.r.t. Higher Education in India)

Aims of NEP 2020 (Based on 21st Century Skills)	
An Indidual Level	*At Societal Level*
• Developing good, thoughtful, well-rounded & creative individuals • study one or more specialised areas of interest • Development of Character, Ethical and Constitutional Values • Development of intellectual curiosity, scientific temper, spirit of service • 21st century capabilities across range of academic disciplines, professional, technical and vocational areas • Personal accomplishment & enlightenment • Constructive Public engagement • Productive contribution to society	• Development of enlightened, socially conscious, knowledgeable and skilled nation • Basis for knowledge creation and innovation • Creation of greater opportunities for individual employment • Creation of vibrant, socially engaged, cooperative communities • Creation of a happier, cohesive, cultured, productive, innovative, progressive and prosperous nation

e) Reaffirming the integrity of faculty and institutional leadership positions through merit-appointments and career progression based on teaching, research, and service;
f) Establishment of a National Research Foundation to fund outstanding peer-reviewed research and to actively seed research in universities and colleges;
g) Governance of HEIs by highly qualified independent boards having academic and administrative autonomy;
h) "Light but tight" regulation by a single regulator for higher education;
i) Increased access, equity, and inclusion through a range of measures, including greater opportunities for outstanding public education; scholarships by private/philanthropic universities for disadvantaged and underprivileged students; online education, and Open Distance Learning (ODL); and all infrastructure and learning materials accessible and available to learners with disabilities.

Institutional Restructuring and Consolidation

The Policy has put forward a number of dynamic measures of institutional restructuring and consolidation to overcome lacunas in Indian higher education system and make it a composite robust system. The following are the main recommendations:

1. *Large multidisciplinary universities, colleges and Higher Education Institutions (HEI):* The policy envisages transforming higher education's scenario by creating large multidisciplinary universities and colleges or HEI clusters; with a student strength of 3000 or more in each such institution; one in every district of the country; inspired from the ancient universities of Takshashila, Nalanda, Vallabhi and Vikramshila. The aim is to bring back the great Indian tradition of vibrant multidisciplinary environments to create well-rounded and innovative individuals, which will bring transformation on other countries as well educationally and economically. A University is defined as 'a multidisciplinary institution of higher learning that offers undergraduate and graduate programmes, with high quality teaching, research and community engagement. The definition of university will thus allow a spectrum of institutions that range from those that place equal emphasis on teaching and research i.e. Research-intensive Universities, those that place greater emphasis on teaching but still conduct significant research i.e. Teaching-intensive Universities'. An Autonomous degree-granting College (AC) is one which is 'a large multidisciplinary institution of higher learning that grants undergraduate degrees and is primarily focused on undergraduate teaching though it would not be restricted to that and it need not be restricted to that and it would generally be smaller than a typical university'. It is envisaged that by 2030 all HEIs will first plan to

become multidisciplinary; and by 2040 all HEIs shall aim to become large multidisciplinary institutions with enrolments in thousands.

2. *Types of Higher Education Institutions (HEIs):* The Policy in its definition as given above, envisages three broader types of HEIs:
   a. Research-intensive Universities
   b. Teaching-intensive Universities
   c. Autonomous degree-granting Colleges

   It also clearly stated that these three broad types of institutions are not rigid, exclusionary categories, but form a continuum. HEIs will have the autonomy and freedom to move from one category to another, based on their plans, actions and effectiveness.
3. *Accreditation System:* The accreditation system will develop and use different norms for each range of HEIs which will be appropriately different and relevant.
4. *Autonomy to colleges:* It is proposed that a stage-wise mechanism for granting graded autonomy to colleges will be established, through a transparent system of graded accreditation. Colleges will be encouraged, mentored, supported and incentivised to gradually attain minimum benchmarks required for each level of accreditation. Over a period of time, each college will develop into either an Autonomous degree-granting college, or a constituent college of a university (i.e. fully a part of the university).The colleges will have the freedom to decide whether they would want to be Research-intensive or Teaching-intensive Universities; with appropriate accreditations.
5. *Access, Equity and Inclusion:* In order to ensure access and equity, the policy advocates creation of at least one high quality large multidisciplinary HEI in or near every district. Steps are to be taken towards developing quality institutions in both public and private sectors with medium of instruction in local/ Indian languages or bilingual. The policy also looks at increasing the Gross Enrolment Ratio from 26.3% to 50% by 2035.
6. *Growth of Public and Private HEIs:* The policy aims at developing HEIs both in the public sector as well as in the private sector. It also proposes to have a fair and transparent system for determining increased levels of public funding support for public HEIs so that they can grow and develop according to pre-announced criteria from within the accreditation norms. HEIs delivering education of the highest quality as laid down will be incentivised in expanding their capacity.
7. *Open Distance Learning (ODL):* The policy has provided that HEIs will have the option to run ODL and online programmes (provided they are accredited to do so) in order to increase the GER and to provide opportunities for lifelong learning (SDG 4). The policy also states that there will be an equivalence in terms of quality and standards between the programmes run by HEIs in ODL or on-campus programmes. Institutions will be encouraged to programmes in online and blended mode.

8. *Phasing out of affiliated and single-stream colleges:* the policy has laid that single-stream HEIs will be phased out over time and all institutions will move towards becoming vibrant multidisciplinary HEI in order to encourage cross-disciplinary teaching and research across fields. The policy envisages that all HEIs be autonomous institutions with full autonomy: academic and administrative; with a vibrant culture. Also the system of 'affiliated colleges' will be phased out over a period of fifteen years through a system of graded autonomy, to be carried out in a challenge mode. It will be the responsibility of every university to mentor its affiliated colleges so that they can develop their capabilities and achieve minimum benchmarks in academic and curricular matters, teaching and assessment, governance reforms, financial robustness and administrative efficiency, gain accreditation and eventually become autonomous degree-granting colleges.
9. *Integrated and coherent ecosystem of Higher Education:* The policy envisages that Indian higher education system be an overall integrated system including professional and vocational education. The present complex nomenclature of different types of universities viz. 'Deemed to be university', 'affiliating university', 'affiliating technical university', 'unitary university' shall be replaced simply by 'University', which worldwide means a multidisciplinary institution of higher education offering undergraduate, graduate and Ph.D. programmes focused on high-quality teaching and research.

Analytical Thoughts and Roadmap for Implementation

As discussed above, the policy strives to bring about systemic reforms in the Higher Education System. The Policy strives to bring India on the Knowledge map of the world and bring back the glory and reputation it enjoyed in the ancient period with world class institutions like Nalanda, Vallabhi, Takshashila etc. It is not just focused on the ancient past, but also visualises realisation of the global education development agenda reflected in Goal 4 (SDG4) of 2030 Agenda for Sustainable Development. Also, considering the demographic profile, the world is also looking at us. The Indian higher education system is facing an unprecedented transformation in the coming decade. This transformation is being driven by economic and demographic change: by 2020, India will be the world's third largest economy, with a correspondingly rapid growth in the size of its middle classes. Currently, over 50% of India's population is under 25 years old; by 2020 India will outpace China as the country with the largest tertiary-age population (British Council, 2014). The main focus on the Policy is towards creating large, multidisciplinary universities and colleges, with at least one Higher Education Institution (HEI) in every district, offering multidisciplinary undergraduate education with medium of instruction being local/Indian languages, faculty and institutional autonomy, revamping curriculum, funding of peer-reviewed research, governance of HEIs by highly qualified independent boards and 'light but tight' regulation. All the recommendations mentioned are ambitious and noteworthy, but the road map to attain these has not been made very clear in the policy. Some analytical points are discussed below:

1. *'Multidisciplinary' Institutions:* The term 'multidisciplinary' has been used in the Policy multiple times; but the exact meaning is not very clear. There are many questions which remain unanswered like how many streams, subjects, courses, programmes a HEI needs to have in order to be classified as 'multidisciplinary'. As depicted in the data in above pages, a huge majority of institutions are single programmes (34.8% of colleges) and there are around 10,725 Stand-alone institutions, most of which would be running one or two programmes/ courses. As per the recommendations of the NEP, all of these colleges will become autonomous multidisciplinary colleges or universities. What kind of and how many additions in terms of programmes/courses need to be there is not specifically mentioned in the policy. Therefore, though the intent of the policy is good, it leaves a lot of loopholes which may, inadvertently be misinterpreted by various stakeholders; and there is a strong possibility that these colleges may perish. Creating such a multidisciplinary institution in every district of the country and having courses and material in all local/Indian languages is a very challenging task, which needs to be undertaken at a massive scale. The government needs to look into this and must define the term 'multidisciplinary' for the benefit of all.
2. *Enrolments in colleges:* Out of total number of colleges, only 4% of the colleges have enrolments more than 3000 as shown in the Table 2 below:

Table 2. Cumulative number of colleges in different ranges of enrolment (AISHE, 2018–19)

College Enrolment	*Number of Colleges*	*Cumulative %*
0–50	2565	6.7
50–100	3642	16.3
100–200	7579	36.1
200–500	10798	64.4
500–1000	6215	80.7
1000–2000	4335	92.0
2000–3000	1509	96.0
>3000	1536	100.0

As we can see in the Table, 6.7 % of the colleges have less than 50 students enrolled; more than 80% of the colleges have less than 1000 enrolled students. Therefore, it will be expected of the remaining 96% of colleges to increase enrolments to a minimum of the 3000; which can be a humongous task in terms of additional requirement land, building, and other physical and human resources therefore, it may risk closure of many HEI especially the smaller ones with enrolments less than 500. This can be very detrimental for students as well as people working in these institutions. Also, as per the official website of Government of India (india.gov.in), there are 718 districts being governed by respective State/ UT governments. According to the policy, there should be a minimum of 718 HEI, one in each district of the country, with an enrolment of 3000 per HEI, which is a very ambitious goal. Proper planning at the state level by state governments is needed for releasing this aim.

3. *GER* at present is 26.3%, which is to be brought to 50% as per the policy. This would also entail increasing the higher education facilities by almost close to 100%. How and from where the funds are supposed to be catered is something which needs to be looked into; especially in light of having large multidisciplinary institutions and the possibility of closing down many of the existing HEIs owing to not meeting the requirements of either being 'multidisciplinary' or 'large'. Public funds may not be sufficient to bring about expansion at such a large scale, and big organisations in the private sector may not be interested in investing in the higher education sector, owing to 'not for profit' clause for educational institutions. This indeed can be a challenging situation and the government needs to relook at its 'not-for-profit' policies, also endorsed in NEP 2020, so that the required expansion may happen in the public as well as in the private sector.
4. *Autonomy:* The policy also advocates giving autonomy to colleges by phasing out the system of 'affiliated colleges' over a period of fifteen years and having a '*light but tight*' regulated by a single regulator. Understanding the dynamics of Higher education in India especially with the share of the private sector is a staggering 78% (AISHE, 2017-18 data). There have been concerns raised over the high instances of commercialisation and malpractices in higher education by the private sector; giving full autonomy may be a contentious idea; giving impetus to complete commercialisation in the higher education sector. Therefore, it is desired that *an equilibrium* needs to be maintained between the desired autonomy and not fueling complete commercialisation. Also the idea of inviting foreign universities has been raising concerns by different strata; wherein it is being speculated that the top league universities may not be interested in setting up their centres in India, and not so good, commercial universities may attract students and drain financial

resources of the country. Allowing entry of only invited universities may be a feasible idea. Also the dynamics of '*light but tight*' regulation need to be elaborated.

5. *Quality Research and Teaching:* At present, only 2.5% colleges run Ph.D. programmes and 34.9% colleges run Post Graduate Level programmes. GER for Ph.D. programmes is very less which leads to less number of high level researches. Also with around 35% of colleges as single programme colleges, there are very few multidisciplinary and interdisciplinary researches happening.

   Also there is a lack of early stage research. In most of the top universities in the world, students even at the undergraduate level are oriented to the basics of researching and are required to write term papers and conduct small research which needs to be encouraged in our HEIs also. Also, generally, we have a habit of spoon-feeding our students even if they are adults and our students are habitual of being spoon-fed. The publication industry is head over heels racing to cater to and fulfill this 'need' of giving ready-made notes, assignments to our students, which make them less involved with their own learning processes. Therefore, the faculty and the entire system need to reorient students towards joys of learning.

6. *Private Sector:* The share of private sector colleges in higher education is a staggering 77.8% and 64.3% of the colleges are private unaided and only 13.5% of the colleges are private aided colleges. Out of these, a huge proportion of institutions are private unaided, though ostensibly working as not-for-profit organisations, it seems preposterous to assume that they will be operating totally on philanthropic principles. The government needs to acknowledge the role of profitability for HEIs and make policies accordingly. Sheer turning a blind eye to revenue sources of private institutions and assuming them to be operating 'with intent of public sector' is highly unrealistic which has been resulting in a lot of malpractices and exploitation of faculty; giving a bad name to the entire private sector involved in education. The government and the regulatory agencies need to ensure that there should be a parity between the expenditures and fee structures to be charged from the students. The private HEIs have to be self-sustaining and at the same time must be in a position to grow themselves. Proper policies will ensure weeding out of unprofessional institutions and coming of reputed institutions in the field. The government also needs to not distinguish between faculty working in the public or private sector as far as giving resources for research purposes is concerned. NPE 2020 has stressed on setting up of a National Research Foundation (NRF) to facilitate research in all areas by providing 'a reliable base of merit-based but equitable peer-reviewed research funding, helping to develop a culture

of research in the country through suitable incentives for and recognition of outstanding research, and by undertaking major initiatives to seed and grow research at State Universities and other public institutions where research capability is currently limited'. Therefore, in the NEP 2020, the stress is on funding of research only in public institutions and leaving private or self-financing institutions totally out of the purview (which at present is at a staggering 78% as already mentioned above).

7. *Gender Distribution:* According to AISHE data, male-female ratio at each level, it is seen that male is higher than female at almost every level, except M.Phil., Post graduate and Certificate. GER for males is 26.3% and for females is 26.4%. However, the proportion of male teachers is 57.8% and female teachers are 42.2% which indicates 73 female teachers per 100 male teachers. The government data do not share the participation of third gender anywhere, at all! This is something that needs to be looked into. The total absence of any data available on third gender is a pointer towards the height of their exclusion in the Indian society. The policy does not highlight the need for inclusion of the one of the most excluded categories i.e. the third gender into the mainstream; which requires not just resources but also transformational shifts in the perception of people. They have been living on the fringes of the society and it was only in the year 2014 that the Supreme Court of India recognises transgenders as the 'third gender' as a historic judgement and ordered the government to provide quotas in jobs and education in line with other minorities, as well as key amenities by considering them as socially and educationally backward sections of society (Pandey, G, 2014). The Transgender Persons (Protection of Rights) Act, 2019 was passed on 5 December 2019 which prohibited discrimination against any transgender person in educational institutions, employment or occupation, healthcare services and gave people the right to have self-perceived gender identity. As far as data pertaining to their education status is concerned, there are not many studies highlighting the status of education among the third gender persons. But it has been conceded by many trans people, that the high school years and beyond are terrifying. They are teased because their behaviour does not conform to that expected of their sex. Therefore, special efforts need to be taken on the government part and also sensitisation programmes at all levels are required to make them an essential part of our society and educational set-up at all levels.

8. *No of colleges in each district:*
   The policy envisages at least one large multidisciplinary HEI in each district of the country. The data as shown in Table 3 shows a high level of disparity between the spread of colleges among districts in the country. More than 10% of the colleges are present only in top 10 districts with

Table 3. Reproduced from AISHE, 2018-19 data

Top 10 Districts having Maximum Number of Colleges	
Districts Name	*Number of Colleges*
Bangalore (urban)	880
Jaipur	566
Hyderabad	463
Pune	450
Prayagraj	343
Rangareddy	332
Nagpur	313
Mumbai	305
Guntur	298
Bhopal	280

Number of District by College Density	
Number of College	*Number of Districts*
Less than 10	153
10–19	102
20–49	174
50–99	136
100–199	94
200–299	26
300–399	4
400–499	2
500–599	2

Bangalore topping the list with 880 colleges. Most of the colleges run under-graduate programmes, 34.9% of colleges run the post-graduate programmes and only 2.5% of colleges run the Ph.D. level programme.

The following Table 4 shows average enrolment per college in all the states as per AISHE data, which shows that in none of the states, average enrolment as on date is anywhere near the desired 3000. The highest average enrolment per college is in Chandigarh with an average of 2034. This points to a very challenging situation indeed before the government given the aspirations of the policy.

9. *Faculty:* The policy points out that a HEI is known by its faculty since faculty is the backbone of higher education. Having the right content knowledge is important, but equally important is the pedagogy/ Andragogy aspect. But it is seen that pedagogues in various academic and professional higher education courses are not oriented towards basics of Andragogy; therefore the faculty, though knowledgeable, may not be able to make a connection with their students; thereby impeding a good educational environment and nurturing future talent and research. The NEP 2020 is silent on this issue of preparing the HE teachers for their job. Various short-time courses or orientation programmes specially based on Andragogy and use of innovative approaches to teaching should be taken up at regular intervals so that teachers in various higher education institutions are able to make use of innovative approaches like Peer Learning, Collaborative and Cooperative Learning, Group and Individual based Projects and

Table 4. Average Enrolment per College (State-wise) (AISHE, 2018-19)

State/UTs	Average Enrolment per College							
	2011-12	2012-13	2013-14	2014-15	2015-16	2016-17	2017-18	2018-19
1	2	3	4	5	6	7	8	9
India	703	715	742	731	721	659	698	693
Andaman and Nicobar Islands	635	659	937	818	888	904	928	914
Andhra Pradesh	490	473	526	516	494	469	493	524
Arunachal Pradesh	1227	1041	1322	1538	1356	695	810	551
Assam	950	908	883	908	942	917	983	971
Bihar	1929	2018	2060	2081	2142	1801	1686	1616
Chandigarh	1376	1530	1682	1741	1871	1964	2052	2034
Chhattisgarh	474	509	510	511	527	531	550	565
Dadra and Nagar Haveli	619	633	645	662	747	668	690	729
Daman and Diu	196	367	395	366	382	382	336	340
Delhi	1292	1311	1440	1506	1527	1501	1531	1562
Goa	575	582	571	526	560	594	640	700
Gujarat	599	604	626	611	585	536	519	513
Haryana	785	730	698	683	646	514	611	610
Himachal Pradesh	513	484	528	549	520	471	553	558
Jammu and Kashmir	1019	947	745	683	644	646	720	799
Jharkhand	2298	1934	1924	2025	1716	1786	1786	1875
Karnataka	401	436	438	434	438	381	416	426
Kerala	538	555	585	517	521	510	554	568
Lakshadweep	0	0	0	0	0	0	0	0
Madhya Pradesh	551	568	582	576	589	575	646	734
Maharashtra	650	489	540	591	628	646	678	681
Manipur	1117	1069	1194	1105	1070	1002	1156	1039
Meghalaya	927	944	950	960	1087	938	1087	1039
Mizoram	586	678	645	669	653	658	612	603
Nagaland	486	433	433	418	416	463	484	497
Odisha	589	616	565	606	661	682	685	682
Puducherry	459	544	571	566	542	549	569	600
Punjab	730	763	708	668	633	580	576	546
Rajasthan	638	661	665	562	551	443	526	521
Sikkim	994	461	520	537	580	586	737	751
Tamil Nadu	772	816	831	854	895	922	919	924
Telangana		561	606	580	574	483	558	554
Tripura	1036	1003	1009	1134	1097	1207	1156	1153
Uttar Pradesh	1029	1119	1143	1011	920	776	816	743
Uttarakhand	1061	1029	842	726	684	508	621	641
West Bengal	1463	1498	1487	1455	1427	1323	1170	1170

Problem-solving, use of ICT (including MOOCs and OERs) and its tools effectively. Only an orientation towards innovative teaching would not be sufficient, equally important are processes of Assessments. Innovative methods of teaching combined with assessments via traditional testing modes will result in disastrous consequences. Use of ICT, which was considered to be an egalitarian practice a few years back, now, because of COVID 19 crises has become essential and the need of the hour. Therefore, in order to realise the vision of the policy, it is extremely important that the most important factor which decides the success or failure of any educational programme, i.e. the teachers/ faculty are duly oriented; especially since NEP 2020 is looking at dynamically changing the entire landscape of higher education.

10. *Private Sector Financing:* In order to curb commercialisation of education, the policy advocates that 'private HEIs having a philanthropic and public-spirited intent' will be encouraged through a progressive regime of fees determination. The 'not for profit' model is also drawing a lot of flak given the proportion of private players in the field, since this has led to a lot of malpractices and ultimately results in overall exploitation of teachers. The policy is positive towards recognising education as a vehicle for attaining social justice. But the present fee structures do not provide for practical functioning of private unaided institutions in an ethical manner. The basic bottom line should be that fee structures of the colleges should be designed in such a manner that an equilibrium is maintained between the HEIs becomes self-sustaining at least on the operating expenses and day to day expenses like covering of prescribed salaries of teaching and non-teaching staff and other operational and/or maintenance expenses and not being operated for commercial interests. The policy needs to acknowledge the importance of 'surplus' for any institution and must provide avenues so that each and every HEI grows into a bigger multidisciplinary institution as envisaged by the policy.
11. *Separation of Research and Teaching:* the Policy talks of creating two types of HEIs: Teaching intensive and Research intensive. Though the policy highlights that there will be no sharp compartments between the two, and the teaching intensive HEIs can choose to become Research intensive, but this may lead to a separation between the two, which is not desirable. Composite HEI worldwide are those where teaching and research go hand in hand. Therefore, it may not be advisable to create separate silos of 'Teaching HEIs' and 'Research HEIs'.

Conclusion

We can conclude that the NEP 2020 is a highly ambitious policy in terms of its vision and recommended structures in Higher Education in all variants: Fundamental disciplines, Technical, Professional or Vocational education. Most of the intent contained in the policy has positive connotations. But the success will depend on the way the policy is actually transacted on ground. Our earlier policies also have been very good on paper, but implementations have been deficient in many ways. The government and the regulatory bodies need to acknowledge that we are not starting from scratch or a blank slate, we already have a huge system in place and to bring about transformational changes in an already existing system is a very challenging task. The NEP 2020 not only demands huge infrastructural demands but also paradigm shift in thinking and orientation of all involved. We, as citizens of the country can keep our fingers crossed for this policy to transpire on ground the way it is intended to be. Undoubtedly, The Policy needs strong pillars of expansion, equity and excellence to bring about the structural reforms as envisaged.

References

Agarwal, Pawan. 2010. *Indian Higher Education: Envisioning the Future.* Sage Publications India Pvt., Ltd. New Delhi

British Council. 2014. Understanding India: The future of higher education and opportunities for international cooperation. Retrieved https://www.britishcouncil.org/sites/default/files/understanding_india_report.pdf

Choudhary, Sujit Kumar. 2008. Higher Education in India: a Socio-Hostroical Journey from Ancient Period to 2006-07. *Journal of Educational Enquiry*, Vol. & No. 1.

Government of India. (1986). A Report of National Policy on Education. Retrieved from http://mhrd.gov.in/sites/upload_files/mhrd/files/upload_document/npe.pdf on 4th Dec., 2018

Government of India. (1992). A Report of Programme of Action: National Policy on Education. Retrieved from: http://mhrd.gov.in/sites/upload_files/mhrd/files/document-reports/POA_1992.pdf on 5th Dec., 2018

Government of India. 2009. National Knowledge Commission: Report to the Nation 2006-2009. Retrieved https://www.aicte-india.org/downloads/nkc.pdf#toolbar=0

Louise Morley & Barbara Crossouard. 2016. Gender in the Neoliberalised Global Academy: The Affective Economy of Women and Leadership in South Asia, *British Journal of Sociology of Education*, 37:1, 149-168, DOI: 10.1080/01425692.2015.1100529

Meghwal, Arjun Ram. 2020. NEP 2020 is a milestone in India's Journey to becoming a knowledge superpower. Retrieved

https://indianexpress.com/article/opinion/columns/national-education-policy-2020-india-eduaction-system-6576627/

Menon, Shyam. 2020. NEP 2020: What is needed is a new kind of thinking. Retrieved: https://indianexpress.com/article/opinion/columns/new-national-education-policy-nep-2020-6544824/

Ministry of Education. 1949. University Education Commission 1950. Retrieved https://www.educationforallinindia.com/1949%20Report%20of%20the%20University%20Education%20Commission.pdf

Ministry of Human Resource Development. 2019. All India Survey on Higher Education 2018-19. Department of Higher Education. New Delhi. Retrieved from http://aishe.nic.in/aishe/viewDocument.action?documentId=263

Ministry of Human Resource Development. 2020. National Education Policy 2020. Retrieved https://www.mhrd.gov.in/sites/upload_files/mhrd/files/NEP_Final_English_0.pdf on 10th Aug., 2020.

Nawani, Disha. 2020. NEP 2020 fails those trapped in vicious cycles of disadvantage. Retrieved:https://indianexpress.com/article/opinion/columns/national-education-policy-2020-nep-6609564/

Navani, Manasi T. 2019. Gender and Higher Education in India: Negotiating Equity with Access. In Neubauer, Deane E and Kaur, Surinderpal (Edr.). *Gender and the Changing Face of Higher Education in Asia Pacific.* Palgrave Macmillan. Switzerland.

Paranjape, Makarand R. 2020. A new educational policy for India: pitfalls and promises. Retrieved:https://www.dnaindia.com/analysis/column-a-new-educational-policy-for-india-pitfalls-and-promises-2760911

PRS Legislative Research (2017). Standing Committee Report Summary. Issues and Challenges before Higher Educational Sector in India. Institute for Policy Research Studies. New Delhi. Retrieved from http://www.prsindia.org/report-summaries/issues-and-challenges-higher-educational-sector-india on 22nd Aug., 2019.

Pandey, Geeta. 2014. India court recognises transgender people as third gender. *BBC News.* Retrieved https://www.bbc.com/news/world-asia-india-27031180 on 1st June 2020.

Singh, L.C. and Mishra, S. (2008). Self-financing Higher Education: Issues and Concerns. In Gupta, A, Levy, Daniel and Powar, K.B. (Eds). *Private Higher Education– Global Trends and Indian Perspectives.* Shipra Publications. Delhi.

17

Rise and Future of Professional Education in India

Asheesh Srivastava

Genesis of Professional Education

It is very often understood that India is a spiritual country and it cherishes spiritual values with a strong idealistic tendency, yet we need to understand that when India chose to put an agenda for itself, it did not want to go back to a spiritual idealistic past, but wished to move ahead with a strong movement towards progress. It strived for egalitarianism based upon a forward-looking tendency of change, transformation based on science and technology and a place where the values of modernity, individualism, professionalism and progress are well conceived. Thus, the planning, policies and programmes of education were casted accordingly. However, implementation of these policies and educational vision soon became a matter of debate and discussion as we have performed less than expected, desired and needed. In a rapidly changing world which we are now calling a 'global village of the 21st century', we all are very well aware of the words like profession, professional and professional education. If we look back to history precisely in the West, there were three recognised learned professions viz. Theology, Law and Medicine which later got increased by recognising professionals from the fields of architecture, engineering, technology, management. With the increasing recognition of professions, it was witnessed that there are several other occupations that demand disciplined, scholarly and skilful training and thus came under the purview of professions such as dentistry, teaching, journalism, agriculture, forestry and nursing. The list goes on.

So far, as the precise definition of the word profession is concerned, the words profession and professional elude precise definitions. All the humans who have prepared for exacting service by a thorough and disciplined training and scholarship and who live and work in the spirit of professional standards and ethics may well be recognised as a member of a profession. Professional education is the process by which human beings prepare for enacting responsible service, accountable attitude in the professional spirit. The term may be restricted to preparation for fields requiring well-informed, disciplined insight and skill of a high order and therefore less preparation

---

Professor & Dean, School of Education, Mahatma Gandhi Central University, Motihari, Bihar

may be designated as vocational education or occupational education or technical education.

Responsibilities of Professional Education

In the words of Professor Elliot Dunlop Smith, "*If our imperilled civilization is to survive our keenest and most disciplined minds and to a very considerable degree this means other professional men must devote their moral energies and intellectual powers to solving current and long-range problems*". All the so-called civilised and modern people, intellectuals of the society, planners and policymakers of the world are confused, perplexed, puzzled and divided as to why intelligence and education do not bring peace and order. They are concerned as to why democratic constitutions do not bring democracy, why religion does not bring brotherhood, why there is so much chaos and disorder in our so-called global village. To respond to all such concerns one reason may be pointed out as that while professional men are women in a large degree are in key positions in the so-called modern society, professional education has failed in entrusting its larger responsibilities of developing overall principles, philosophy, morality and accountability through which these professional men or women must stand, live and work; even to the extent that their purpose and philosophy lack in true spirits. So, the engineer may be at the service of anyone who will pay him well, regardless of the social worth of his/her services; the lawyer's skill may be for sale for right or wrong; the physician may seek the place of largest income, rather than that of greatest service. While each may have high skill, the total effect may be great internal stress and even social deterioration. The foundation of professional education should not only be related to technical skill or competence but must also imbibe a sense of social responsibility, an appreciation of social, human values, and relationships and disciplined power to see realities without any bias, prejudice or blind commitment. While professional human being largely set the pattern of national life, that pattern is much influenced by their earlier intellectual and moral experiences, especially their professional training. The standards and motives of professional practice in time to come are by and large being made in the present professional schools. Re-educating the professionals to increase their sense of social responsibility is not going to solve the purpose rather the whole process of professional education, for specifically in method and spirit needs serious attention resulting in young human being entering the professions shall be living and working in the spirit of the new India.

As far as professional education is concerned, National Educational Policy 2020 starts with, "*Preparation of professionals must involve an education in the ethic and importance of public purpose, an education in the discipline, and an education for practice. It must centrally involve critical and interdisciplinary thinking, discussion, debate, research, and innovation. For this to be achieved, professional education should not take place in the isolation of one's specialty*". Researches suggest that when professional students are taught the humanistic, social and basic science subjects with the methods of professional education, it increases the power and zest for learning in some measure as compared to that which characterises the shift from the textbook learning of law medicine to the case and clinical methods. Rigid compartmentalisation, stand-alone institutions, rigid separation of disciplines, segregation in expertise are few of the reasons which have affected professional education severely. The problem of professional teaching is one of content as well as diluted pedagogy that has added to the already poorly functioning of professional education. If the professional aspirant can acquire wisely selected basic knowledge and the professional way of thinking which is related to working with representative increments of particular knowledge then the aspirant will be in a position to acquire the particular knowledge to their specific need from time to time along with other necessary skills. If the aspirants can master the art of using fundamental knowledge to get particular knowledge, the amount of particular knowledge s(he) must accumulate is greatly reduced and time is made available for the teaching of fundamentals. However, the reverse is not true. If their time is spent in cramming the facts the very process may make her/him less competent to work with fundamentals. Each practitioner of professional stature knows that human and social problems are inherent in all measures of professional questions which must be dealt with. We must understand that when such problems will be tackled, only then a professional can accept moral responsibility for his own professional conduct and determine for himself what values his technical competence will serve, instead of leaving this to be determined by outsiders.

Since the very early days, Professional Studies are so demanding that until and unless the spirit and habit of seeing the total problem, professional, human and social are in the very spirit and texture of professional pedagogy, human and social considerations will tend to fade into the background with the memories of adolescence. Consequences, in general, will be on losing the human motive and purpose to be part of professional training. We can see a fundamental unity between scholarly thought and professional thought and for the students it is necessary to recognise this unity and therefore teachers must have with the breath of mind and outlook to work out and to use in their courses, common expressions of the common fundamentals of effective thinking and learning. For this reason, various professional schools in higher education institutions might work together at developing these fundamentals. By having such common explorations, the stature and quality of all professional pedagogy might be enhanced. The common basic methods for using fundamental knowledge in solving a particular problem on being applied in widely divergent fields, may become so characteristic of Higher Education Institutions that its students will absorb those methods as one learns the mother tongue. And similar analogies can be made to all professional fields. The professions can understand and cooperate with each other akin to the professional pedagogy, the development of fundamental methods in one profession which will tend to serve all professions.

National Education Policy 2020 has explicitly expressed its concern on agricultural universities, legal universities, health science universities, technical universities. It very clearly says that professional education is an integral part of the overall higher education system and stand-alone agricultural universities, legal universities, health science universities, technical universities, and stand-alone institutions in other fields are a serious concern which must be transformed into multidisciplinary institutions offering holistic and multidisciplinary education. National Education Policy says that all institutions offering either professional or general education will aim to organically evolve into institutions/clusters offering both seamlessly, and in an integrated manner by 2030.

Let us take a few of the aforesaid mentioned concerns of professional education in little detail.

Agricultural Education

If we look back in the historical frame, going back earlier to the eighteenth century, Indian agriculture had an indigenous organisation and structure which quite reasonably served the Indian requirements of the time having more or less self-sustained villages. But the invading of British rule followed by industrial revolution with a profit economy as a general acceptability led the old village structure to almost a breakdown. The strong foundation of Indian agriculture can be best understood in the words of Dr. J.A. Voelcker of the British Royal Agricultural Society, who was sent to study, Indian Agriculture in 1889, who wrote in his report, "*Certain it is that I, at least, have never seen a more perfect picture of careful cultivation, combined with hard labour, perseverance, and fertility of resource than I have seen at many of the halting place in my tour.*" This statement is more than sufficient to understand that the then farmers were well informed and skilled for their very purpose of agriculture. During his visit to India, a conference on 'Agriculture' was held which paved the way for the appointment of agricultural chemists followed by an appointment of Inspector-General of Agriculture and a mycologist after a gap of ten years, later an entomologist was also added in 1903. This was the same time when Pusa Research Institute was established using a donation of 30,000 pounds by Henry Phipps of Chicago. Somehow, it was gaining attention and in the year 1905 'Central and Provincial Departments of Agriculture' were expanded followed by the constitution of 'Indian Agricultural Services' in the year 1906. In spite of all such initiatives, their gross effect on Indian Masses remained to be questionable in debates. Moving ahead, in 1928, a 'Royal Commission on Agriculture in India' was appointed to study agriculture and rural life which presented an exhaustive report on research, marketing, financial credit and rural welfare. It may be a note of interest here that the major recommendation of its outcome was to establish a 'research institution', thereby placing a great emphasis on research. It was of the view that without research support any organisation would be a 'house built on sand' and therefore 'Imperial Council of Agriculture Research' was inducted in 1929. During the first half of the 20th century, agriculture gained some attention, which can be put under the umbrella term 'professional'. A number of developments have provided the beginning of agricultural programmes and policies. During this phase, only twenty-one institutions for higher educational work in agriculture had been established. This is interesting but unfortunate to know that in this period it was informed by heads of agricultural institutions that not more than two or three per cent of the students returned to agriculture communities. It is also interesting to note that the areas where influence of Agricultural Research has been felt were largely those in which industry has so directly connected and therefore the demands of industry affected the overall agricultural practices. Several institutions of interest were established viz. Indian Institute of Fruit Technology, Central Agricultural Marketing Department, Imperial Bacteriology Laboratory, Indian Veterinary Research Institute, Indian Dairy Research Institute, Rice Institute, etc.to name a few so far as research in agriculture is concerned.

What do We Need to do Now?

Keeping in view the insistence of National Education Policy 2020 on converting all stand-alone Institutions into a multidisciplinary University will be paving the way for a more integrated, holistic and professional attitude not only in agriculture but also in all the other branches of disciplines and therefore this is the high time when we need to recognise agricultural education not only with highly professional attitude but also as a major National issue. Study in agriculture must be organised and given high priority from primary education itself to make the future generation aware of its importance on national economic planning. This is a high time when we need to take on board all the persons who have first-hand experience, penetrating knowledge of agricultural life, professional outlook and accountable attitude in the planning and formulating of curriculum, pedagogy, assessment or so to say any other policy related with agriculture. The whole process of agricultural education must be conducted in a true setting, be it a rural or urban setting so that it may include direct participation and experience with agricultural life. Keeping all infrastructure in place will have its immense value so far as output of agricultural education is concerned and therefore without any further delay human resources, physical resources, financial resources, etc. must be given high attention. All the proposed 'Multi-Disciplinary Education and Research Universities' (MERUs) must be equipped with all branches of agricultural education, in particular, to give professional education, in general, all prerequisite resources to make it a real success.

Legal Education

It is a commonly acknowledged fact that Legal Education throughout the globe and especially in Europe and America has long occupied a high niche among the learner and curricula. India also is not an exception so far as the influence of Legal Education on the masses is concerned. As very rightly mentioned by the University Education Commission that, "*in the range of subjects studied in our universities there are some like mathematics and philosophy which are studied for their value as cultural disciplines; others like medicine and Engineering have a definite vocational end in view. Law stands midway between these two groups. There are some who take law as part of a liberal education; others because they wish to enter the legal profession after graduation. Many who would enter public services, International organisations or business concerns would like to read law at the universities.*"

Content and output of the study of Legal education have risen to positions of distinction in public service and therefore Legal education may be seen on an elevated plane and teachers of Legal education enjoy high respect. We can witness many eminent practitioners as well as excellent judges in our surrounding itself who are no other than the output of Legal education which is organised very professionally. It is Legal education only which has also given us great leaders and persons having high social importance. Needless to mention here the most celebrated name of our father of nation (Rashtrapita) Mahatma Gandhi emerged from Legal Education. On the other hand, it is also unfortunate to note that we have very less internationally known expounders of jurisprudence and legal studies. Our very few Institutions of legal studies which hold a place of high esteem, profound scholarship and enlightened research in the field of Legal education are till date do not hold important status globally. The importance of Legal education can be best understood by knowing the fact that faculty of law were among the first established in the early modern universities such as Universities at Calcutta, (now Kolkata), Bombay (now Mumbai) and Madras (now Chennai). However, the opportunity for original and stimulating studies in Legal education hardly existed. Most of our universities set up their colleges of law but they readily succumbed to the general policy of using the universities as training grounds for government services, which we need to change now under the intents of National Education Policy 2020, which says, "*Legal education needs to be competitive globally, adopting best practices and embracing new technologies for wider access to and timely delivery of justice. At the same time, it must be informed and illuminated with Constitutional values of Justice – Social, Economic, and Political – and directed towards national reconstruction through instrumentation of democracy, rule of law, and human rights. The curricula for legal studies must reflect socio-cultural contexts along with, in an evidence-based manner, the history of legal thinking, principles of justice, the practice of jurisprudence, and other related content appropriately and adequately. State institutions offering law education must consider offering bilingual education for future lawyers and judges – in English and in the language of the State in which the institution is situated.*"

Healthcare Education

Formal healthcare education has existed in India for over two centuries. In fact, if we look back at the history, it may easily be observed that even before the universities were instituted in 1857, colleges of medicine granting what were called degrees, were existing three major centres viz. Calcutta (now Kolkata), Madras (now Chennai) and Bombay (now Mumbai). The bulk of the practitioners trained in medicine, however, went through medical schools which were existing in different parts of the country. Some of the schools were being maintained by the state, while others were under the control of private agencies largely missionaries. This was the same time when we deviated from the indigenous knowledge of India, which used to exist in different forms. The Healthcare education was narrowed down in many ways as the existing schools of the time we are intended to train a set of practitioners who would function as assistants and would have no individual responsibility in the treatment of any of the major complaints and therefore only a set of people who were known as hospital assistants, latter known as sub-assistants were created. These sub-assistants were given training for a duration of four years restricted to the subjects of clinical interest only. In the later years, medical schools revisited there curricula and gradually tried to improve on them. So far as the degree courses in Healthcare education is concerned, some of the Indian institutions had two different grades, the L.M.S. and the M.B.B.S. Entry to both of the courses remained the same. Equivalence, parity and the relevance of the different programmes leading to degree, diploma or certificate started having certain dichotomies and inconsistencies and therefore General Medical Council made its entry in order to ensure recognition and standards at different levels. Soon, General Medical Council was resented by Indian universities. Controversies were increasing day by day and therefore Indian Medical Council was established in the year 1931 with the objective of laying down minimum standards for qualification and teaching. The demand for Healthcare education was increasing rapidly which posed a pressure so far as the number of individuals entering into the Healthcare institution is concerned. This resulted in a demand to increase the number of Healthcare institutions. We all are aware that the establishment of a Health Care institution by no means is an easy task as apart from financial implications it needs to address the need of highly professional, trained and experienced personnel. After independence, India has taken a giant leap by establishing many highly equipped healthcare institutions throughout the country, however, lack of number in having such institutions is a matter of great concern even till date. Medical education has expanded greatly by entering into several specialisations across the discipline of medicine itself. The overall situation regarding health care education as well as institution has become a matter of great concern even in 21st century and therefore National Education Policy 2020 must be incorporated in letter and spirit when it says that, "*Healthcare education needs to be re-envisioned so that the duration, structure, and design of the educational programmes need to match the role requirements that graduates will play. Students will be assessed at regular intervals on well-defined parameters primarily required for working in primary care and in secondary hospitals. Given that people exercise pluralistic choices in healthcare, our healthcare education system must be integrative meaning thereby that all students of allopathic medical education must have a basic understanding of Ayurveda, Yoga and Naturopathy, Unani, Siddha, and Homeopathy (AYUSH), and vice versa. There shall also be a much greater emphasis on preventive healthcare and community medicine in all forms of healthcare education.*"

Technical Education

National Education Policy 2020 says that, "Technical education which includes degree and diploma programs in Engineering, Technology, Management, Architecture, Town-planning, Pharmacy, Hotel Management, Catering Technology etc. are critical to India's overall development", and therefore we need to be very cautious so far as planning and execution of technical education.

Engineering Education

If we look back to history, we can see that engineering education, unlike other types of professional education, does not have a long history. Having said this, we are not overlooking the period of ancient and mediaeval India which had numerous monuments that can be put under Civil and Hydraulic engineering, as a part of empirical knowledge only. The formal branches, in addition to the classical branches (Civil and Mechanical) also emerged as professional discipline in the 19th century. It now included, civil engineering, viz. architectural, building and construction, irrigation, sanitary, railway, civil, mechanical engineering viz. aeronautical, railway mechanical, automotive, electrical engineering viz. communications, chemical engineering viz. ceramics, fuel technology, metallurgical, mineral processing, petroleum; geological engineering viz. mining, geophysical prospecting; public health engineering, industrial management, industrial engineering, agricultural engineering etc.to name a few. As we all know that technology and engineering are products of fundamental discoveries in basic sciences, and it is also well known that these developments started taking shape in late 19th century and in 20th century which witnessed greater variety than ever before, therefore in independent India, a dire need was felt to groom the generation squarely and professionally so far as different branches of engineering education is concerned. However, the number and quality of such institutions is a matter of great concern even till today. This is the high time when we need to understand that effective engineering education requires work experience for practice along with academic history and therefore, we need to integrate it very carefully and meaningfully.

Technological Education

The technological institutions in pre-independent India were used to tackle with chemical, textile, leather, mining, dyes, applied chemistry, plastics and paints, oil, pharmacy, food and drugs, glass and ceramics, sugar technology, metallurgy, Aeronautical, Applied Physics, etc. These institutions were of different types, some were part of universities, some were polytechnics and others of a lower standard but in post independent India scope of technological education expanded rapidly and started to be delivered through the variety of institutions, however, number, scope, quality, performance and output of majority of such institutions soon became a matter of concern.

Management Education

In the last few decades, management institutions have burgeoned in the country rapidly in particular and worldwide in general. The multi-national companies actively seek out management graduates to fill its rank and file and groom them to become future leaders. This has led a vast majority of Indian students aiming to get degree in 'Management Education' to make their career in this field and therefore, management education received high retention, as a result world class institutions in the form of Indian Institute of Management were established in different parts of India. However, to cope up with the masses infiltration of poorly planned and managed institutes for providing management, education spoiled the spirit of management education. In the past few decades, we have witnessed thousands of stand-alone institutions providing management education. In the era of liberalisation, privatisation and globalisation well planned and executed management education is the need of the hour, integration of stand-alone institutions into a multidisciplinary institution will be of immense value in this regard.

Hotel Management

There are numerous college and university programmes throughout the country and the world-at-large offering two and four-year undergraduate degrees in hotel management and tourism preparing students for hospitality industry careers. Educating future hotel managers and executives poses a greater challenge, given the number of different operational segments included under the rubric of hospitality industries. All unique entities share common hospitality and tourism elements: restaurants, hotels, travel, attractions, conventions, and leisure. For industry-based programmes such as hospitality, part of a student's experience and collegiate preparation includes practical experience and an understanding of how the industry operates in a professional setting. To garner industry exposure and experience for students, many collegiate programmes offer internships or cooperative-learning experiences to provide valuable experience within controlled and monitored industry, for students to be successful, hotel management programmes must meet the needs of both students and industry, developing skill sets needed in the industry while achieving the academic rigour demanded by institutions. Students may be encouraged to obtain industry-based skills beyond an internship by holding a part-time job while completing their studies; students and graduates who do not gain extra experience may be inadequately prepared for the work and demands of the hospitality industry.

Catering Technology

We all understand that Catering technology stands for the application of science to the art of catering, which is an integral part of hotel, restaurant, online demands, etc., and therefore for this purpose catering is taken to mean the feeding of people in large groups and includes restaurants, hotels, work canteens, school's canteen, hospitals, train's pantry, etc. which suggest us its inherited strength for professional outlook which is needed to take care of its overall functioning.

Conclusion

For the last more than two centuries the so-called modern society is advancing having plenty of branches of specialisation, with specific reference to post-independent India in general and post LPG era in particular, needs and demands are rapidly varying and therefore, National Education Policy 2020 rightly emphasised, when it says, *"There will not only be a greater demand for well qualified manpower in these sectors, it will also require closer collaborations between industry and higher education institutions to drive innovation and research in these fields. Furthermore, the influence of technology on human endeavours is expected to erode the silos between technical education and other disciplines too. Technical education will, thus, also aim to be offered within multidisciplinary education institutions and programmes and have a renewed focus on opportunities to engage deeply with other disciplines. India must also take the lead in preparing professionals in cutting-edge areas that are fast gaining prominence, such as Artificial Intelligence (AI), 3-D machining, big data analysis, and machine learning, in addition to genomic studies, biotechnology, nanotechnology, neuroscience, with important applications to health, environment, and sustainable living that will be woven into undergraduate education for enhancing the employability of the youth."*Therefore, all possible linkages between industry and higher education institutions must be explored followed by a deterministic approach towards a strong sense of profession, professional education and committed professional attitude.

References

Rao, D.B.: *National Policy on Education: Towards on Enlightened and Human Society.* Discovery Publishing House, New Delhi, 2005.

Rao, K.S. (ed.): *Educational Policies in India: Analysis and Review of Promise and Performance.* NIEPA, New Delhi, 2002.

Reddy, G.S. (ed.): *Current Issues in Education.* Neelkamal publication, Hyderabad, 2007.

Rai, B.C.: *History of Indian Education and Problems.* Prakashan Kendra, Lucknow 1999.

Rawat, P.L.: *History of Indian Education.* Ram Prasad & Sons, Agra, 1953.

Chandola R.P.: *The Real Problems of Indian Education.* Book Enclave, Jaipur, 2003.

Chandra, S.S.(ed.): *Indian Education; Developments Problems, Issues & Trends.* R. Lal Book Depot, Meerut, 2002.

Graves, F.P.: *A History of Education (Vol. 2).* Vidya Vihar, Kanpur, 1993.

Garg, B.R.: *Policy Document on Indian Education.* The Associated Publishers, Ambala, 2001.

Govt. of India: *The Report of University Education Commission.* 1948-49. Published by Govt. of India Press.

Govt. of India: *The Report of Indian Education Commission,* 1964-66. Published by Govt. of India Press.

Govt. of India: India Vision 2020: The Report. Planning Commission, Govt. of India. Published by Academic Foundation, New Delhi, 2004.

Kaushik, V.K.: *Principles of Education.* Anmol Publication, New Delhi, 2001.

Ministry of Education: *Challenges of Education: A Policy Perspective.* Published by Ministry of Education, 1985.

MHRD: *National Policy on Education* 1986. Published by MHRD, 1986.

MHRD: *National Policy on Education* 2020. Published by MHRD, 2020.

18

NEP's Vision on Strengthening Adult Education and Lifelong Learning

Nisha Singh

Whenever anyone talks of an Adult– a picture of a mature, supposedly responsible, independent person pops up in our mind. As human beings, we go through four stages of development – childhood, teenage, adulthood and old age. Adulthood is the stage where a person spends most of his/her life. It is the longest, most productive and directional stage of one's life wherein blooming of a flower takes place. Thus, if we look across the evolution of human civilisation, this stage has contributed to growth, transformation and transmission of cultures over the ages. In fact, the more innovative the adults of the society were, the more progressive and stronger had that historical period been. As we say, education is a never-ending process, therefore, to put it simply, the entire education received by, and spread over the adulthood of any individual is nothing but adult education. A question that may be bothering you could be why we should talk of adult education as education is a lifelong process and all efforts for teaching children have been done since time immemorial. If children get education, why are we talking of adult education? If it is the higher education given in colleges and universities to the youths, then why do we have to call it adult education? The probable answer is though the age group of some may be the same as in higher education, adult education comprises efforts to teach groups of people who have missed the bus of educational opportunities as a child.

Adult education is a practice in which adults engage in systematic and sustained self-educating activities in order to gain new forms of knowledge, skills, attitudes, or values. Adult education is distinct from child's education as the way adults process knowledge is different from how children do it. Therefore, the methodology used to teach children, called pedagogy, cannot be applied to adults. The age and maturity level of adults matter when we are devising ways of teaching and learning. For example, the way we teach school children is different from college or university learners. In the same way, the teaching methodology of the adults is different and is known as Andragogy.

Adult education takes its meaning from the fact that even in the last census, in 2011, the number of illiterates (7+ age group) was 282.70 million which was a decrease from census 2001 figures of 304.10 million. If we look at the

Deputy Director, Centre for Onlie Education, IGNOU

literacy figures in our country as per the latest Census (2011), we do see a good percentage of above 70% as it stands at 72.98%, a good jump of 8.14% over the figure of 64.84% in 2001. Three states/union territories achieved the literacy rate of more than 90% which is really commendable: Kerala (94%), Lakshadweep (91.85%) and Mizoram (91.33%). There are rural (67.77%)-urban (84.11%) disparities beside the gender and other disparities in literacy rate.

Though the male literacy rate has grown less than female as it has been 5.62 per cent points (75.26% in 2001 and 80.88% in 2011) whereas female literacy rate 10.96 per cent points (53.67% in 2001 and 64.63% in 2011), but still the female literacy lags behind male literacy by 8 points.

Adult education and lifelong learning have continuously strived to eradicate illiteracy from our country. Let us try to look at some efforts through the policy.

Adult Education in our Policies

Independence gave wings to all our dreams and education was one of them. Education is looked upon as a means to all round development and the children are looked upon as the future of any country. Therefore, the major thrust in the educational policy and initiatives in the first three decades of planning and vision for the education system was the growth in the formal system of education. Elementary education was focused and through it the future of India was being insured. It was implied that the education of children will take care of adult education as these children mature. Thus, the issue of adult education was hoped to be solved in the investment in education of children.

It was only after 1977 that policy makers took into consideration that if illiteracy has to be eradicated, we must also address the other side of the spectrum as well, i.e. adults, thus focus came on literacy of adults as well. National Adult Education Programme (NAEP) (Ministry of Education and Social Welfare, 1979) was initiated for the illiterates of the age group of 15-35 years for a period of six years (1978-84). The focus of NAEP was not merely literacy but social awareness as well. It was envisaged to be implemented through voluntary agencies, educational institutions (universities and colleges), local bodies (for example, panchayats and municipalities) and the central and state governments with administrative and organisational support at all levels. As often happens with mass level programme planning, the implementation goes amiss, so happened with NAEP and it became rather limited as an Adult Education Programme (AEP) without achieving any significant dent in eradicating illiteracy as envisaged. It was the year 1986 the National Policy on Education (NPE), (and its revised version in 1992) wherein we see the emergence of a serious and systematic approach to address adult education. The plan aimed to eradicate adult illiteracy in a planned, systematic and concerted manner. It widened the scope of Adult education to provide flexible learning opportunities to out of school youth and adults. It made provisions for non-formal vocational education and training for workers of the unorganised sector through the existing institutions and agencies like Industrial Training Institutes (ITIs) and for divergent groups (workers, youth, farmers, etc.) to upgrade their knowledge and skills to improve their productivity and their skills. It gave impetus to continuing education for neo-literates, school dropouts and even for higher levels of formal education through advocating distance and open learning.

It was felt after NPE that a mission mode is required to eradicate illiteracy. It was in 1988 that the National Literacy Mission (NLM) was launched to impart functional literacy to 80 million adult illiterates in the age group 15-25 years. This was again a diverse group and emphasis was made for women, scheduled castes and scheduled tribes and other disadvantaged groups through mass mobilisation and support of the wider sections of society. It was not merely the three R's but also developmental literacy with social awareness, values like national integration, environment conservation and also acquisition of relevant skills for productive life. Success in the adult literacy campaign in Ernakulam district in Kerala in 1990 under NLM programme led to adoption of the campaign approach and Total Literacy Campaign (TLCs) was introduced. It was based on conviction and assumption that an intensive campaign approach will ring in total eradication of illiteracy. The strong and unique features of TLC strategy were in its use of local ways for mass mobilisation like use of Kala Jathass, personal contact, radio and television, folk media so that the need for literacy emerged in the society. Thus, a decentralised approach both administrative and organisational through Zilla Saksharata Samiti was roped in. These samitis were also responsible for internal evaluation of Learning Outcomes as per the NLM norms wherein functionaries and volunteers were actively involved.

In 1999, the NLM adopted a sustainable threshold literacy rate (75%) and expansion of continuing education programmes to cover all districts by 2007. The ninth and the tenth Plan strategised the NLM approach for sustainable functional literacy and its matching with the Education for All (EFA) 2000 Dakar Declaration wherein education for all was the goal across the world. Now with the effectiveness of TLC, the percentage of the adult literate population was increasing. At this stage some changes were observed like the volunteers were replaced by paid workers and people's movement character faded away. TLC at this time became more or less like other target oriented programmes. Thus, the post literacy phase came in under a project called 'Literacy Campaigns in Operation Restoration'. It was looked at as a seamless integration of TLC to post literacy programmes so that it becomes one learning continuum. This was further linked to continuing education programmes wherein the whole initiative of adult literacy was linked with real life situations through imparting relevant technical and vocational skills.

The NLM went for expansion through creation of State Literacy Mission Authorities for sanctioning literacy-related and continuing education projects thus adopting decentralisation especially in administrative and financial aspects. NGOs were continued to be roped in for environment building for TLC and also in continuing education programmes. Also, State Resource Centres (SRCs) were strengthened for a larger role in continuing education programmes. Similarly, the activities of the Jan Shiksha Sansthan (JSS) were also made to act as repositories of vocational/technical skills in urban and rural areas for the adult literacy as well as the youth and workers.

So in short, the steps taken for adult education took baby steps through the National Literacy Mission (NLM) from 1988-2009, wherein Saakshar Bharat Programme (2009 -2017) was launched to make it a more comprehensive programme which aimed to go beyond the '3' R's (i.e. Reading, Writing and Arithmetic). Besides functional literacy and continuing education, it also aimed to create awareness of social disparities and a person's deprivation on the means for its amelioration and general well being. The objective of this programme was achieving 80% literacy level at national level, by focusing on adult women literacy seeking to reduce the gap between male and female literacy to not more than 10 percentage points. The four objectives which it focused on were extension of earlier literacy programmes: i) imparting functional literacy and numeracy to 70 million non-literate adults in the age group of 15 years and beyond especially of women, SC, ST, minorities and others; ii) acquiring equivalency to formal educational system; iii) imparting relevant skill development programme; and iv) promote a learning society by providing opportunities for continuing education. The targets were 410 districts belonging to 27 States/UTs of the country. (https://www.mhrd.gov.in/saakshar_bharat).

And the most recent being the Padhna Likhna Abhiyan is a leap forward for achieving the goal of total literacy by 2030. It is a new scheme with Centre and States collaborating to reach the target group of 57 lakh learners for making them literate in financial year 20-21wherein centre's share is Rs. 148.74 crore and State has share of Rs. 76.2 crore. The distinguishing features of the scheme are:

- Basic Literacy component in a four months cycle; priority will be given to aspirational districts.
- Both rural and urban areas, target and budget. States/UTs will distribute targets to Districts.
- Flexible approach and innovative methodologies such as involving school and college students and other volunteers of NCC, NSS and NYKS, for imparting Basic Literacy.
- Project Approval Board (PAB) at the national level to approve the Annual Plans of States/UTs. Secretaries of Education will present their Annual Plans, based on district plans, on the portal being developed by NIC, in the PAB meetings.
- Convergence with projects of M/o Rural Development (MGNREGA), Skill Development, Culture, Information Technology, Finance, Sports

and Youth Welfare (NYK), schemes of NCC and NSS, NGOs/Civil Society and CSR sector may be taken up.

- Formation and involvement of SHGs, Voluntary and User Groups and other community based organisations may be encouraged.
- Basic Literacy Assessment under the scheme will be conducted by National Institute of Open Schooling (NIOS) for adult learners, thrice a year.(http://seshagun.gov.in/adult-education)

The policies and the government have been striving for literate India and it looks achievable if concerted efforts are taken. The National Education Policy (NEP) 2020 is a vision document which has come to give a meaningful direction to all fields of education.

National Education Policy 2020

The NEP 2020 is a vision document and intertwines all the aspects of education for a growing, glowing India. The adult literacy finds its first mention in Chapter 3.0 wherein the policy talks of ODL programmes at school level by NIOS and SIOS to address adult literacy (3.5, NEP). Also, when talking of HEI offering teacher education programmes, it encourages HEI to network with schools, both government and private in adjacent areas so that prospective teachers can also participate in adult education programmes. A whole chapter (21) is dedicated to Adult Education and Lifelong Learning. It begins with utmost and urgent need for foundational literacy, education and abilities to pursue a livelihood as basic rights of a citizen. This reflects on the acknowledgement of the undeniable role of literacy and education in a human being's life, irrespective of the age. The functional literacy of childhood if missed due to any reason should not be the reason for being lagged behind throughout life. Literacy and basic education though appear to be individual matters but have a larger perspective as it is a nation's loss as well. Literacy opens up a world of knowledge, new learning opportunities and the way a person interacts with knowledge brings in innovations which have individual and commune benefits. Literate persons tend to make informed choices for collective goals. The NEP (21.1) also talks "At the level of society and the nation, literacy and basic education are powerful force multipliers which greatly enhance the success of all other developmental efforts. Worldwide data on nations indicate extremely high correlations between literacy rates and per capita GDP"

Having established the need for literacy for development, it categorically and elaborately talks about the disadvantages of illiteracy in real life; how a person is at loss in all domains of life and is bereft of the benefits the technology interlaced in the modern-day society. Policy document simply builds a picture of society today and how being literate is essential for one's own growth and development (section 21.2). To be able to overcome the disadvantages, it also hints at the state to adopt innovative measures for adult education. Over the years, the adult education has been seen as teaching adults the way children are taught. The way the teaching-learning process of adults is designed is discussed under Andragogy and needs to be practised.

The policy document credits the involvement of the community, the spirit of volunteerism and mobilisation (21.3) in the success of the adult literacy programme. This has been recorded by extensive field studies and analyses, both in India and across the world (NEP 2020). This when supported by the governments with proper planning, financial support, organisational structure had been very effective, involvement and commitment of volunteers. It is so rightly said that "Successful literacy programmes result not only in the growth of literacy among adults, but also result in increased demand for education for all children in the community, as well as greater community contribution to positive social change". The role of 'The National Literacy Mission' was also appreciated for significant rise of literacy in India "when it was launched in 1988, was largely based on the voluntary involvement and support of the people, and resulted in significant increases in national literacy during the period of 1991–2011, including among women, and also initiated dialogue and discussions on pertinent social issues of the day".

The NEP in the field of adult education and lifelong literacy clearly outlines steps as a directional way to go for 100% literacy. The policy asks the governments to take "strong and innovative" initiatives (21.4, NEP) for adult education using two of the most powerful ways-community involvement and integration of technology. In the entire NEP document, the technology role in ensuring effectiveness and efficiency of any system is reflected. The vision in the document is futuristic.

The Steps proposed by NEP 2020 are:

First Step: Realising and appreciating the role of NCERT in education of children in India, the policy calls for NCERT role in Adult education. It suggests the creation of a new and well supported constituent body of NCERT, dedicated to Adult Education. The proven efficiency of NCERT, its huge and wide ranging pool of expertise should be roped in to develop an adult education curriculum framework. NEP at the same time praises the existing expertise of NCERT in drafting curricula for the children of the nation. This is very important as it will give a structured guideline to the coverage of literacy, numeracy, basic education, vocational skills and other relevant areas (21.5, NEP). It further suggests that the Adult Education Curriculum Framework should cover a minimum of the five types of programmes with clearly defined outcomes:

(a) foundational literacy and numeracy;
(b) critical life skills (including financial literacy, digital literacy, commercial skills, health care and awareness, child care and education, and family welfare);

(c) vocational skills development (with a view towards obtaining local employment);
(d) basic education (including preparatory, middle, and secondary stage equivalency); and
(e) continuing education (including engaging holistic adult education courses in arts, sciences, technology, culture, sports, and recreation, as well as other topics of interest or use to local learners, such as more advanced material on critical life skills).

A close look at these areas show us that a comprehensive and all-round development is being envisaged at the adult level. The adults may have missed the education at their younger stage in spite of all the initiatives by the government– like they were not fortunate to get education at the right age of childhood. But nobody should be left behind and thus even in adult age, the goodness of a holistic curriculum should not be missed. Here in the teaching-learning processes should be adult based i.e. andragogy should be applied and not the pedagogy. As this was the element missing earlier, NEP says "The framework would keep in mind that adults in many cases will require rather different teaching-learning methods and materials than those designed for children."

Second step recommended by NEP (21.6) is the next logical one with infrastructure which should not be merely name sake. Appropriate infrastructure is almost basic to the success of any academic endeavour and should be made available to anyone, in this case interested adults who want to be educated should have access to welcoming and simple infrastructure for adult education and lifelong learning. Now how to get the infrastructure, where to establish and, of course, the budget.

NEP does not leave the question unanswered and recommends the optimum use of already available infrastructure in the country. It recommends "to use schools/ school complexes after school hours and on weekends and public library spaces for adult education courses which will be ICT-equipped when possible and for other community engagement and enrichment activities."

Sharing of infrastructure will not burden the budget allocation and at the same time will bring in the spirit of interdependence and efficiency. The school, higher, adult, and vocational education, and for other community and volunteer activities should ensure "efficient use of both physical and human resources as well as for creating synergy among these five types of education and beyond". Thus, the Adult Education Centres (AECs) should be created within other public institutions such as HEIs, vocational training centres, etc. (21.6, NEP).

Third step suggested by NEP is the main force behind the success of the Adult education programme, i.e. the educators or the instructors. They will be the ones who will be transacting the deftly designed curriculum to mature learners, they will be implementing the five types of adult education and how they do it is pivotal for the success of the whole programme. The instructors will not be effective if they are not adequately trained, so need to be trained. NEP suggested that it should be done by "National, State, and district level resource support institutions to organise and lead learning activities at Adult Education Centres, as well as coordinate with volunteer instructors" (NEP, 21.7). It should not be left to the designated resource centres but the HEIs and other qualified persons should be roped in in the cause of adult education and lifelong learning. These interested and committed people should be encouraged and organising "short training courses" could make them more apt as adult education instructors. As volunteers they can make the movement a success and "will be recognised for their critical service to the nation". It is like looking deeply around and catching on to all the ways, opportunities and organisations like NGOs and other community organisations to work for adult education and lifelong learning.

Fourth step as the policy unfolds is to ensure that the community is involved. As already mentioned, until the community support is elicited. As in transportation we try to bridge the last mile connectivity similarly in adult education we should also capture the strength of community leaders, community and social workers to identify the persons in need of adult education and lifelong learning. The identified data about the adults who are illiterate or have dropped out of the earlier efforts to educate is shared with AECs and the connection between the two –the educational abode and the persons in need of the education –are connected. In this, the local AECs have a very crucial role to play. They have to provide a welcoming warm environment for the adult learners who may be reluctant, wary and not interested in the education. This may be due to many reasons. Also, the obvious question as to how it will help them, needs to be answered by linking it to a better quality of life. The NEP in 21.5 has clearly mentioned it to be linked to vocational skills and thus livelihood. An adult learner's foremost interest is livelihood for oneself and the family. So if vocational skills and its link to livelihood is provided, it will have more impact on the movement. Also having some kind of alumni group which can set a living example of how adult education and lifelong learning has added value to their lives will be more motivating than other things.

As today is the time of media and advertisements, this medium should also be used as quoted in NEP, 21.8) "Opportunities for adult education will also be widely publicized, through advertisements and announcements and through events and initiatives of NGOs and other local organizations".

Fifth step is inculcating the habit and culture of reading. This is equally important at a young age and has been emphasised for young children at school stage too in the document. It happens that schools and colleges have stock of books and it is not thought about in case of adult learners.

The NEP suggests "improving the availability and accessibility of books" (21.9, NEP) within reach of adult learners like the community, associated educational institutions. which will help in inculcating the habit of reading in adult and lifelong learners. NEP (21.9) recommends that "all communities and educational institutions – schools, colleges, universities and public libraries – will be strengthened and modernized to ensure an adequate supply of books that cater to the needs and interests of all students, including persons with disabilities and other differently-abled persons". As it is an all-encompassing endeavour, the central and state governments should guarantee the accessibility of age and level appropriate books across the country. Efforts should ensure nobody, no area, no section is left out. It should be like that for everyone at any place.It may not be as easy as it may sound, it will need the collective strength of both public and private sector agencies/institutions. This can only be implemented in true spirit if we have attractive and good literature published in all Indian languages. One would agree that ensuring availability of good interesting attractive literature in local and Indian languages attracts young minds to read rich text. The planning of strategies to improve the quality and attractiveness of books published in all Indian languages should be taken up. The world of online can help in strengthening the libraries. The world of Open Educational Resources (OERs) can also be used to enrich the libraries. These are free and open source educational material for anyone to access and get benefitted from. There are many initiatives by the Government of India to make books available through one single portal. The National Digital Library (NDL) is one such initiative. It is full of books for all levels. These initiatives should be extended to adult education and lifelong learning too.

NEP talks of "vibrant libraries in communities and educational institutions, it will be imperative to make available adequate library staff and also devise appropriate career pathways and CPD for them. Other steps will include strengthening all existing libraries, setting up rural libraries and reading rooms in disadvantaged regions, making widely available reading material in Indian languages, opening children's libraries and mobile libraries, establishing social book clubs across India and across subjects, and fostering greater collaborations between educational institutions and libraries".

Sixth and final step, the NEP reiterates the strengths and the advantages of using technology to reach the unreached. All the initiatives should be made stronger by capturing all kinds of affordable technology. As today is the time of modular learning opportunities, app-based reach, satellite-based TV channels, online repositories, books and many such technology based connect to reach the target. Similarly, all these should be explored and made available for adult education and lifelong learning in AECs. Let it be equipped with these "Quality technology-based options for adult learning" (21.10). The new world has shown us ample examples where philanthropic initiatives, crowd funding and other such innovative initiatives have been used to fund the common good. The government support should always be provided for these AECs to be continuously trying to achieve the goals of adult education and lifelong learning.

Conclusion

Adult education and lifelong learning, though appear to be niche areas of discussion in academic circles, have a very crucial role in the development of India. It is by addressing this domain that we can achieve total literacy. Total literacy is not merely ornamental and tag but has implications in society. Informed choices for selection of government being the basic to good governance. The rights, roles and responsibilities will be better understood if the non-literates will not have to depend on others for interpretation of policies, rules and so on. Of course, with 72% literacy we should have been a in a better governed, more rationale society, whereas we see decline of social values, intolerance and other evils in society, so though adult education will not be a magic wand and once achieved, we will enter Ram Rajya or a fairy land or Utopia. But it is a step towards all round development of an adult so that a dignified, humane existence can be achieved. The NEP very carefully points of five areas which if we look carefully covers all angles of a dignified human existence.

19

Governance and Leadership in Higher Education

Saroj Sharma and Akshita Bahuguna

Education is a chariot which takes the nation to the journey for overall development. Education is considered to be a powerful instrument of bringing desirable changes for the betterment of the society and world. Hence, it is indispensable to individuals and Society.

The National Education Policy 2020, which is on the fore, now provides insight for reforms at all levels of education from school to higher education. With increased focus on following key aspects:

1. India Centric Education
2. Sustainability
3. Access
4. Equitable
5. High Quality.

The policy also points towards transparency, accountability, community participation, social integration, research and innovation, critical thinking and analytical ability, public financial management reforms and development. The overall vision tries to develop synergy between school education, teacher preparation and higher education with overhauling the complete reforms in governance and regulation.

The policy also tries to focus on creating a good teaching-learning environment and bringing innovation through new ideas. The 21st Century Millennium 2030 goals of UNESCO are at the centre stage of this policy with Indian ethos and grassroot realities. It aims to proper implementation of policy with local and global vision altogether in educational reforms.

The entire policy document has to be seen in light of universalisation of Education with the four foundation pillars in current as well as our ancient Indian knowledge and traditions. These can be categorised as:

1. Education –from Veda to contemporary period
2. Skills – from Basic education or *Nai Taleem* of Gandhiji to modern soft and vocational skills at early stage of education

[1] Chairperson, National Institute of Open Schooling (NIOS) and Professor, Guru Gobind Singh Indraprastha University, New Delhi

[2] Research Scholar, School of Education, Guru Gobind Singh Indraprastha University, New Delhi

3. Self-dependency – Economic reforms through local resources (swadesi) and employability which was proposed by Gandhi ji in his book *Hind Swaraj.*
4. Value based education – From UPNISHADAS to UNESCO's Millennium 2030 goal.

Contemporary Higher Education and Need of Paradigm Shift

Higher education in India plays a pivotal role in the process of fostering and nurturing an individual to become a critical thinker so that he/she will be able to find the logic behind the phenomena and explain it in a systematic, scientific and meaningful manner. Creating new knowledge and epistemology, acquiring new capabilities and competencies, producing innovative, critical, and analytical thinkers will ultimately help in making a pool of intelligent human resources. Also, for giving solutions to global challenges higher education systems have to make a bridge between theory, research, and the industry as per the need.

Higher education today must teach more about how to learn rather than what to learn. It would be better if education to the student is given in such a way that the student is without fear, and with a free mind vis-à-vis, it helps the student to know about his/her self-capabilities and self potentialities.

After a long aperture of 34 years, on 29 July 2020, the Union Cabinet approved the National Education Policy 2020. Aim of policy is to prepare the way transfiguration ameliorates in school as well as higher education systems in the country. Also, the cabinet has approved the renaming of the Ministry of Human Resource Development to the Ministry of Education. It addresses some of the major issues faced in the Indian higher education system, including a fragmented sector; the big gap between research, industry, and education per se; graduates lacking employability skills; low student enrolment from marginalised groups; bureaucracy laden institutional governance and leadership.

Since the last two decades, there has been a proliferation of new universities, but because of issues in quality management, many end up being of inferior quality. There is a confusing pool of names for these such as, 'deemed to be universities' or 'affiliating technical universities'.

Taxonomy for Action Proposed in NEP 2020

NEP 2020 defines a university as a multidisciplinary institution of higher learning that offers programmes with high-quality teaching, research, and community engagement. It then proposes three domains of universities: research-intensive universities that collaborate teaching and research; teaching-intensive universities that emphasise teaching but still conduct some research; and autonomous degree-granting colleges focusing primarily on undergraduate teaching.

The NEP 2020 has emphasised the need for "large multidisciplinary universities". Focus on multidisciplinary education in contrast to fragmented over-specialised professional institutes/ universities can be seen to promote globally competitive education that meets the contemporary demands of industry and innovation.

NEP has suggested remedies for building robust systems to support quality research and innovation, generate skilful professionals, and promote a culture of meritocracy. The policy thus recognises that though not higher education institutions can be expected to provide both teaching and research of high quality, it is an inherent purpose of all of them to meet the educational needs of learners and professional needs of faculty employers, and this classification is what India needs.

The construction of a National Research Foundation to actively seed research and to fund outstanding peer-reviewed research is how NPE suggests promoting meaningful research and innovation.

Entrepreneurial Leadership among Teachers

All the progressive looking vocabulary, the advanced technologies, Artificial Intelligence, Internet of Things (IOT), Machine Learning, Robotics, Sustainable Technologies 21st Century, Innovation entrepreneurship, change, evolution, etc. attract our attention and we feel a dire need to adapt these. Our industries, business houses and society are looking towards these and they all have a direct impact on our education system. In a country like India that has uniqueness of diversity in culture, religion, ethnicity, practices, faith, geography, climate, environment, soil, distribution of resources, finances and lifestyle, the education system needs to focus on multiple factors of effectiveness, which operate at different levels and have both direct and indirect effects on student's self-reliance and synergy with self and society. A nation with approximately 1000 universities, 45000 colleges, 16 lakh schools, one crore teachers and 33 crore students' needs a dynamic education system that can accumulate the progressive century and unique characteristics of the nation cultivated by Saints, Rulers, Britishers, Priests, Gurus, Social Leaders, Industrial Leaders, Business Leaders and many more.

India has seen different types of leaders like spiritual leaders, technological leaders, social leaders, political leaders, academic leaders, business leaders, motivational leaders, transformational leaders, inspirational leaders. One profession that expects all this present in one is teaching. We call such teachers entrepreneurial leaders. Looking at statistics of the number of teachers and students in India we may say India has one teacher for 33 students. If each one teacher is educated to lead then, one crore teachers will be able to lead the students with grit, courage and values needed to lead the world and create a family like ecosystem called "vasudhaiv kutumbkam" on the earth. Teachers need autonomy and entrepreneurial qualities to lead the future.

We believe teachers need to be progressive and forward-looking personnel who can visualise change well in advance and can prepare the youth for his future life.

Common belief accepts teachers in higher education to be more reliable and; logical with respect to preparation for professional, vocational and societal life and the teachers in school education need to be more academic and value oriented. Having worked in both we, at times, feel disappointed in looking at celebrations of mediocrity and lack of leadership to groom excellence. An entrepreneurial leader among teachers has the academic, administrative, intellectual and financial capacities to build the global humane human for future. Teachers in school need to be more visionary and capable of long-term planning.

Not only research but teacher education institutions have been working in silos that have developed a traditional idealistic leadership based on character and sacrifice. Whereas the teacher in the 21st century needs entrepreneurial leadership that is based on values with mutual gains. The organisations working in silos developed digression and depression from social, technological and international leadership and concentrated only towards academic leadership. The problems in teacher education have most of the time been viewed with coloured glasses of international philosophers and westernised pinch, whereas the issues faced in the practical classes are indigenous. Hence, there is a gap in what is taught and what is practised. The New Education policy has brought a clear roadmap for inclusion of international standards of global leaders with indigenous ingredients. A welcome shift in teacher education is envisioned in the National Education Policy 2020 by jacketing higher education teachers into teacher education and a smooth transfer from academic excellence to professional development would certainly imbibe entrepreneurial traits among people employed in teaching. The concept of accountable autonomy is again an appreciated initiative that will lead to an overall development of the teachers across the country. The objective performance appraisal of teachers will give insights for professional development among the faculty which can compete at the global level.

The common person believes what they hear and read without researching the facts. An Entrepreneurial leader has the courage and fortitude to do research before accepting what is told. Teachers need to have grit to question obsolete and outdated practices and interact with management and administration to bring about the change needed.

Leadership is not everybody's cup of tea. It requires muscle to voice, capacity to support and grit to lead. An entrepreneurial leader has power to lead and empower the subordinates to lead. Leader has the grit to take the responsibility of each failure and encourage subordinates with success and appreciation. An entrepreneurial leader has to be free from callousness and recognise true leadership and empower them to take charge.

Teacher education is the basis of any education system where teachers are pillars and foundation of the educational structure of the nation. The systematic and sustainable changes and amendments in teacher education reflects in the whole education system. The New education Policy 2020 has constructed the whole system with raw materials of creativity, innovation, critical thinking, entrepreneurial skills, interdisciplinary subjects, multidisciplinary institutions, vocational education and liberal arts education held together with a strong teacher education and research mind-set.

A teacher in the 21st century does not need to be a mere academic leader but an entrepreneurial leader who is a jack of all traits who can facilitate sustainable learning for the students. Curiosity, creativity, innovation, entrepreneurship knowledge generation, wealth generation and research attitude are no more disjoint. These are all subsets of skills and values in any profession and a must for teaching profession.

Restructuring the Higher Education Institutes: Governance and Leadership

Good governance is needed both in the public and private sectors of higher education. NEP has adequately highlighted the importance of governance and leadership in the administration and institution-building efforts. It is seen to impact productivity and quality improvement directly. The NEP 2020 identifies not only the challenges in the field of higher education but also a vision for opportunities in it.

Aim of HEIs in India will become independent self-governing institutions pursuing innovation and excellence. Each college will either be an autonomous college or part of the parent university. This will ensure that course design, instruction, and assessment are in sync within each Higher Education Institute [HEI]. The current system, in contrast, has all three domains delinked from each other, and this adversely impacts quality teaching and learning experience.

Upon receiving the appropriately graded accreditations that deem the institution ready for such a move, a Board of Governors (BoG) shall be established. Equity considerations will also be taken care of while selecting the members. The BoG of an institution will be empowered to govern the institution free of any external interference. It is envisaged that all HEIs will be incentivised, supported, and mentored during this process and shall aim to become autonomous and have such an empowered BoG by 2035.

The BoG shall be responsible and accountable to the stakeholders through transparent self-disclosures of all relevant records. It will be responsible for meeting all regulatory guidelines mandated by HECI through the National Higher Education Regulatory Council (NHERC).

The BoG of each HEI will anchor the preparation and implementation of a strategic plan of action, namely: Institutional Development Plan (IDP). The IDP shall be the basis on which institutions will develop initiatives, assess their own progress, and reach the goals set therein, which could become the basis for further public funding. The IDP shall be prepared with the joint participation of Board members, institutional leaders, faculty, students, and staff.

The NEP 2020 intends to provide academia its long due. All leadership positions in institutions will be offered to persons with high academic qualifications and demonstrated administrative and leadership capabilities along with the abilities to handle critical and complex circumstances. Leaders of an HEI will reveal strong alignment to constitutional values and the overall vision of the institution, along with attributes such as a strong social commitment, belief in teamwork, pluralism, ability to work with diverse people, and a positive outlook. The selection shall be carried out by the BoG through a rigorous, impartial, merit-based, and competency-based process led by an eminent expert committee (EEC) constituted by the BoG.

Implementation

NEP 2020 acknowledged the challenges of implementation of the proposals in India. COVID-19 has further deepened hardly surfacing issues. The New Education policy envisions the increase in meagre public expenditure on education from about 4.6% of gross domestic product (GDP), to 6% of GDP. It discusses about the strong self-governance and merit based appointments of institutional leaders to be catalytic force and strong tool to achieve this goal. It aims towards a suitable system of graded accreditation and graded autonomy, all HEIs in India to become independent self-governing institutions pursuing innovation and excellence over a period of 15 years.

While visualising and aiming the above we should also have a glance at the contemporary practice in this area:

1. Entrepreneurship in education Sector
2. Collaborative and Community participation
3. Transparency
4. Public Private Partnership (PPP) and Corporate Social Responsibility (CSR)
5. Institutional autonomy and accountability
6. Regulation, Monitoring and Compliance
7. Total Quality Management (TQM) in education.

In the process of synergising current educational leadership and governance practices with the new roles suggested by NEP 2020, we must focus upon its establishment in following domains:

1. New leadership roles, challenges, and prospects.
2. Redefining models of leadership styles at individual and institutional levels.
3. Developing leadership skills and insights for values, vision and moral purposes in educational leadership

In continuation to above to bring quality in the teaching-learning process with good governance the concept of multidisciplinary instruction needs to be addressed at both policy and practice levels. A clear guideline is needed on how disciplinary institutions must be converted into multidisciplinary institutions and the role of main stakeholders in the process.

University departments must be engaged actively in planning and executing the professional development programmes. Efficient task force must be constituted in a multi layered fabric keeping in mind the various dimensions involved in it.

In the area of online mode of teaching, learning the new tools and techniques accordingly needs to be chalked out where participation of different stakeholders is also involved so that governance becomes more efficient, acceptable and mass-friendly. This process must be phase wise and planning and organising strategies with better coordination in a cost effective manner must be the inherent principle.

The local governance must be based on grass root realities and local needs must be kept in mind while implementing the policy vision in thrust areas. This policy talks of energising the CERT in education, so more and more trustees are needed to take it further with new areas of research and innovation.

New institutions established with skill-oriented and vocational courses to meet the need of employment are in need of the hour now. Various areas of employability and job opportunities must be identified according to the local needs and related courses must be launched with training and development as essential course components. Credit transfer provision must be a part of interdisciplinary and industry academia interrelation in the curriculum transaction process.

Development of entrepreneurship skills among students should be encouraged and a cadre of academic leaders as well as technocrats must be developed. Experts of concerned skills of vocational training must be made part of the academia-industry interrelation in training, monitoring, evaluation and feedback mechanism. Identification of employment and employability through experiential execution mechanism should be developed to take a note of the optimum utilisation of resources. Participation of different stakeholders must be ensured to give it a more functional edge and to bring efficacy.

When we are talking about good governance and related efficient leadership models then we must also devise plans for special zones and demographic mapping in rural sector, hills, tribal areas and other remote areas and these sectors must be given proper attention at priority to address their local issues and challenges. Physical, financial, and human resources must be adequate and timely proximity of these resources must be ensured through better execution and governance. A strong monitoring procedure must be developed to take it up at another level with forecasting and analysis where experience, practice and implementation gaps are looked after to bring efficient local educational governance in tune with the national and global levels.

Concluding Words

With the introduction of Education Policy 2020 we as stakeholders of the education sector have to think rationally and critically over the past experiences and future prospects. Considering the desired changes, a complete paradigm shift in the education sector is needed in terms of quality, access, retention and employability for the students in all the dimensions and levels of the education sector.

India is a country which is leading in youth power globally. Hence, the students and teachers must be skilled, value-oriented and devoted to the goal of nation-building. Unless we are self-reliant and progressive, we cannot lead the knowledge society. Today quality expansion is sought in all the sectors of education which can meet the needs of society. Value based education can lead the society towards human dignity and social coexistence. Autonomy and accountability have been the thrust areas in this policy and with this initiative in India through this policy, concerns of bringing quality and taking responsibility will be ensured.

Creating a good teaching-learning environment and bringing innovation through new ideas should be the utmost goal of today's educational scenario. Use of ICT with professional ethics will definitely change the conventional system of Education into a more updated and advanced education system in tune to global education.

The NEP 2020 is a very positive step in rejuvenating Indian education. We have a firm opinion that before implementing the policy initiatives, there is a dire need to identify the gaps and challenges of previous policies. It will give a clearer foresight and smooth path to this academic endeavour. Proper implementations of policy with local and global vision altogether in educational reforms, the desired changes can definitely move towards success.

20

Preparing for e-Education through Online and Digital Resources

Amit Kauts

Due to Covid-19 pandemic, there is a need to reassess the education models by keeping in view the challenges of the global economy. COVID-19 has not only brought academic activity to a standstill but has also challenged the system of education that we have been practising for several years. This situation challenged the education system across the world and forced educators to shift to an online mode of teaching overnight. To create a more inclusive, cohesive and productive nation, MHRD (which is now MOE) unveiled National Education Policy 2020 in July 2020. Under the NEP 2020, the focus areas of the reforms seek to cultivate '21st-century skills' among students, including critical thinking, problem-solving, creativity and digital literacy. The policy has a balanced and inclusive outlook, with a diminished line of difference between arts and STEM courses, in addition to blended, multidisciplinary learning. It recognises the need to bridge the gap in education through technology and digitisation.

India is a global technology leader in information and communication. The Digital India Campaign is helping to transform the entire nation into a digitally empowered society and knowledge economy. While education will play a critical role in this transformation, technology itself will play an important role in the improvement of educational processes and outcomes; thus, the relationship between technology and education is bi-directional. The policy recognises the importance of technology intervention as an integral part of its charter and stresses upon specialised learning, character development, blended learning, interdisciplinary methods, outcome based learning, creative thinking and the skills which are necessary to dwell in the 21st century.

It will be interesting to see how the education industry and academia at large leverage the various opportunities laid out by the government to impart quality education with edTech as a medium. The policy envisages the creation of a dedicated unit for the purpose of devising the development of digital infrastructure, digital content and capacity building to supervise e-education needs of both school and higher education.

Professor and Dean, Faculty of Education, Guru Nanak Dev University, Amritsar

Provisions of Online and Digital Education in School Education, Higher Education, Professional Education and Technical Education

School Education

a) Online question banks of higher order questions will be made available to teachers and students.
b) Virtual labs will also be set up to give the students a hands-on-experience.
c) A rich variety of educational software will be developed and made available for students and teachers at all levels. All such software will be available in all major Indian languages and will be accessible to a wide range of users including students in remote areas and with disabilities.
d) Teaching-learning e-content will continue to be developed by all States in all regional languages, as well as by the NCERT (including CIET), CBSE, NIOS, and other bodies/institutions, and will be uploaded onto the National Teacher's Portal. This platform may also be utilised for e-content related to Teacher's Professional Development, etc.
e) Video-viewing equipment will be made available to teachers at all schools so that teachers can suitably integrate open educational videos into teaching-learning practices.
f) Particular attention will need to be paid to emerging disruptive technologies that will necessarily transform the education system and what it teaches to students. In school, the study of current affairs and ethical issues will include a discussion on disruptive technologies. Appropriate instructional and discussion materials will also be prepared for continuing education.
g) Other disruptive technologies that are expected to change the way we live, and therefore change the way we educate students, including those relating to clean and renewable energy, water conservation, sustainable farming, environmental preservation, and other green initiatives; these will also receive prioritised attention in education.
h) The policy recognises the importance of technology in aiding teachers, bridging the language barrier between students and teachers, creating digital libraries, popularising language learning as well as ensuring greater access to education (specifically for differently abled children).
i) Efforts to teach languages to school students will be dovetailed with efforts to enhance Natural Language Processing for India's diverse languages.

Higher Education

a) Universities will play an active role not only in conducting research on disruptive technologies but also in creating initial versions of instructional materials and courses (including online courses) in cutting-edge domains and assessing their impact on specific areas such as professional education.

b) Once the technology has attained a level of maturity, autonomous colleges can scale these teaching and skilling efforts. Disruptive technologies will make certain jobs redundant and hence approaches to skilling and deskilling that are both efficient and ensure quality will be of increasing importance to create and sustain employment. Institutions will have autonomy to approve institutional and non-institutional partners to deliver such training, which will be integrated with skills and higher education frameworks.
c) All universities will offer Ph.D. and Masters programmes in core areas (such as Machine Learning) as well as multidisciplinary fields ("AI + X") and professional areas (healthcare, agriculture and law). They may also develop and disseminate courses in these areas via platforms, such as SWAYAM. For rapid adoption, HEIs may blend these online courses with traditional teaching in undergraduate and vocational programmes. The colleges may also offer targeted training in low-expertise tasks for supporting the AI value chain such as data annotation, image classification, and speech transcription.
d) Higher Education Institutions have been encouraged to set up start up incubation centres and technology development centres.
e) National Research Foundation is proposed to set up to cultivate a culture of research.
f) An Academic Bank of Credit shall be established which would digitally store the academic credits earned from various recognised HEIs which can also be transferred and counted as a part of the final degree.

School Education + Higher Education

a) An autonomous body, the National Educational Alliance for Technology (NEAT), will be created to provide a platform for use of technology to enhance learning, assessment, planning, administration, and so on, both for school and higher education. The aim of NEAT will be to provide on a single portal various educational technology solutions that are tested for their robustness for improving the learning experience, with a special focus on the needs of the students with disabilities. An expert body within NEAT would facilitate decision-making on the induction, deployment, and use of technology, by providing to the leadership of educational institutions, state and central governments, and other stakeholders, the latest knowledge and research as well as the opportunity to consult and share best practices with each other.
b) NEAT will have the following roles: (i) provide best educational technology to the students using a portal; (ii) build intellectual

and institutional capacities in educational technology; (iii) provide independent evidence-based advice to Central and State governmental agencies on technology-based interventions, through its expert body; (iv) envision strategic thrust areas in this domain; and (v) articulate new directions for research and innovation. To remain relevant in the fast-changing field of educational technology, NEAT, through its expert body, will maintain a regular inflow of authentic data from multiple sources including educational technology innovators and practitioners, particularly at the grassroot level, and will engage with a diverse set of researchers to analyse this data. It will act as a forum for harnessing the distributed energy that democratising technology can unleash, particularly among the youth of the country who continually prove their capacity to innovate and lead, while also bringing a scholarly emphasis to ensure that the overall impact of these efforts is positive. To support the development of a vibrant body of knowledge and practice, NEAT will organise multiple regional and national conferences, workshops, etc. to solicit inputs from national and international educational technology researchers, entrepreneurs, and practitioners.

Professional Education

a) The need to embrace technology in professional education as well as the incorporation of technology to expedite the aim of achieving 100% literacy has been put forward. The policy recognises the importance of technology in addressing various societal challenges and seeks to promote interdisciplinary research and innovation.
b) Policy also notes that technology can be an effective tool in facilitating teacher education and encourages the utilisation of technology platforms for online teacher training.
c) There are several other initiatives that are introduced specifically for training of teachers in school and higher education. One is to train them in digital technology with the help of nationwide agencies and centres in each district.
d) the main other development is introducing courses in education via B.Ed and a mandatory certified education in teaching pedagogy during Ph.D enrolment for aspiring professors.
e) It also recommends pilot studies for online education and encourages the use of e-learning platforms such as SWAYAM, DIKSHA, etc. Under it, teachers will undergo training to use online platforms which will help them in improving skills and learning content.

Technical Education

a) Technology-enabled education is another issue that has been highlighted in NEP. Internet based activities like quizzes, competitions and assessments will be developed. Creation of online communities, building smart classrooms and providing digital content are some of the highlights. In the higher education sector, institutions will have the option to run open distance learning and online programmes.

b) Use of technology and its integration with school and higher education curricula, more in the context of digital India campaign, it will create a sound knowledge economy. Also, the policy has rightly underlined the need to use technology in education during the pandemic like Covid-19, which disrupted traditional teacher-in-class education.

c) Lok Vidya will be made accessible to students through integration into vocational education courses. NETF (National Educational Technology Forum) shall operate as a platform for free exchange of ideas on the use of technology to enhance learning, assessment planning and administration for school and higher education.

d) The policy recognises the challenges arising on account of the widespread use of Artificial Intelligence (AI) and highlights the need to adopt changes occurring on account of increased use of Artificial Intelligence across sectors.

e) As the cost of Artificial Intelligence falls, Artificial Intelligence will be able to match or outperform and therefore be a valuable aid to even skilled professionals such as doctors in certain predictive tasks.

f) National Research Foundation (NRF) will initiate or expand efforts in the technology including fundamental research in the domain, development of the technology and assessment of socio-economic impact. In the context of Artificial Intelligence, NRF may consider a three-pronged approach: i) advancing core AI research, ii) developing and deploying application based research, and iii) establishing international research efforts to address global challenges in areas such as healthcare, agriculture, and climate change using AI.

Challenges in the Way of Digitalisation

a) As per a survey conducted by the government for the period of July 2017 to June 2018 and published in November 2019, in rural India, only 4.4% households have computers as against 23.4% of urban households, and nearly 14.9% of rural households have Internet facilities as against 42% of urban households.

b) In rural areas, among persons aged 5 years and above, 9.9% were able to operate a computer as against 32.4% in urban areas and 13% of rural users were able to use the Internet as against 37.1% in urban areas.

c) Digital education is not about videos of lectures on blackboard by teachers on the Internet. It is about the appropriate platforms, technology, tools, interactivity, curation, content and a lot more. We are completely underprepared for it.

d) Government schools and colleges do not have the resources to provide digital education. Private schools and colleges are not different. However, they all want parents to pay full fees to be able to pay their staff and maintain facilities.

e) The financial model for education is falling apart everywhere during this pandemic. In India, the situation is even more complex because of lack of proper policy on digital education, infrastructure and multiple languages.

f) Merely moving classrooms online would not mean effective remote learning. One-to-one interactions among peers and teachers are very important for learning. On a digital platform, how students learn and communicate with others is largely dependent on the readiness of both teachers and students to accept digital learning. In the case of distance education, the onus of learning is more on students, which requires discipline.

g) There are many other challenges for the parents beside fees for services which schools and colleges are not equipped to provide like,
   - Who will assure uninterrupted broadband connectivity for several hours a day?
   - Who will pay for the data?
   - Is there any adequate space and peace at home for the students to concentrate?
   - What happens when the power goes out?
   - How to train kids at home to follow digital discipline.

   These are huge problems for working parents and poor people in slums and rural areas.

Measures for Effective Implementation

a. In the context of education, it is important that each student in urban and in rural areas has access to digital hardware, whether in the form of smartphones, computers or tablets exclusively for their use.

b. Government should create a better structured digital infrastructure which is no longer seen as luxury. So that poor people can afford it properly and their children can be at a par with other children in the society.

c. As the flow of uninterrupted electricity is a big issue in India, to implement digital and online learning, government will have to make some arrangements to provide the electricity 24x7 in all villages and rural places.

d. Government can tie up with the telecom service provider companies to make the Internet pack affordable, so that a common man can take advantage to attend the online classes.

e. Academicians and teachers can organise seminars or workshops for parents about how to attend online classes like how to handle computers, mobile phones, educational apps etc. so that they can train their children at home about digitalisation of education.

f. Policy makers can make a policy on digitalisation of education by keeping in mind the constraints of technology.
g. The implementation plan has to be developed involving not only academicians and educational experts but also some of the top-notch technology education companies that are providing end-to-end technology solutions to oversee schools and universities. For e.g. Mysuru's Excelsoft technologies are already hand holding Government schools in technology enabled education. In fact, the company's own school has built benchmark e-learning processes in school education.
h. The strategy to tie up with industries and institutes of repute, both in India as well as abroad, should be chalked out that would not only enhance our core strengths but also provide the yardstick to assess our own strengths and weaknesses.
i. There is a need to develop competence among the faculty to effectively implement a blended mode of learning. The competence to develop instructional designs for various instructional strategies, designing learning outcomes of courses and specific classes, developing self-instructional modules, developing and editing of audio content, video content and animated content. Along with these competencies, teachers need to develop competence to use various Learning Management Systems and a variety of various softwares for developing various evaluation strategies and tools for interactive learning.
j. Teachers in higher education need to be developed with respect to various online pedagogy, collaborative and cooperative learning strategies for ensuring the achievement of learning outcomes failing which the whole initiative of learning outcome based curriculum in NEP 2020 would remain on papers. The restructuring of higher education would be able to yield desirable outcomes only if it brings out quality in terms of student employability skills, innovative outlook and sense of commitment to society and excellence. As opposed to listening to lectures by teachers in classes, the students will listen to audio/video lectures at home to be able to get the content to records, remembrance, understanding and application. Similarly, as opposed to doing homework at home one can do homework with others in the classrooms. But all this requires a new mindset and framework.

Conclusion

In nutshell, we can say that to take place effective implementation of digital and online education proposed by NEP 2020, government will have to seriously lay down the foundation of infrastructural facilities, think of a policy for affordable sustenance of such facilities in institutions and for students, implementing blended mode of education by providing regulations to be inserted in the ordinances for curriculum transaction, which means blend of offline and online education. In this scenario, special regulations needs to be developed for curriculum transaction with respect to LMS, online and innovative pedagogy by UGC and specific directions to different professional development agencies like HRDCs, schemes of PMMMNMTT, ICSSR/ UGC/ CSIR sponsored programmes for systemic and sustained efforts for capacity-building among teachers in higher education and such.

References

Ministry of Human Resource Development (2020). *National Education Policy.*

Survey conducted by National Statistical Office titled 'Key Indicators of Household Social Consumption on Education in India.' Retrieved from http://www.mospi.gov.in/sites/default/files/NSS75252E/KI_Education_75th_Final.pdf

21

Education for Sustainability: One of the Pillars of Quality Education

Seema Dhawan[1] and Ashu Roulet[2]

Concept of Quality Education in SDG4

In pursuit of a better and sustainable future for all, the United Nations General Assembly proposed 17 global goals, generally called Sustainable Development Goals (SDG), intended to be achieved by 2030. Approved and adopted by UN General Assembly Resolution vide 70/1 on 25 September 2015 is a supremely ambitious and transformational plan of action for people, planet and prosperity. It envisions health, prosperity, peace and wellbeing for all. United Nation identified various challenges to sustainability including poverty, gender inequality, menial living status, natural disasters, spiraling conflict, violent extremism, terrorism, environmental degradation, etc. Among various challenges, education is one of the goals which works as a foundation stone for our sustainability. The agenda in SDG4 endeavours to provide equal access of quality education to all without any discrimination on the grounds of gender, race, ethnicity, caste or creed thus ensuring inclusive and equitable quality education and promote life-long learning opportunities for all. The ten-target bullets within the goal emphasise the need for quality education so that all learners acquire the knowledge and skill and lifestyle needed to promote sustainable development. Let us have a look at SDG4 and its targets.

Goal 4- Ensure inclusive and equitable quality education and promote life-long opportunities for all. The ten targets set are as follows:

1. By 2030, ensure that all girls and boys complete free equitable and quality primary and secondary education leading to relevant and effective learning outcomes.
2. By 2030, ensure that all girls and boys have access to quality early childhood development care and pre-primary education so that they are ready for primary education.
3. By 2030, ensure equal access for all women and men to affordable and quality technical, vocational and tertiary education including university.

[1] Professor, Department of Education, HNB Garhwal Central University, Srinagar, Uttarakhand

[2] Assistant Professor, HNB Garhwal Central University, Srinagar, Uttarakhand

4. By 2030, increase the number of youth and adults who have relevant skills, including technical and vocational skills, for employment, decent jobs and entrepreneurship.
5. By 2030, eliminate gender disparities in education and ensure equal access to all levels of education and vocational training for the vulnerable, including persons with disabilities, indigenous people and children in vulnerable situations.
6. By 2030, ensure that all youth and substantial proportions of adults, both men and women achieve literacy and numeracy.
7. By 2030, ensure that all learners acquire the knowledge and skill needed to promote sustainable development, including among others, through education for sustainable development and sustainable lifestyles, human rights, gender equality, promotion of a culture of peace and non-violent, global citizenship and appreciation of cultural diversity of culture's contribution to sustainable development.
8. Build and upgrade education facilities for promoting gender sensitivity and provision of safe, non-violent, inclusive and effective learning environments for all.
9. By 2020, substantially expand globally the number of scholarships available to developing countries, in particular least developed countries, small island developing states and African countries, for enrolment in higher education including vocational training and information and communication technology, technical engineering and scientific programmes, in developed countries and other developing countries.
10. By 2030, substantially increase the supply of qualified teachers including through international cooperation for teacher training in developing countries especially least developed countries and small island developing states.

SDG4 and NEP 2020

The Government of India has envisaged inculcation of SDG4 and its goals in NEP 2020 through effective recommendations concerning the entire educational structure. The government shows strong will power to bring quality of life to its citizens through promoting the aforesaid goals. Revamping the educational structure to bring the entire target population into consideration. The policy has tried to integrate the education system in 5 + 3 + 3+ 4 with flexible approaches and interconnectedness to prepare the students for further studies at higher levels through proper orientation. The policy envisions free, compulsory, and universal access of secondary education throughout the nation thereby accomplishing target 1 of the SDG4. The policy also talks about the need of Early Childhood Care and Education (ECCE) to be an integral part of the existing education system. The most provocative time of child development is the first five-years school time period from pre-primary to Grade 2, which was considered trivial, but now it has gained sufficient attention in the policy moving one step ahead in attaining target 2 of the SDG4. Orienting vocational education, the policy has made vocational education an inseparable part of school and higher education. The sole focus is on producing a skilled workforce and preparing human resources for specific occupations. The policy also lays emphasis on the development of higher order thinking skills in learners so that the product could be competent enough on global parameters. Moreover, it also discusses various issues like inclusive education, adult education, assessment techniques, GER, teacher training etc. which are the pillars of a quality education system.

It is stated in the NEP that education is a public service and access to quality education must be considered a basic right of every child. Education is fundamental for achieving full human potential, developing an equitable and just society and promoting national development. Providing universal access to quality education is the key to India's continued ascent, and leadership on the global stage in terms of economic growth, social justice and equality, scientific advancement, national integration, and cultural preservation. The NEP 2020 provides prospects to ensure equal access for all women and men to affordable and quality technical, vocational, and tertiary education. The principles of NEP 2020 highlight the importance of recognising and identification of distinctive capacities of each student while focusing on the flexibility in choosing the subject of study as per her/his interests. It talks about holistic development of students including the development of life skills viz. communication, cooperation, teamwork, and resilience. The policy realises teachers and faculty as the heart of the learning process. One of the prime concerns in the policy is 'quality'; that is quality teachers, quality curriculum, quality teacher-education and quality of education at all levels. To understand the concept of 'quality' in NEP we need to understand the quality parameters first.

Quality Parameters

Determining quality parameters in education is challenging and generally disputable. People around the globe could not reach general consensus on the concept of quality education, and it still remains elusive. Pirsig (1974, p. 163-164) states, "Quality you know what it is, yet don't know what it is." Perhaps, the parallax exists due to the purpose nations serve in education, individual's perception and society as a whole. In its report, the World Bank has tried to define the quality of education by stating "Quality in education is difficult to define and measure. An adequate definition must include student outcomes". Most educators would also include in the definition, the nature of educational experiences that help to produce outcomes, from the learning environment (World Bank, 1995, p. 46). The World Bank dealt with quality and policy issues in education. Coombs (1985) describe quality in his book *The*

World Crisis in Education as 'customarily defined and judged by student learning achievements, in terms of traditional curriculum and standards'. Quality also pertains to the relevance of what is taught and learned to how well it fits the present and future needs of the particular learners in question, given their particular circumstances and prospects. It also refers to significant changes in the educational system itself, in the nature of inputs (students, teachers, facilities, equipment and supplies), its objectives, curriculum and educational technologies and its socio-economic, cultural and political environment (Coombs, 1985, p. 105).

Parameters of Quality Education must include:

- *Quality of Inputs:* Teachers, books, libraries, curriculum framework, infrastructure, facilities, etc. is a vast source of input into education. The quality of input will certainly influence the quality of the final product. Low quality teachers, books and curriculum will fail to produce competent and qualified students. Such products may suffer inability to thrive and sustain in society. For quality teachers, in the NEP 2020 it has been described that the high respect for teachers and the high status of the teaching profession must be restored so as to inspire the best to enter in the teaching profession. The teachers should be motivated and empowered to ensure the best possible future for the children and the nation and the practice of excessive transfers of teachers will be minimised with full transparency. Local knowledge and professions will be promoted to provide opportunities to local people realising their potential in varied fields as local arts, vocational crafts, entrepreneurship, agriculture, etc. The policy also emphasises on Service Environment and Culture for teachers.
- *Quality of Process:* Process in education largely pertains to the time in which the taught interacts with the teacher and gains all learning experience within the institution premises. It is based on teacher-taught relationship which incorporates physical and behavioural aspects of human resources in education. In fact, input and process in education together can create large institutional differences, begetting student's choice and rankings of the institutions. For this reason alone, many universities, colleges and institutions are top ranked and admissions in them is a cut-throat competition. Somehow this has caused a deep trench leading to hierarchical stratification of the education system. Why our education system is not able to impart equitable quality education to all? Why should there be discrimination on the institutional grounds? Migration in pursuance of quality education has to stop and equity regarding quality education has to be established.

  Quality in education is not just the concerns about grades and numbers; actually, it is more or less about the education process and the experiences of learning. Thus, the character of school life and human relationship are important aspects of the education process. A school or college where pupils are fearful, abused, and unhappy and made to feel inferior because of their caste, religion, race, ethnicity, disabilities, family, social or cultural life can hardly be called a good quality educational institution, even when it ranks top among all educational institutions. Further, varied learning opportunities should be provided to the students to explore, inspire, critically analyse, and reflect. First time, the NEP 2020 highlights the significance of 360-degree assessment and self-motivated learners.

- *Quality outputs:* The final output which is not only confined to examination scores or grades but also reflects in behavioural aspects of learners. They should be holistically developed having critical and high order thinking skills. Also, they should think divergently, indicating creativity and novelty perspectives. They should perform like self-motivated learners and promote self-directed learning. Moreover, quality education is perceived by individual stakeholders from their own perspective indicating contextualisation of quality output. Therefore, company hiring engineer from a technical institute may not only demand excellence in academics as parameter of quality education but also the way an engineer communicates and collaborates, behaves, manages, thinks critically and creatively, and presents himself to others through best use of soft skills adding to the benefits of the company. In such a way, it is possible that someone who graduated from the top rank institution may not fit well into the perception of a company hiring engineers. Thus, it totally depends upon the perception the stakeholders develop for any academic or professional course. But still, we need to carve a common framework of quality education for all types of courses in compliance with Sustainable Development Goals 4, meeting individuals' as well as society's needs. Broadly, quality education can be visualised from two perspectives:
  a) *Micro Perspective*: Micro perspective is a narrow concept of quality education. It generally talks about quality in education which supports personal development. It includes supporting individual wellbeing, livelihood generation and integration into society, empowering the learners and building resilience. It is more or less associated with target 4.4 and 4.7 of SDG4 which emphasises sustainability of life through technical and vocational skills. Outcomes of quality education through micro perspective not only include knowledge and hard skills but also soft skills like attitudes, attributes, habits, values, critical thinking, awareness and tolerance, which are highly individual and personal.
  b) *Macro Perspective*: On broader terms quality education helps in improvement and development of society preparing productive and participatory citizens supporting sustainable development and

common good. Whatever an individual learns has to be linked with the good of the society. Maybe it is in a form of economic and social development, health and hygiene, poverty eradication, political stability and resilience or administrative efficiency. The macro perspective considers a larger sect, state, or society as a whole. Thus, when the learners have completed their formal learning, they should be ready to enter into the workforce and work for the good of society, nation and the world as well.

Factors Affecting the Quality Education

As it is clear from the above description that quality education does not depend on a single factor; rather it takes many factors into consideration, including a variety of inputs, processes, institutional arrangements, outputs and contextual factors. The developing world is facing the challenge of access and quality in education simultaneously, which seems like two opposite things not meeting each other at any point. Contemporarily, the governments should merge both access and quality together through long-term plans and strategies. The unprivileged group of people still needs proper access while talking only about quality can leave marginalised out because quality comes with cost. There are several factors affecting quality education which need close observation. In fact, there is no single golden key to open the treasure of quality education. To unlock these factors, we will have to move back on the parameters of quality education, i.e. the input, process and output. The contributors to these parameters identify the factors influencing the quality education. The New Education Policy 2020 clearly mentions that the objective of education is to develop among the students, knowledge, skills, values, and dispositions that support responsible commitment to human rights, sustainable development and living, and global well-being, thereby reflecting a truly global citizen.

Teachers' Training

The teacher plays a key role in contribution towards quality in education. The Sargent Commission (1944) emphasised that quality of school education should be improved but it could not be improved without improving quality of teacher training (Sharma, 2010 p. 7-8). The quality teacher enhances the knowledge, skills and contributes to the learning experiences of students positively. SDG4 target 4.c emphasises the supply of quality teachers through international cooperation of teacher training. To prevent hampering education because of the learning crisis (UNESCO, 2014) teacher training becomes necessary. Learning crisis is a condition when a teacher fails to understand students and students fail to understand their teacher. The lag occurs due to hampered pedagogy and low quality training. In our country, we have made tremendous growth in enrolling children, but the learning outcomes are still poor. The reasons may be attributed majorly to the failing teacher education system in the nation, putting 370 million at risk (Verma, 2012). The reports suggested that

85% of teachers fail the post-qualification competency test (Central Teacher Eligibility Test, CTET). The teacher education institutions (TEI) inspections found institutions with only a foundation stone for infrastructure but with a 99% pass rate. It was observed that faculty was paid 1/8 of the prescribed norms, which shows menial perspective for teacher educators. To look into the matter, Justice Verma Commission was set up by the Supreme Court of India in the year 2012, which listed comprehensive list of reform proposals in four major thrust areas:

1. Quality of Pre-Service Teacher Education
2. Quality of In-Service Teacher Education
3. Teacher Performance and Teacher Audit
4. Strengthening of the Regulatory function of the National Council for Teacher Education (NCTE).

The commission gave following recommendation regarding improvement of Teacher Education (TE):

1. The government should increase its investment for establishing Teacher Education Institutions (TEI) and increase the institutional capacity of teacher preparation especially in the deficit states.
2. The government may explore the possibility of instituting a transparent procedure of pre-entry testing of candidates to the pre-service Teacher Education Programmes (TEP), keeping in view the variation in local conditions.
3. Teacher Education Programme to be part of the higher education system and the duration of the programme needs to be enhanced with reference to the Education Commission (1966).
4. Existing TEI's may be encouraged to take necessary steps towards attaining academic parity with the new institutions.
5. Current TEP may be redesigned keeping in view the recommendations of National Curriculum Framework for Teacher Education (NCFTE, 2009).
6. In keeping with the recommendations of the Education Commission (1966), every pre-service TEI may have a dedicated school attached to it as a laboratory where student teachers get opportunities to experiment new ideas and have their capacities to become reflective practitioners.
7. The degree/diploma in TE should be offered only in face-to-face mode.
8. There is a need to establish a national level academic body for continual reflection and analysis of TE programme, their norms and standards, development of reading material and faculty development and teacher education.
9. The institutional capacity should be increased for preparation of teacher educators. There is a need to make the Masters in Education Programme of two years duration with the provision of specialisation in curriculum

and paedagogic studies, foundation studies, management, policy and finance and other areas of emerging concerns in education,

10. All the existing TEI's imparting in-service teacher education will be strengthened, including DIETS and SCERT.
11. There is an urgent need to develop comprehensive programmes for continuing professional development of secondary school teachers.
12. The central government in consultation with the state government and other stakeholders may develop a framework for assessment of teacher performance, keeping in view the guidelines suggested in the report.
13. The NCTE needs to review the existing norms and standards for the various teacher education programmes and create a standing committee for periodic review of curriculum and the norms and the standards of the programme.
14. The NCTE should develop comprehensive guidelines for innovative TEP for grant of recognition.
15. The NCTE should develop a new framework undertaking inspection of the recognised institution, with enhanced focus on process parameters to ascertain the quality of the institutions and take appropriate action to improve the overall quality of the teacher education system. Apart from these recommendations, there were lots of other recommendations given to improve the teacher education system.

NEP 2020 on Quality Teacher Education

As per reports of Justice J.S. Verma Committee 2012, there has been continuous degradation in teacher education and the very cause has been imputed to '*mediocrity and rampant corruption due to commercialisation*' (MHRD, J.S. Verma Committee, 2012). There has been unexpected mushrooming of the teacher education institutions everywhere in the nation. Reflecting on above recommendations, the NEP envisages major reforms in the area of Teacher Education. The regulatory bodies at national and state level have proved to be a failure in preventing terrific downfall in the system. Resultantly, different aspects of teacher education have been severely affected which needs immediate assessment through the lens of NEP 2020.

The new education policy emphasises to re-establish teachers, at all levels, as the most respected and essential members of our society, because they truly shape our next generation of citizens. The teachers should be empowered and helped to do their job as effectively as possible. The new education policy aims to recruit the very best and brightest to enter the teaching profession at all levels, by ensuring livelihood, respect, dignity, and autonomy, while also instilling in the system basic methods of quality control and accountability. The Policy strongly suggests a multidisciplinary approach in the teacher education system, which is the most important aspect for quality. B. Ed integrated course is proposed to take over one- and two-years teacher education courses by 2030, which means that the course will not be perceived in separation rather as an integral part of academic courses. The policy recommends highest quality in content, pedagogy and practice by moving the teacher education system in multidisciplinary colleges and universities, establishing a four-year integrated teacher education course as the minimum eligibility to be a school teacher. This also signifies the eradication of substandard teacher training institutions which mushroomed overnight to commercialise the noblest job of teaching. The policy clearly writes "Corrupt and substandard institutions, cannot and must not be allowed to run. They must be shut down." The policy further suggests "TEI's that do not meet basic educational criteria must be closed".

Libraries and Books

Libraries and books play a vital role in the development of quality education among the students. Libraries and books disseminate knowledge and human information resources. They contain labour of years of knowledge exploration and a wide range of experiences. A well designed and equipped library must contain books and literature pertaining to science, arts, philosophy and current research. It should give maximum exposure to quality knowledge and resources, so that students do not miss any opportunity to access. Thus, the libraries create favourable conditions for improving students' comprehensive quality, developing professional technology education, and improving scientific and cultural quality (Yang, 2011).

Curriculum

Curriculum is an important pillar of quality education. Imagine a gym where there is an instructor but no machines to work out. The curriculum has the same role as machines have to the gym. Instructing alone would not help any customer to build physique or maintain health. Similarly, for all round development of students, i.e. development of all three domains, *viz. cognitive, affective* and *psychomotor domain*, quality curriculum is essentially needed. A good quality curriculum is able to meet the needs of all the stakeholders and is always constructed on their high expectations aligned to state standards. Viewing the global dynamic technological and scientific transitions it is expected that curriculum should instigate critical thinking and essential skills to cope with the challenges of the 21st century. A strong and quality curriculum does not put content into watertight compartments but provides a vertical and horizontal alignment between grades in order to scaffold or build the learning experiences. Moreover, it does not coerce the students to feel the pain of being asked to recall information they never learned in a way they were never taught. It gives freedom to learn in a healthy environment.

A high-quality curriculum allows teachers to:

- Provide enough opportunities for students to engage in all types of scholastic and non-scholastic activities.

- Provide various opportunities to develop thinking strategies and models that would foster innovation and creativity among teachers.
- Provide a bridge between different levels of learning and grades.
- Design assessments that are reflective of grade level standards
- Provide opportunities for the development of meaningful professional capacities.

A high-quality curriculum allows students to:

- Achieve their goals through academic mastery.
- Develop excellence in character, skill, knowledge and thinking.
- To develop ideas and concepts related to their own lives.
- Build into a rational, sound and expressive personality.

Infrastructure

The infrastructure is one of the important aspects of education. It includes buildings, classrooms, laboratories, libraries, teaching-learning equipment and all types of crucial elements of the learning environment in the educational institutions. Because a child spends maximum time in schools, infrastructure becomes a very important factor behind how a child sees the world as he/she grows up. There is strong evidence that high quality infrastructure facilitates better teaching learning environments and helps in improved student outcomes, reduced dropout rates and other benefits in the teaching-learning process. The research show that infrastructural design affects learning through three interrelated factors:

a) *Naturalness*: factors related to natural surroundings like light, sound, temperature, air quality, links to nature, etc.
b) *Individualization*: factors pertaining to ownership, flexibility and connection
c) *Level of Stimulation*: factors associated with complexity and colour (Barrett, *et al.*, 2016)

Many educational institutions across the globe use piecemeal or fragmented approaches towards the infrastructure. This approach is driven by adhoc needs and limited funding availability rather than a strategic approach. Such situations cause schools to run without science laboratories, libraries, playgrounds and sometimes essential facilities like drinking water, chairs, tables, benches, fan, lights, black boards and toilets or separate washrooms for boys and girls.

To summarise, schools are the frontlines of overall development of children which ensures not only academic learning but mental and physical wellbeing of learners too. Educational institutes with poor infrastructure and facilities tend to be poor in terms of students' achievement and personality development. Sometimes, in developing nations like India, it becomes a prime cause of dropouts. The NEP 2020 embarked upon the issue with a highly momentous approach. It foresees effective and sufficient infrastructure so that all students have access to safe and engaging education at all levels from pre-primary to Grade 12 (NEP 2020).

Quality Education in India

India has made significant progress in the field of education. Besides quality education, there are other challenges which have been haunting our education system. Dropout rates, gross enrolment, gender issue, retention rates, poor infrastructure, lack of teachers, etc. are some of the burning challenges which are hurdling the quality education in the nation. Other reasons which contribute to the hike in poor quality education are the absence of teachers which is 25% every day (Jeevan & Townsend, 2013). The government is trying to improve quantitative growth and to certain extent has reached the universalisation of education at all levels accomplishing one of the targets mentioned in SDG4 but the quality education is incomplete without taking the other targets into account. Although, private sector in India has commercialised education, they are far more progressive in providing quality education as compared to the government agencies. On one side, the nation is inching closer to the universalisation of education but on the other side, the quality of education has been questioned in the government-run school system. The government is trying to pursue the targets mentioned in SDG4, initiating various programmes and movements like UEE, RMSA, RUSA, SSA, sub-programmes like *Padhe Bharat Badhe Bharat*, *Hello English* and sometimes using incentives like mid-day meal, scholarships, reservations, etc. The NEP 2020 has also emphasised on reintegrating dropouts and ensuring universal access to education with the sole aim to achieve access and participation in free and compulsory quality school education for all children from age group of 3 – 18 years by 2030. (NEP 2020).

Roles of Key Stakeholders

To achieve the targets projected in SDG4, key stakeholders and agencies will have to work in close partnership and cooperation. It is a joint venture of all stakeholders and without cooperative efforts, it would be hard to achieve the goals. Therefore, it becomes important to chalk out the roles and responsibilities of key stakeholders.

Role of Government and Non-Government Agencies

Government and non-government agencies have potential to change the face of education with their firm determination. Agencies can undertake the system and de-commercialise it providing equal opportunities to all without any discrimination. Why can't students from economically weaker sections take advantage of quality education? Why don't all have equal opportunity to access quality education? If the private sector has thrived and succeeded to impart quality education why can't government agencies do so? The governments can provide solutions to these questions by framing strong policies and programmes. It should be the responsibility of the state alone to provide equal opportunities of quality education to all. On the other hand, non-government agencies should be empowered to adopt and reach the areas where the government fails to cover.

Role of a Teacher

Teachers are the masons of nation-building. Without their participation, nation-building is impossible. Being in such a key position, they should always take their responsibilities diligently and be accountable to whatever and wherever appointed to serve. Moreover, a good teacher, as a Scottish student in grade 2/3 thinks "is *very clever, doesn't shout, helps you every day, is not bossy, has faith in you, is funny, is patient, is good at work, tells you clearly what to do, helps you with mistakes, makes your work, helps you to read, helps you with spellings and has got courage*" (Mac Beath *et al.*, 1996, p. 55).

No one is born a teacher; good teaching is a result of quality education, quality training and the rich teaching experiences. Moreover, teaching competencies can be enhanced if they empower these three thrust areas:

Quality awareness (or self-evaluation): A teacher should be able to reflect on their own teaching methods, strategies and the ways of teaching. A teacher can improve quality in education and skills after diagnostic self-evaluation and corrective teaching.

Personal Ethics: Every profession has a set of laws to be followed which are called professional ethics. Some of the countries have professional ethics expressed in legal documents with certain rights and obligations of a teacher while in some countries, it is in the form of agreement between government agencies and organisations. These set of rules are followed strictly in order to establish certain standards of profession. The ILO / UNESCO recommendations concerning the status of teachers' professional ethics are referred in paragraph 73 states *"codes of ethics or of conduct should be established by the teachers' organisations, since such codes greatly contribute to ensuring the prestige of the profession and the exercise of professional duties in accordance with agreed principles".* It also declares that teachers shall "justify public trust and confidence and enhance the esteem in which the profession is held by providing quality education for all students" (Education International, 2001 a).

In absence of teaching ethics, the whole society can be ruined. In fact, teachers who are free from obligations tend to escape teaching-learning activities which is fatal for the educational health of children. Reports suggest that teachers' absence is one of the causes of degradation of quality education.

Professional Freedom: It is one of the important aspects in developing quality in education. It is not about literal freedom of educational personnel but about the freedom to switch on to the different ways and methods of teaching which can create an optimal learning experience for the students. Professional freedom comes when teaching is free from all kinds of economic, political, ideological and religious influences. This encourages teachers to become more innovative and creative.

The quality in teaching is positively correlated with the quality of teacher in following five dimensions:

a) Knowledge of substantive areas and content
b) Pedagogical skills
c) Reflection and ability to be self-critical
d) Empathy and commitment to the acknowledgement of the dignity of others
e) Managerial competencies within and outside the classrooms (OECD, 1994, p. 13-14).

Role of Community

Community here is referred to as an umbrella term for all the stakeholders of education other than teachers and government. The parents are the first teacher of a child, so it becomes crucially important for them to be well aware of the quality of education imparted at educational institutions. Improving quality in education requires consistent involvement of parents in all academic and administrative activities of the institutions. Responsible parents must take part in meetings organised by schools, colleges and other institutions from time to time, providing suggestions to ensure best practices fostering quality education.

The lay leaders of the community must take issues which are necessary and of prime importance in education. 'What can be included in the curriculum' can be well suggested on the part of the leaders of the community. Other stakeholders should also raise their concern regarding the quality of service and products in education. The community can suggest the curriculum which prepares a product well fitted into the needs of society.

Thus, the community can play a vibrant role in shaping the quality educational structure of the country. The best example is our neighbouring country Nepal which has made a significant growth in its education system by active involvement of its community. The community has never waited for the government to take initiative in the field of education; instead, the community itself acted first to establish new schools and hire teachers in their areas. People voluntarily gave their lands, funds, labourers, construction material and hired teachers for their schools. Most of the educationists thus seem to be convincing community involvement for quantitative and qualitative growth in education is unavoidable.

Conclusion

Quality education is not only the demand of the United Nations under SDG4, but it is now the demand of the time to equip our generation for future challenges to survive on the blue planet. We need to talk and write publicly on the issue not because the quality is lowering for last few decades or it is a burning global concern forcibly loaded on the nations or because it is a process of restructuring the public sector (Synder *et al.,* 2004), but instead we should look into the matter concerning the graveness and gravity of the issue connected to the threat of our sustainability on the earth. All the nations and the stakeholders need to come together in order to prevent nations and generation from destruction and equip our coming generations with best knowledge, skills and behaviour even if we have achieved milestones in education. 'UNESCO International Commission on Education for the 21st century' generally called as Delors' Commission, concluded that a great focus on quality is desirable everywhere even in the countries, where all the children are enrolled in the basic education (Delors, *et. al.,* 1996 p. 120) Moreover, if the lag continues, one day the world will divide in two halves of high-quality education class and low-quality education class. The high-quality education class will take the advantage of their education where the low-quality education class will suffer for their sustainability.

India is striving hard to achieve the Sustainable Development Goals 4 on sustainable education and lessen the educational gap between the people of different economic classes. The NEP 2020 is designed keeping all such views in consideration. It takes various issues like dropouts, universalisation of education, equitable and inclusive education, regulation and accreditations, institutional restructuring and consolidation, learning environments, Teacher Education etc. into account which is a certain indication for achieving SDG4 and all its targets. The NEP 2020 has bought a positive hope for quality education and better tomorrow.

Every policy is made with positive intentions but fails on the ground when it is not followed in its spirit. It needs strong political will power and mass cooperation for best implementation and success. So, let us come together in one accord, pursuing targets in SDG4 and defending our degrading education system by implementing quality education and taking up our roles and responsibilities faithfully.

References

Barrett, P., Davies, F., Zhang, Y., & Barrett, L. (2016). *The Holistic Impact of Classroom Spaces on Learning in Specific Subjects.* Sage Publications. doi: 10.1177/0013916516648735

Barrett, S.A. (2017/02/23) *Characteristics of a High-Quality Curriculum.* Stand For Children, https://stand.org

Coombs, P. H. (1985). *The world Crisis in Education: The view from the Eighties.* Oxford: Oxford University Press.

Delors etal, (1996). *Learning: the Treasure Within. Report to UNESCO of the International Commission on Education for the Twenty First century.* Paris: UNESCO

Education International (2001 a). *EI Declaration on Professional Ethics.* Brussels: Education International

General Assembly resolution, 66/288, the 2030 Agenda for Sustainable Development, A/RES/70/1 (15 September, 2012), available from https://undocs.org/en/A/RES/70/1

Government of India, Ministry of Human Resource Development. (2012). *Report of The High -Powered Commission on Teacher Education constituted by Hon'ble Supreme Court of India,* Vol. 1

Government of India, Ministry of Human Resource Development. (2019). National Education Policy

ILO, UNESCO, EI and WCT (2001). *EFAFlagship on Teachers and the Quality of Education. Memorandum of Understanding between Partners.* Paris: UNESCO

Jeevan, S., & Townsend, J. (2013/07/17). *Teachers: A Solution to Education Reform in India.* Stanford Social Innovation Review, https://www.ssir.org

Mac Beath, J., Boyd, B., Rand, J., & Bell, S. (1996). *Schools Speak for Themselves: Towards a framework for self-evaluation.* London: National Union of Teachers

OECD (1994). *Quality in Teaching.* OECD, Paris

Pirsig, R.M. (1974). *Zen and the art of Motorcycle Maintenance,* Bantam Books, New York

Quality Standards in Education– Discussion Summary, E-discussion by the Common Wealth Education Hub, June, 2016, Retrieved from https://thecommomwealth-education-hub.net

Sharma, R.A. (2010). *Teacher Education and Pedagogical Training,* Surya Publications, Meerut.

Snyder, K., Fredrikkson, U. & Taube, K. (2004). *Measuring quality, learning and knowledge in the knowledge society.* Paper presented at the 32nd conference of the Nordic Education Research Association. Reykjavik, Iceland. March 2004

Teixiera, J., Amoroso, J., & Gresham, J. (2017/09/03). *Why Education Infrastructure matters for Learning. World Bank Blogs,* https://blogs.worldbank.org

UNESCO (1996). Recommendation concerning the status of teachers. Paris: UNESCO

World Bank (1995). *Priorities and Strategies for Education.* Washington D.C: The World Bank

Yang, E. (2011). *Orientation and Function of Library in Quality Education of College,* International Education Studies, 4 (2), Doi:10.5539/ies.v4n2p195

https://www.mhrd.gov.in

https://www.ssa.nic.in

Abbreviations

CTET – Central Teacher Eligibility Test
DIET – District Institute of Education and Training
ILO – International Labour Organization
NCFTE – National Curriculum Framework for Teacher Education
NCTE – National Council for Teacher Education
NEP – National Education Policy
RMSA – Rashtriya Madhyamik Shiksha Abhiyaan
RUSA – Rashtriya Uchchatar Shiksha Abhiyaan
SCERT – State Council of Educational Research and Training
SDG4 – Sustainable Development Goal 4
SSA – Sarva Shiksha Abhiyaan
TEI – Teacher Education Institutes
UEE – Universalization of Elementary Education
UNESCO – United Nations Educational Scientific and Cultural Organization

Contributors

The Editors/Contributors

Professor Pankaj Arora has been serving in the Department of Education (CIE), University of Delhi for around twenty-four years. Presently he is working as Director, Institute of Life Long Learning, University of Delhi. He is serving UGC as Member of various Expert Committees with regard to implementation of NEP 2020 at National level. Prof. Arora has authored numerous articles, and presented research papers in various national and international conferences.

Professor Arora has eight books to his credit. He is one of the prominent Experts on National Education Policy 2020 and has delivered many Keynote address/ Inaugural Address/ Eminent Speaker for various Webinars/ workshops/ FDPs on different aspects of National Education Policy 2020.

Professor Arora's areas of specialization include Pedagogy of Political Science, Adolescence Education, Social Science Education and Democratic Education.

Professor Arora has published more than 19 research articles in indexed/ peer reviewed Journals at national and international level and writes for National Newspapers' Editorials. He has made 69 presentations at various Conferences/ Seminars across the world. He is serving various committees at NCTE, NCERT, ICSSR, SCERT and different Central and State Universities.

Professor Arora is associated with various publication houses as part of their academic team member at National and International level.

Professor Arora has led various major and minor research projects funded by UGC, ICSSR, and University of Delhi.

Professor Haneet Gandhi teaches in the Faculty of Education (commonly known as CIE), University of Delhi for over fifteen years. She is a part of various National Policy making bodies such as NCERT and NCTE. She had been the Co-convener in the Under-Graduate Curriculum Revision Committee of University of Delhi and is holding the position of Deputy Dean in the Admission Branch of University of Delhi.

Having done her Post Graduation in Mathematics from Indian Institute of Technology (I.I.T., Delhi) and master's in Education from Jamia Millia Islamia, Professor Gandhi completed her Doctorate in the area of 'Problem Solving in Mathematics through Strategic Content Learning Approach: Promoting Self-Regulated Learning' from University of Lucknow.

Professor Gandhi engages in the area of Mathematics Education, Quantitative Methods in Educational Research and Assessment for Learning by having published over 30 research papers in various National and International journals of high repute. Most of her work is concentrated in understanding and promoting Stochastic Thinking among adults and children. She also has 6 books to her credit spanning in the areas of Assessment for Learning, Mathematics Pedagogy and Hands-on Mathematics. She has made over 54 presentations, delivered various Keynote addresses, and given Invited talks at National and International Conferences and Congresses. She is also a part of Editorial and Reviewer Teams of renowned Journals such as Voices of Teachers and Teacher Educators, NCERT; At Right Angles, Azim Premji University; Educational Quest; and Statistics Education Research Journal, International Association for Statistical Education (IASE).

The Contributors

Professor Amit Kauts is Dean, Faculty of Education, Guru Nanak Dev University, Amritsar. He is doctorate in Education and has 27 year experience of teaching with research focus on educational development, ICT based pedagogy and various dimensions of Teacher Education. He has mentored one Postdoctoral research, 16 doctoral researches and has authored over 87 research papers, 14 book chapters and authored/edited 2 books. He coordinated 3 UGC and ICSSR sponsored Research Projects and is also serving for Ministry of Education funded project 'School of Education' at GNDU under PMMMNMTT, MHRD as Coordinator.

Professor Anjali Bajpai is a Professor in Faculty of Education, BHU, possessing M.Sc. (Botany), and PhD degree from BHU. Her areas of specialization are Science Education, Assessment and Curriculum Studies. She is currently looking after the Centre of curriculum development and advance research. She has successfully guided 15 PhD Scholars and has published more than 30 research papers in national journals, contributed 7 chapters in various books, and edited 3 books.

Professor Asheesh Srivastava is an alumnus of University of Lucknow & DAVV, Indore. He has served University of Lucknow, Amity University before getting appointment in BHU & Visva-Bharati. Presently Prof. Srivastava is Founder Dean, School of Education, Mahatma Gandhi Central University. Prof. Srivastava is engaged with different assignments of National Bodies. He has been awarded the Maya Gold Foundation Award for 'Excellence & Service as a Young Academic Leader', USA.

Dr. Ashu Roulet is an Assistant Professor, Department of Education, HNB Garhwal Central University, Srinagar, Uttarakhand

Dr. Chandan Shrivastava is an Assistant Professor in the Department of Teacher Education, School of Education, Central University of South Bihar, Gaya. He is Ph.D. in Education, M.Phil. (Education), M.Ed. and B.Ed. from Department of Education, University of Delhi. He has completed Post-Doctoral Fellowship under ICSSR for research on Digital Learning in Indian Classrooms. In addition to his academics, he has contributed in developing various Teacher Education programmes, CPD modules and school textbooks at National and State level.

Professor Chand Kiran Saluja took voluntary retirement in the year 2013 after teaching and doing research work for about 27 years in the Department of Education (C.I.E), University of Delhi. Since then he has been working as the Academic Director in the Sanskrit Promotion Foundation. Dr. Saluja has obtained Master's degree in four different subjects, along with being a Doctorate and D. Lit. Degree in Education. He is known across the country and internationally for his teachings in the area of Language pedagogy. He is an expert in Educational planning and Policies. Currently, he is associated as a consultant in various educational institutions of the country.

Dr. Geetika Datta is the Founding Principal of Bhavan's Leelavati Munshi College of Education, Bharatiya Vidya Bhavan, New Delhi. She has a rich experience of working with in-service and pre-service teachers and educators for more than 19 years. Her areas of interest are Educational Psychology, Inclusive Education, Contemplative Educational Practices, Assessments, Higher Education, Business Education and Curricular Issues.

Her academic pursuits include content writing and video lessons in collaboration with institutions like IGNOU, NIOS and MHRD Swayam Prabha and publications in Journals of national and international repute.

Professor Jyoti Sharma is a Professor at Cluster Innovation Centre, University of Delhi. Presently, she is teaching M.Sc. (Mathematics Education) program in the university and has an experience of teaching in B.El.Ed and B.Ed programs of DU. As a mathematics pedagogue, she closely works with pre-service math teachers, students, in-service math teachers and math educators at policy level and in the practice. She is actively involved in research and innovation in the field of Mathematics Pedagogy and Education of Gifted Students. She is also involved in developing innovative strategies to mentor high ability students.

Professor Kaushal Kishore is a Professor in the Department of Teacher Education, School of Education, Central University of South Bihar, Gaya. He is also the Coordinator of National Resource Centre (NRC) for Education established by MoE, GOI. He has more than 16 years of experience of teaching and guiding research at various levels and more than 35 papers and articles published in various International and National Journals. He has, contributed in 3 books as author, editor and translator. His areas of interest are Assessment and Evaluation in Education, Research Methodology in education.

Professor Navleen Kaur teaches in the Department of Community Education and Disability Studies, Panjab University, Chandigarh, and her areas of Specialization are Educational Psychology, Guidance and Counselling, Inclusive Education, and Learning Disability. She has a Masters degree in English, Sociology and Education. and Ph.D. in Education. She has authored a close to 22 books on varied psychosocial issues, edited 2 books on Higher Education and Inclusive Education, published 42 research papers in international, national and online journals and has presented 43 papers in Conferences.

Dr. Nisha Singh was the Deputy Director, Centre for Online Education, IGNOU. She held a Bachelors and Masters degree in Science, Instructional Design & Technology (MIDT) and Education, M.Phil. in Buddhist Studies and Education, and Ph.D. in Education from Jamia Millia Islamia.

Dr. Pawan Sinha is Spiritual Preceptor and Associate Prof., MLN College, University of Delhi. He has founded *'Rishikulshala'*, where more than 1100 marginalised children are getting free education. Author of many articles & books, he is the recipient of 'National Ved Vyas Samman' given by the Govt. of M.P. in the field of education and U.P. Govt.'s prestigious D.C. Kothari award for his book *'Shiksha ke Dwand'*.

Professor P. K. Misra is Professor of Education in the Chaudhary Charan Singh University, Meerut. He has received several prestigious international research scholarships that includes Commonwealth Academic Fellowship of CSC, UK; Doctoral and Senior Researcher Scholarship of DAAD, Germany; Erasmus Mundus Visiting Scholar Scholarship of European Commission; National Scholarship of Slovak Republic; MASHAV Scholarship of Israel Government; and Research Exchange Scholarship of FMSH, France.

Dr. Pranita Gopal works with teachers to create engaging classrooms for both teachers and students. She works as an Instructional Coach and Educational Consultant. She is also an avid crafter who finds that art always cements in learning experience. Her area of interest focuses on enhancing the technological, pedological and content knowledge of teachers.

Professor Saroj Sharma is Professor of Education at Guru Gobind Singh Indraprastha University (GGSIPU), New Delhi is presently serving as Chairperson, National Institute of Open Schooling (NIOS) on deputation. She is involved in many academic and administrative activities today at National and International levels at different capacities to bring qualitative change in present academic scenario.

Professor Seema Dhawan, Ph.D. (Forestry & Education) is serving in the Dept. of Education, HNB Garhwal Central University, Srinagar, Uttarakhand. Her expertise is in the areas of Education for Sustainable Development, Educational Technology and Research. She has teaching experience of 25 Years including administrative works. She has published 5 books, 7 resource books, 127 research papers. Has delivered 140 invited lectures and received 9 awards.

Professor Usha Sharma has been doing research, content creation and training at NCERT, New Delhi for the last 14 years. Presently, she is holding the charge of National Literacy Centre-Cell, NCERT. She has published about 25 research papers, edited ten books. Apart from being the academic editor of the children's magazine 'Firki Children's' and research-journal 'Primary Teacher' published by NCERT. Professor Sharma is continuously contributing in the field of language education, basic literacy, adult education and lifelong learning as well as early childhood care and education, teacher education, value education.

Professor Yukti Sharma teaches at the Department of Education and is also the Academic Secretary at the Institute of Lifelong Learning, University of Delhi. She has done M.Sc. (Botany) and M.Ed in which she was gold medallist from University of Delhi. She is involved in teaching and guiding research in the area of inclusive education, science education, environmental education, giftedness and creativity at the department. She has conducted several research projects awarded by renowned bodies like NCERT, ICSSR and has presented papers in national and international conferences. She has to her credit several publications in acclaimed international journals. She has authored textbooks, edited books, contributed chapters, and developed MOOCs and OERs for several organisations such as NCTE, NIOS, IGNOU, NCERT and CBSE.